FROM THE CRUSADES TO GULAG AND BEYOND

VALERY G. YANKOVSKY

"FROM THE CRUSADES TO GULAG AND BEYOND"

was first published in Russian in the year 2000. The publishers were the M.Gorky Scientific Library (Section of rare Books and Manuscripts) of the town of Vladimir.

Author	V.G YANKOVSKY.
Editor	A.A. KOVZUN.
Publishers	M.Gorky Scientific Library (Section of rare Books and Manuscripts).
ISBN	5-93787-011-5.

Vladimir, Russia   2000

EDITORIAL COMMITTEE OF THE ENGLISH EDITION

Translator	Michael HINTZE
Proof Reader and Layout	Eileen M. HINTZE
Reviewer	Larissa N. WATERSON (nee HINTZE)
Technical Editor	David "Prilezhny" WATERSON

Sydney, Australia	June 2000
Reprinted with corrigenda	August 2000
Second Edition	August 2001

Copyright © 2007 Elliott Snow
All Rights Reserved
ISBN: 978-0-6151-4851-9

Front Cover

Main Picture :   the Author Valery G. Yankovsky.
Mountain Scene : Yuri (George) Yankovsky hunting with dogs.
Bottom Left :   Yuri (George) Yankovsky with trophies.
Bottom Right :   Novina Deer farm.

Back Cover

Photograh by Natalie B. Hintze, 1936

Arseny Yankovsky once made a prophetic statement to his elder brother, Valery… "Many years hence, when we are all dead and gone, an old Korean will walk past Novina, stop for a short rest and say: 'Chone ennere I Koran e nenooni ran maudgha-dori al-sarasso!' ['Many years ago some Russians we nicknamed 'the four-eyed' lived in this valley. And how well they lived!']

Valery Yankovsky concludes : "Here he is, the old Korean who has probably just walked past Novina."

VALERY G. YANKOVSKY.

Valery G. Yankovsky was born in 1911 in the Russian Far East, near the town of Vladivostok, into a well-to-do family. His father, Yuri (George) M. Yankovsky was a successful horse-breeder and deerfarmer prominent in local affairs .

The Russian Revolution and Civil War forced the family to flee to Northern Korea in 1922 where Yuri Yankovsky rebuilt his lost fortune with the active help of his wife and young family (three sons and two daughters). Valery's childhood and youth were dedicated to that task.

At the end of the Second World War Russia occupied North Korea which resulted in another destruction of the family's fortune and imprisonment of most of its members in the infamous Gulag in 1946.

Valery has survived that holocaust and is currently living with his wife, a former "white slave" of the Gulag, in the town of Vladimir, near Moscow. They have a grown-up son and a granddaughter.

V.G. Yankovsky has been writing articles in Russian magazines for several decades and is an author of a number of books, all written in Russian (**"Nenooni The Four-Eyed"**, **"Tigers, Deer and Gingseng"**, **"A Long Return",** and others). They deal with the history of his family and many episodes of his life in Korea, and as a prisoner of the Gulag and an exonerated citizen in Russia.

FROM THE CRUSADES TO GULAG AND BEYOND is the first of Valery's novels to be translated into English. It gives a broad overview of the Yankovsky-Novina clan and provides a fascinating insight into the senseless brutality of the Gulag slave labour camps.

FOREWORD TO THE ENGLISH EDITION.

Valery G. Yankovsky comes from an ancient family of Novina - Yankovskys, Polish nobles whose origins can be traced to the Crusades.

During the latter half of the 19th and most of the 20th century the Yankovskys interacted with the rulers of Russia, often with disastrous results. In this book Valery Yankovsky traces the origins and the history of his family and describes his personal sufferings at the hands of the Russian Communists, which included imprisonment in the infamous Gulag.

However, in addition to tragic events, the book contains many humorous stories based mainly on the life in Novina and Lukomorye, two holiday resorts established by the Yankovskys in what is now North Korea, after the family's escape from Russia in 1922.

The reader will be fascinated by stories of hard work in an attempt to rebuild a lost fortune, of hunting expeditions, of love, romance and adventure.

The impression left at the end of the novel is of a boundless optimism of a man and a family who survived against all odds and triumphed in the face of adversity.

Valery's exposure of the senseless brutality of the Gulag confirms the wisdom of a saying attributed to Edmund Burke (1729--1797):

" It is necessary only for good men to be silent, for evil to triumph."

Valery G.Yankovsky is a good man who has spoken out....

CONTENTS

PART I	1
CHAPTER 1. THE ORIGINS.	3
CHAPTER 2. PROSPERITY	10
CHAPTER 3. THE SECOND GENERATION AND THEIR OFFSPRING.	11
CHAPTER 4. EXODUS.	16
CHAPTER 5. GULAG MEMORIES	19
CHAPTER 6. POTPOURRI OF THE FAMILY HISTORY	21
CHAPTER 7. KOREA. GETTING ON OUR FEET.	25
CHAPTER 8. KOREA. THE TURNING POINT.	34
CHAPTER 9. NOVINA AND LUKOMORYE ---VARIOUS EPISODES	36
1. BUTAMOCHI	36
2. THE HISTORY OF LUKOMORYE.	39
3. CHINA AND JAPAN.	39
4. "PUSSYCAT"	41
5. THE BUTTERFLIES.	43
CHAPTER 10. THE STORY OF THE SHEVELEV FAMILY	46
CHAPTER 11. DEER FARMING IN NOVINA.	49
CHAPTER 12. IVAN KUZMICH RESNYANSKY AND DAIRY FARMING WITH A DIFFERENCE.	51
CHAPTER 13. NOVINA'S HAPPY DAYS. LARISSA.	83
1. LARISSA	84
CHAPTER 14. THE CLOUDS ARE GATHERING BUT LIFE GOES ON.	93
1. A TRIP TO HARBIN	94
2. BACK TO NOVINA	97
CHAPTER 15. THE FIRST CLAPS OF THUNDER -BUT LIFE GOES ON.	99
1. A CLASH OF RIVAL ARMIES	99
2. THE CYCLONE AND A GOOD SAMARITAN.	100
3. VERA BELAYA ("VERA THE BLONDE ")	105
4. NOVINA RECOVERS	108
CHAPTER 16. SHANGHAI IN 1941 - VARIOUS EPISODES.	110
1. I TRAVEL TO SHANGHAI.	110
2. AUNTIES GELYA AND TATA.	111
3. TARZAN IS BEING SHOWN THE SIGHTS.	113
4. A CLOSE CALL.	115
5. WELL SUITED.	116
6. EUGENE ("ZHENKA") ELLERS.	117
CHAPTER 17. THE LAST FEW YEARS OF NOVINA.	123
1. TIGER KILLERS.	123
2. FATHER TAKES A BRIDE	125
CHAPTER 18. A NEW BEGINNING.	127
1. THE TIGER HAMLET.	127
2. A SECOND FATAL WEDDING.	128
3. THE TIGER HAMLET COMES OF AGE	133

CHAPTER 19. THE HOLOCAUST. 135
    1. THE LIBERATORS. 135
    2. SERVING THE MOTHERLAND 135
    3. NORTH KOREA'S NEW LEADER. 137
CHAPTER 20. GULAG. 140
    1. THE BETRAYAL. 140
    2. UNDER INVESTIGATION. 142
    3. CONDEMNED. 145
    4. HOME SWEET HOME. 146
    5. ESCAPE. 149
    6. RETRIBUTION. 153
CHAPTER 21. BEYOND GULAG. 158
    1. THE FIRST TENTATIVE STEPS. 158
    2. A TRIP INTO THE PAST. 159
    3. HONOURING THE FAMILY NAME. 160
    4. THOSE WHO ESCAPED GULAG. 161
    5. WE HAVE OVERCOME. 163
CHAPTER 22. ACKNOWLEDGEMENTS. 164
CHAPTER 23. CONCLUDING REMARKS IN LIEU OF AN EPILOGUE. 165
    1. CREATION OF NOVINA 165
    2. THE DEATH OF NOVINA. 166
    3. SUMMARY OF THE YANKOVSKY FAMILY'S HISTORY. 167
    4. ARSENY YANKOVSKY'S STORY 169
PART TWO 171
CHAPTER 24. A CAR CALLED "STARYA" (THE OLD BOY) AND ITS MATES. 173
CHAPTER 25. A POISONOUS SNAKE (MEDYANKA). 178
CHAPTER 26. MORE ABOUT MY ANCESTORS. 186
CHAPTER 27. SKIPPER GEK AND HIS DESCENDANTS. 189
CHAPTER 28. DISCOVERY OF LONG LOST RELATIVES. 191
CHAPTER 29. FYODOR PAVLOVICH SOLOMAKHIN. 193
CHAPTER 30. MY COUSIN TANYA. 196
CHAPTER 31. MORE ABOUT LIFE IN NOVINA AND ITS ENVIRONS. 199
CHAPTER 32. DE TEMPORA ET MORES. 202
    1. KOREAN CUSTOMS. 202
    2. A KOREAN WEDDING. 202
    3. RESTAURANTS AND BATH HOUSES. 203
    4. HANGYABY. 203
    5. RESTAURANTS. 204
    6. BATH HOUSES. 205
    7. BUSINESS ACUMEN. 207
    8. THE YANKOVSKY LEGACY. 208
CHAPTER 33. THE SHEVELEV FAMILY. 210
CHAPTER 34. HISTORY OF THE PIONEERS OF THE USSURI REGION. 214
CHAPTER 35. OUR JAPANESE AND KOREAN FRIENDS. 216
CHAPTER 36. BEYOND GULAG. I REVISIT VLADIVOSTOK AND SEDEMI. 219
CHAPTER 37. FALSIFIERS OF HISTORY. 225

CHAPTER 38. THE TRUTH 229
CHAPTER 39. THE NEAREST AND DEAREST OF MY AUTUMN YEARS. 232
    1. MY WIFE IRINA AND HER FAMILY. 232
    2. EXTRACTS FROM IRINA YANKOVSKY'S MEMOIRS. 233
    3. MY SONS. 235
    4. BEYOND GULAG. 236
CHAPTER 40. EPILOGUE. 238
CHAPTER 41. APPENDIX. 240
CHAPTER 42. FAMILY TREES 243
CHAPTER 43. PHOTOGRAPHS. 251
CHAPTER 44. MAPS 313
CHAPTER 45. INDEX. 317

Part I

Chapter 1. THE ORIGINS.

My grandfather, Michael Ivanovich Yankovsky ("Son of Ivan" - actually "Jan" in Polish) was a hereditary Polish nobleman. The history of our ancient clan was recorded on a parchment, which we kept in a cover made of lead. It was, alas, lost when we fled Russia to settle in Korea. From it we knew that our ancestors took part in the Crusades whose aim was to rescue the Lord's casket from "The Infidels". It also told us that back in the 14 Th Century our ancestor Tadeusz Novina - Yankovsky saved the life of the Polish King during a battle with Teutonic knights, having lost a leg during that encounter. This earned him the title of a knight and an attendant family crest consisting of a blue flag on which were depicted a shield and a short sword, called "Novina" in old-Polish. Above the sword was a drawing of a helmet with ostrich plumes and just below it --a gilt-edged black knee-guard, symbolising the nature of his feat, which cost him his leg. A bow (a symbol of a marksman), located below the knee-guard, completed the design. All that is left of this crest is a photograph of my father Yuri M. Yankovsky and his two sons (myself and brother Arseny) holding the unfolded ensign.

When my grandfather was a student of the Gory-Gorets Agricultural Institute (which was located near the city of Mogilev), he took part in the Polish Rebellion of 1863. The insurgents were defeated. The leaders of his detachment were executed by firing squads, with rank and file members being sentenced to various terms of imprisonment. Michael was sentenced to eight years penal servitude and his personal possessions were confiscated by the court. He was sent to Siberia together with a large contingent of other prisoners. The journey from Smolensk (Central Russia) to the Transbaikal Region (Eastern Siberia) took about eighteen months because the prisoners had to cover the distance on foot. Upon arrival at their destination the prisoners were assigned for work in abandoned mines where the "Decembrists" (members of an army uprising in St Petersburg in December 1825) served their punishment. They were also required to build timber-carrying barges on the Amur River. Luckily for them, the Tsar declared an amnesty in 1868, which allowed the convicts to become free settlers within the confines of Eastern Siberia (they had no right to return to Europe). Michael Yankovsky accepted this opportunity and found work in the goldmines located on Olekma (one of the tributaries of the River Lena).

A fellow convict by the name of Benedict Dubovsky, a recently imprisoned former Professor of Biology at the University of Warsaw, wrote to him in 1872 with an interesting proposal. Dubovsky had an offer from the Imperial Russian Geographical Society to explore the Amur River Basin all the way to the shores of the Pacific, and was inviting his compatriot to join him in that venture.

Michael made up his mind at once. He immediately resigned from his job, gathered his modest belongings, his rifle and shotgun and hurried to meet his friend at the town of Chita, taking as his only companion his favourite dog by the name of Bars ("Snow Leopard"). Another former political prisoner by the name of Viktor Godlevsky joined the two men in Chita. The trio travelled from there to a Cossack village called Sivakovo located on the River Ingoda where they used to build barges in their convict days. Their present task was to build a sturdy boat for their travels along the River Amur. Despite his upbringing as nobleman Michael displayed remarkable abilities as a carpenter. With the aid of his friends he built a skiff equipped with sails and oars, which was destined to become their home for the next two years. They christened it "Nadezhda" ("Hope") and used it to navigate the rivers Ingoda, Shilka, Argun and Amur after which they entered the mouth of the Ussuri River where they spent the second winter of their adventure. They left "Nadezhda" in the local Cossack village of Kazakevichevo and made for the then military station of Vladivostok, having first forwarded their collection of fish, birds and insects, as well as animal skulls, furs and samples of mineral ore to the capital of Eastern Siberia, Irkutsk. They reached Vladivostok via the River Sungacha and Lake Khanka.

During his stay in Kazakevichevo my grandfather received and accepted an invitation to become a manager of a rich gold mine on Askold Island, located in the Sea of Japan, some 50 miles from Vladivostok. He held that position from 1874 to 1879. The mine belonged to a Vladivostok businessman by the name of Kuster. Michael combined his managerial duties with scientific work, having acquired considerable knowledge in the field of biology during his work with Professor Dubovsky.

The Island of Askold is a natural stopover point for various butterflies and birds during their migration along the Pacific seaboard of Russia's Maritime Provinces, and this enabled my grandfather to assemble invaluable collections of these creatures. He forwarded many of his entomological and ornithological finds to Warsaw, St Petersburg, France and Germany. Many newly discovered species and subspecies of butterflies, bugs and birds were named after him, and Yankovsky becomes known within a wide circle of European scientists. The Imperial Russian Geographical Society rewarded him with a silver medal for his article entitled "The Island of Askold".

However, his main ambition was to introduce a hardy breed of horses to this far-flung outpost. His forebears were the King's horsemen and from them he inherited his passion for horses. But the horses he encountered on this fringe of The Empire were quite appalling. The local Asian horses were far too small, whereas the imports, which reached that region by sea or land (via Siberia), could not tolerate the humid seaside. Instead of thriving, they suffered from various diseases.

This descendant of noble horsemen decided to breed a horse suitable for the climate of the Far East through interbreeding between the local and imported horses. He hoped that such a crossbreed would eventually become acclimatised, resulting in a unique local breed. In order to explore the area around Vladivostok, he sailed in a junk to the Korean border returning on horseback along the shores of the ocean. During his trip he discovered a magnificent mountainous peninsula which was located on the western shores of the Bay of Amur, within twenty nautical miles of Vladivostok. This is how he described it in one of his articles in the "Journal of The Society for the Exploration of the Amur Region": "It is an uninhabited peninsula with marvellous bays full of fish and crabs, with sandy beaches and clear springs and, above all, with first class pastures. Ever present sea breezes guarantee an almost complete absence of gadflies and mosquitoes --this scourge of cattle breeders of the Ussuri Region"

He asked the permission of the Military Governor whose name was Erdman to buy a tract of land and to be given a long lease on the whole peninsula. The Governor thought that this enthusiastic man was capable of creating a stud farm, using only his own resources. As far as Michael was concerned, he realised that he needed a companion to accomplish this task. Another necessity was a female manager, because he recently lost his companion, a widow of a soldier, who died giving birth to their son.

Michael went to Vladivostok in search of a fiancée. However, the task was proving difficult because he had no friends or relatives in that small settlement. He was advised to seek help from the only photographer in town, by the name of Karl Ivan Schultz who proved very helpful, having supplied the prospective groom with an album containing photographs of prospective brides. There were a total of fifteen candidates but Schultz knew each one of them and was able to give a detailed description of their individual merits.

The hapless searcher confided in a letter to his friend Dubovsky that having gone to bed after his visit to the matchmaker he saw in his dreams all fifteen prospective brides who, however, would not talk to him despite all his efforts to engage them in conversation.

He finally settled for a poor girl without a dowry, by the name of Olga Kuznetsova who worked as a domestic for her uncle. Having received the permission of the girl's grandmother, he married Olga and journeyed with her to Askold in a whaling boat equipped with sails.

People and materials were being shipped to the gold mine where Michael worked, by a whaler and skipper who was well known in the Far East, a free settler by the name of Friedholf Gek. Yankovsky told him about the fabulous peninsula in the Bay of Amur and offered him a share in its development. Having visited and inspected the site, the prospective partners came to the following agreement: The sailor is to take up residence on the shores of the bay (which was later named after him) and the future stud owner was to settle in a valley which was protected from storms by a low ridge. Clean springs abounded in the valley and it had a river, which fed a lake large enough to supply drinking water for hundreds of heads of cattle.

However, Yankovsky was unable to move to the new location because his employer held him to his contract as a mine manager. It was therefore decided that captain Gek would be the first one to build a house on the shores of Sedemi Bay, a name given to it by the aborigines, members of a tribe calling themselves "The Udegei". Gek made frequent visits to Michael and his young bride. He told them of the riches abounding on the peninsula: about shoals of herrings frequently entering the bay, about the abundance of flounder, navaga (local fish) and red-fish, about schools of salmon using the mouths of local rivers as spawning grounds. A lagoon separating the peninsula from the mainland was a home to ducks, geese and swans; the surrounding hills were a haven for pheasants and wild deer. Gek said that he and his family (a wife and a six-year-old son) were anxious for the Yankovskys to join them.

In 1878 the Yankovskys adopted Michael's ex-nuptial child Alexander (his Russian diminutive was "Shoora"). In the same year Olga Yankovsky gave birth to a daughter they named Elizabeth. The young husband was delighted with his wife. Here is part of what he wrote to his friend Professor Dubovsky:

"She is always happy, always satisfied with her surroundings. The ugly malaise of boredom, which is infecting the educated Russian society, is completely foreign to her. She is a magnificent house manager..."

Their son Yury (my father) was born in April of 1879. And in June of that year they were finally able to move to the peninsula, which was later named after my grandfather. From that time on all maritime charts have referred to it as "The Yankovsky Peninsula". There is also a 449 - meter high "Yankovsky Mountain" on the mainland, very close to the Peninsula.

Captain Gek transported his future neighbours in his schooner "Anna". They were accompanied by Olga's parents, the couple's children and staff. Cattle, agricultural implements and tents were also loaded on the vessel. Everybody was full of happy expectations...However, a disaster awaited them upon arrival. Gek's house was looted and burned down, his wife was brutally hacked to death and hanged on a hook, which supported a lamp, murdered farm workers were thrown into the basement. Escaped cattle were roaming on the mountains and there was no trace of his six-year old son.

Korean farmers who lived within twenty kilometres of Sedemi arrived at the scene of the disaster on their tiny skinny-legged mounts and told the new settlers that the atrocities had been perpetrated by Manchurian bandits, known as Hung Hu Tse ("Red Beards"). They regarded the Peninsula as their bailiwick from which they conducted their criminal activities. During the murderous raid the "Red Beards" also robbed the Koreans, took hostages and confiscated horses in order to get a ransom. The farmers who were also experienced hunters and scouts, offered to join the Russians in tracking down and fighting the bandits.

Olga who was an excellent shot armed herself with a carbine and stayed on board the schooner to protect the children, with the "International Brigade" setting out in pursuit of the outlaws. They caught up with them on the border with Manchuria and routed them in a gun battle. All of the band's prisoners, except for Gek's little boy, were freed unharmed. There was no sign of the poor child, and the surrounding blue hills are harbouring the secret of his demise to this day. The distraught father made many trips to China in his boat, looking for the flaxen-haired head among the black-haired Chinese kids, but, alas, in vain...

Michael nearly perished during the encounter with the Hung Hu Tse. Their leader hid behind a large tree and ambushed my grandfather. Luckily Michael sensed the trap and being a first-class marksman dispatched the felon before he could take a shot at him. That duel created an enduring legend because superstitious Koreans came to the conclusion that Yankovsky had two pairs of eyes: one on the forehead and another one at the back of the head; how else could he see his would-be assassin? My grandfather became known by an honorary title of "Ne Nooni" which means "The Four-Eyed" in Korean. This title, or nickname, stayed with three generations of our family. The Koreans called my father Yury "Ne Nooni Atiri" (with the letters "I" pronounced as in "hip") which meant "The Son of The Four-Eyed". His three sons were known as "Ne Nooni Sondja" (with the "O" as in "Ron")—"Ne Nooni's Grandsons".

By 1880 my grandfather completed the construction of the farmhouse, a veritable fortress equipped with thick walls, made of adobe bricks, which were impervious to bullets. The same year saw the establishment of a stud farm. A stallion called "Ataman" ("The Leader") was not very large but towered over the Mongolian, Manchurian and Korean mares. During the winter of 1880 tigers killed four mares and all young foals but a start had been made. Every year saw an increase in the height of the new offspring and at the same time they were becoming well acclimatised. Grandfather kept the horses outside throughout the year because there was not enough room for them in the stables. As a result they did not succumb to either the cold weather or cold viruses. "They were washed by the rain and dried by the wind"- wrote Michael in his memoirs - "and they looked as if they had been looked after by the best of grooms".

The farm boasted cows, sheep, pigs and poultry. The family friend Dubovsky visited the farm in 1883 and later praised his compatriot in his book "Siberian Reminiscences". He was very proud of Michael's achievements and proclaimed that he had never met a more efficient establishment anywhere in the Far East. This was particularly commendable because for the first few years the farm was mainly family-run. The only assistants were Olga's brother Simon and two retired soldiers. Skilled Korean shepherds were grazing the cattle. These lads later became independent farm owners. The rapidly growing children of the couple enthusiastically helped their parents. The farm was turning into a large stud.

Every autumn the Defence Ministry bought a number of select sturdy half bloods for the needs for its cavalry and artillery units. In the summer of 1890 the Yankovskys were visited by the Governor of Eastern Siberia, Baron N.A. Korf who inspected the herds of horses and expressed his general approval of the stud. However, the Governor was not too happy with the height of the mounts, saying that an extra hand or so would be very desirable. To show his appreciation, he promised Michael an official pardon, since despite his contribution to the development of the region my grandfather was still treated as a former convict and was subject to police surveillance. Korf kept his promise. The Emperor granted his request in the following terms: "Following a humble request from the Minister for The Interior, His Imperial Majesty has on this, the fifth day of June of 1890, graciously consented to grant a pardon and the removal of police supervision to one Yankovsky".

For his part, Michael kept the promise to increase the average height of his stud. He made thorough preparations for a long trip required for the accomplishment of that task and summoned his brother-in-law, Simon, from the town of Irkutsk to act as manager of the stud during his absence.

In November of 1891, taking advantage of the cold weather and fresh snow, he embarked on a long journey in a "troika" (three-horse) sleigh, accompanied by an assistant, a retired warrant officer by the name of Afanassy Antipov. They were heading for the far-away Siberia, which was familiar to Michael from his convict days, when he crossed it on foot.

My grandfather was taking a great risk. He sold many of his young horses and borrowed money from the bank for this uncertain venture. After all, the distance from Vladivostok to Irkutsk is five and a half thousand kilometres, a return trip of eleven thousand!... Bad roads.. Wolves...Bandits.. And absolutely no guarantee of success, only a dogged reliance on one's own strength and wits.

They reached Irkutsk after the New Year. There they bought six full-blooded colts and thirty-six mares of the "Tomsk" (a town in Siberia) breed from state-run studs and thriving private farms of the Kuznetsk Region.

The horses were formed into a herd, which was driven back to Sedemi. It was spring, Lake Baikal was becoming dangerous to cross, the ice being full of water holes, and they had difficulty in negotiating it. By the time they reached the River Selenga, the ice on it had begun to break and they nearly drowned during the crossing. From the Cossack settlement of Sivakovo, which was well known to them, they took to rafts for the journey along the rivers Ingoda, Shilka and Amur. A huge flood caught them along the way; they were unable to reach dry land to buy oats, and the horses began to starve. The men cut down branches of willows, which they found on the islands and used them instead. Three of the weakened mares fell into the waters of the Amur and drowned.

Finally, a steamboat took them between the towns of Blagoveshensk and Khabarovsk and into the mouth of the Ussuri River. Then - another trip overland along the shores of the River Sungacha and the shores of Lake Khanka, this time through dangerous swamps. That section of the journey saw the horses' hooves affected by a fungal disease which made them lame.

My grandfather was forced to stop in the town of Nikolsk for a whole month before they recovered.

It was only in September of 1892, after ten months of a truly heroic expedition, that six stallions and thirty-three large Tomsk mares stepped on the firm soil of the Sedemi Peninsula. The promise my grandfather gave to Korf as well as his own ambition were satisfied, and future generations of his horses acquired the desired height.

Chapter 2. PROSPERITY

The farm grew and prospered despite the need to ward off attacks from wild animals, such as tigers, leopards and wolves, from the Hung Hu Tse and smugglers. My grandfather saved herds of spotted deer from extinction, first on the Askold Island and later on Sedemi. He saw to it that they were protected from predators and given fodder. Their fawns were captured, reared on cows' milk and domesticated. Occasionally the deer crossed the isthmus and vanished into the thick forest (known as "the taiga"). However, they invariably returned in search of protection from preying animals and humans. Michael erected a fence across the isthmus, which consolidated all the deer into a seven hundred - strong herd grazing in a park. It exists to this day as a state farm called "Amursky".

Soft deer antlers (known as "pantui"), used as medicine by the Koreans, were beginning to bring in rich profits...But to top it all off, Yankovsky was the first Russian citizen to have established a plantation of wild ginseng which he grew on the slopes of a hill called "Proseka" ("A Forest Cutting").

His stud farm played a very important role in the region. P. F. Unterberger, the Governor-General of the Region, spoke very highly of it in his work called "My Notes". Here is what Michael wrote about his farm in a large article, which was published in a magazine called "Stud Farming in the Ussuri Region":

"If I wanted to, I could have followed the example of many resourceful merchants and used the money I made on the Askold Island to purchase land and build houses in Vladivostok which would made me a millionaire. But that would have meant that I would have had to forego any investment in the development of many generations of my horses, in other words, I would not have achieved something which escaped even the almighty Americans, or holders of huge capital. Nobody achieved the same results as I, in mere five to ten years, except, perhaps, some rabbit or pigeon owners."

In the same article he writes that in the first fifteen years of the existence of the farm, more than fifty of his horses and untold numbers of dogs, pigs and cows were killed by tigers, which he referred to as "the scourge of cattle breeding". My grandfather personally killed nine tigers whilst defending his horses and deer. That number did not include a female tiger, which killed a foal during grandfather's absence on business. When a group of riders started pursuing her, she attacked one of them -Michael's assistant, a retired bombardier, a giant by the name of Platon Fedoroff. She dragged him from the saddle but luckily two young Yankovskys, Yuri (my father) and my uncle Alexander, shot her dead. Nevertheless, their favourite mentor Platon received a severe mauling.

Chapter 3. THE SECOND GENERATION AND THEIR OFFSPRING.

Michael and Olga had a large family. In addition to Michael's ex-nuptial son Alexander who was born on the Askold Island, Olga bore her husband another six children: Elizabeth, Yuri (my father), Anna, Yan (Ivan), Serge and Paul.

Serge died in infancy. Lisa married very young. Her husband was a Russian of American descent by the name of Powers. They had nine children. Powers turned out to be a drunk, and Lisa was forced to care for the family, which led to her untimely death. Her younger sister Anna took over the upbringing of her orphaned nephews.

Anna was a sturdily built brown-eyed and brown-haired girl, with a cute upturned nose. She was brave and daring. When she was fourteen years old, she amazed her travelling companions during a journey on the Amur River (there was no railway at the time). When the boat docked for the night, young passengers lit fires and indulged in dangerous jumps over the fierce flames. Anna joined the boys in these games, jumping ever higher, but suddenly her foot got caught in a burning branch and she collapsed into the inferno like a nocturnal butterfly into the flame of a candle.

Everybody was aghast expecting her to turn into a flaming torch at any moment. But Anna quickly jumped out of the fire and dived into the river having sustained only a few superficial burns. The worst damage was to her dress...

The parents sent her to a Western convent in the Japanese town of Yokohama where she became proficient in French and English and acquired a good general education. Nevertheless, she never shunned any work on the family farm. When my father, who was grandfather's right hand man, left for the United States on a three-year study trip, Anna took his place and acquitted herself well. She spent the whole day in the saddle, looking from a distance like a smallish lad. She visited the horse herds, which were scattered over hills and dales of the peninsula, supervised the Korean herdsmen by day and at taught them at night to write in Russian.

The Koreans were not the only people she was educating. She was very close to my father Yuri at that time of her life, and both of them, being avid readers, rather naively hoped to turn all the farm-hands into connoisseurs of the written word.

The quarters of the unmarried stable hands working on the farm were located in a single - storied brick edifice with a pompous name "The Castle". One fine night the young democratically- inclined siblings made their way to that structure armed with a number of what they considered were interesting books.

They were welcomed with open arms. A stable hand by the name of Mitookov was particularly hospitable, making sure that they were seated close to a table lamp. He was a well-built lad, with a well-kept light- brown beard. His hobby was the consumption of copious quantities of methylated spirits.

"Well, Annie and Yurik", he said, "Out with your books! We are all ears!"

My father opened what he thought was an interesting and easily understood novel by Mayne Reid, made himself comfortable at the table and started to read. When he thought that the tale reached a climax, he observed that the audience appeared to be quite attentive although everybody was quietly going about their customary chores, such as mending of clothes. Yuri made a slight pause and looked at Mitookov expecting to be asked to continue. Instead of that, the amiable chief stable- hand said quite nonchalantly:

"You are reading very well from this book, Yura! Let's see if you can read just as fluently from another one!" My father was flabbergasted. He hastily gathered his books and said to his sister: "Let's go, Nita, it seems that our audience is too tired after a hard day's work".

They went outside. The moonlit summer night was warm and peaceful.

"You know, dear sister," said Yuri, "There is absolutely no point in reading to them and I am no longer going to waste my time ". ' Now read from another book ', he mimicked - "they obviously did not understand a thing ".

"Suit yourself", replied Anna. "I will continue reading to them, but the books have to be less complicated ".

"This is entirely up to you. I have other plans now and hope that you will support my request to 'papa' to let me go to America to study the farming business". I know that mother is quite happy with it. And you can promise him to take my place; how about it?

Anna agreed, and kept her word. Yuri was away for three years. He studied progressive farming methods as well as English. He bicycled through several states, worked as a cowboy in Texas and attended the St Louis Agricultural College as a "miscellaneous" student (i.e. one not proceeding to a formal degree).

The Russo-Japanese War started soon after Anna's brother returned to Russia, and our daring aunt hurried to the front, having first completed a nurses' course. Braving bullets and bombs, she rescued the wounded in battle, but survived unscathed, having, however, been infected with the virus of Marxism from which she suffered for the rest of her days.

During the Revolution of 1905 she was racing around with a red flag, took part in meetings and acts of civil disobedience which earned her a prison sentence. She escaped from detention and turned up at the farm of her parents who hid her in a hut in a nearby forest. Somebody alerted the police who searched for her without success. She escaped to Korea in a barge belonging to some Korean friends, from where she caught a boat to Japan. She returned only after the Tsar proclaimed amnesty and settled on the peninsula bearing her father's name.

When her elder sister Lisa passed away, she left behind a wayward husband who neglected his orphaned children. It was left to Anna who never had children of her own, to take on that unfortunate brood. At about that time she became known as "Comrade Galya", which turned into her new first name and all the family started to call her "Galya".

My father who became the principal owner of the greatly developed family farm after grandfather's death, built his sister a separate homestead based on her design. It was located in a so - called "Ozernaya" ("By the Lake") valley with an oblong lake which was separated from the sea by a rocky outcrop and consisted of a two-storied house, a cow - shed and a poultry yard. It was named "Galya's Nest".

Galya married her first cousin who was known as "Victor Piotrovsky The Elder" whose name had a rather interesting origin.... The elder sister of our grandmother, Stepanida, was, like her sister, married to a Polish exile, whose name was Konstantin Piotrovsky (who was the first cousin of Victor Piotrovsky). Their first son was born in 1880. In 1900 he went to fight the Chinese in a war which became known as "The Boxer Rebellion "and disappeared without trace. Their second son was born at the time of Victor's disappearance, and the parents also named him Victor, in memory of their first - born whom they regarded as having fallen in battle. However, "Victor -The - Elder" was merely imprisoned and returned from the war a year later! That's how the family acquired the two Victors.

Auntie Galya gave her affectionate heart to her seven nephews and nieces, affectionately known as "Powersyata" ("Little Powers"), although their upbringing was organised along strictly spartan, revolutionary -proletarian lines.

When I was growing up, three of the them--Olya, Katya and Masha were no longer little kids, but the rest of the "Poweryata "--Vassili, Phillip, Augusta ("Gusta") and Vladimir ("Dodik") were our constant companions. We frequently saw each other, played cowboys and Indians, went fishing together. In winter we used to literally fly our toboggans down the hill from their home to the ice- covered lake where a specially built centrifuge would whirl them in a large circle.

From age four I was an accomplished fisherman. There was a wide road from our home to the seashore, to the horse - shoe shaped Sedemi Bay, which had three jetties. The middle one belonged to our family where our steam launches "Prizrak" ("Phantom") and "Wllis" used to dock. To the right of it was the Brynner jetty, the home of their launch "Voyevoda" ("Commander"). The left jetty was located opposite the estate of the late legendary freedom - loving Captain Gek. It was known as the "Vasyukevich Jetty" because Gek's daughter married a Captain Vasyukevich whose four sons were our childhood friends. Jetties had white swimming enclosures, each complete with a ladder, which led into the water, and a diving board.

I often used to fish from one of them, usually in the company of one of the adults, spending long hours sitting patiently with my fishing rod and bucket. I used to catch a lot of red-fish, smelt, bullheads, and "dog fish" which used to swell up like a balloon after being landed. They would grind their teeth, and often managed to bite through the fishing line. Schools of scamber were some of the rarer visitors to those shores.

One fine day I was being supervised by auntie Galya who was suffering from rheumatism which she contracted as a result of her ordeals during the war and imprisonment. The treatment of her malaise consisted of hot sea water baths. To that end, a railway trolley without wheels, complete with a bath, was installed on the beach opposite the Vasyukevich jetty. The water in the bath was kept warm by a fire. Aunt was lying down on the hot sand feeding the fire, which was burning, under the bathtub; when the water was hot enough she would immerse herself into it up to her neck, at the same time keeping an eye on me.

As for myself, I walked to the edge of the long jetty and made myself comfortable in the swimming enclosure having taken up a position on the top rung of the almost vertical ladder leading into the water. The sea was calm and my float made of cork and kept in position by a goose feather, was peacefully floating on its surface. I never left my eyes off it. On rare occasions when I glanced at the beach I saw auntie's head in a white scarf about forty paces away. She was having her hot bath in the crimson- coloured railway trolley.

All of a sudden, I felt that I was rolling at great speed down the ladder into the water. I cannot tell what caused that accident: it could have been a large fish taking the bait or simply the result of my falling asleep in the hot sun. Be as it may, I found myself rapidly sinking to the bottom. All I can remember is being surrounded by green water and seeing air bubbles above my head. I had not yet learnt to swim but instinctively started to thrash around with my hands and legs, which brought me to the surface. I do not remember whether I unleashed a yell but do remember quite clearly the sight of auntie Galya, her skin red from the hot bath, racing towards me over the timber decking of the jetty. In the meantime, I kept bobbing up and down like a drowning pup, sometimes completely disappearing underwater, swallowing huge quantities of salt water but somehow staying close to the surface, just like my float.

I have no clear recollection of how Galya grabbed me by the scruff of the neck, dragged me out of the water and got me ashore. All I remember is that she was simultaneously berating, undressing and wiping me with a towel, finally drying me in the sun. I heard later that her rheumatism was aggravated as a result of diving into the cold water to rescue me.

Like all Yankovskys she was passionately fond of animals, particularly the spotted deer. And amongst her favourites was a powerful stag called "Krasavets" ("Handsome"). He grew up in a spacious enclosure located next to the house, accepted food out of human hands, allowed to be scratched behind the ears and stroked. His antlers were cut off in autumn, to produce the famous health - giving "Pantui" so valued by the Koreans, after which he was let out into the park occupying two thousand hectares of the mountainous terrain of the Sedemi Peninsula.

After one of his absences in the wild he appeared quite unexpectedly near "Galya's Nest", and Anna ran towards him.

"How are you, Krasavets!" she exclaimed.... Nobody knows what was bugging him, but all of a sudden he attacked Galya in a way reminiscent of a bull charging a toreador during a corrida. He knocked her to the ground and started to gore her with the stumps of his antlers, which were quite hard by that time. If it wasn't for my auntie's upbringing and training he could have quite easily gored her to death. But she managed to escape having slithered like a lizard under the trunk of a fallen tree, which saved her life. Her injuries took quite a while to heal. Her husband was beside himself with anger at "Krasavets" who was practically a domesticated animal. Not being able to forgive him his transgression, he stalked and shot the stag.

Chapter 4. EXODUS.

I was eleven years of age when the Civil War in the Far East forced my parents to consider fleeing abroad. Across the bay from us, in Vladivostok, one uprising followed another: Reds, Whites Chechs and the Japanese --all kept being involved in a never - ending kaleidoscope of horror!

In 1922 the Whites were in retreat, with the battle - front getting ever closer to us. My father, accompanied by his interpreter, a Korean by the name of Ivan Magai went to Seoul to see the Governor - General of Korea, which had for a long time been a Japanese Protectorate. Following his visit he was able to send his half- brother Alexander ("Shoora") in the launch "Prizrak" ("Phantom") to the Korean port of Seisin (now Chongjin) to acquire some dwellings for the family, and others who might have wanted to follow him. My eight-year old brother Arseny and I were making plans for a temporary (of course!) trip to Korea, because everybody was convinced that the emergency was going to last not longer than three years.

In the meantime, our house was being armed to the teeth. Twenty battle-ready "three-line" calibre and "Mexican" rifles, well stocked with ammunition, were stored in my late grandfather's study. They were supplemented by one heavy and two light "Lewis" machine guns and two grenade launchers. The defendants of the peninsula rode every day around its twenty-five-kilometre perimeter. Ussuri Cossacks who were invited to join the defendants, and young family members kept constant watch in concealed dugouts located on the slope of a hill overlooking the bridge over the canal. It was expected that the Hung Hu Tse or Red guerrillas would launch an attack from that direction. Brother and I paid frequent visits to the dugouts, having armed ourselves with short Japanese carbines. We practised our marksmanship on a specially equipped rifle range located under "The Observatory Hill".

During one of the fine days of the summer of 1922 I was returning home from either a fishing trip or after visiting the Brynners (can't remember now). I got to the top of the hill from which I could see the tower of the white castle with a singing harp in the shape of a mermaid located on the top of a mast, together with a fluttering flag with the "Novina" ensign. To the left of it was the figure of auntie Galya dressed in a white blouse and wide black trousers, with a white scarf on her head. She opened the garden gate separating the deer park from the road. It seemed that she was on the way from her "Nest" to the main homestead, perhaps to visit my grandmother. She stopped after noticing me. I caught up with her and we started walking together. Auntie gave me a strange, defiant look.

"Well, I hear you have also decided to go to Korea!", she said.

I muttered:

"Of course; everybody is going ".

EXODUS

Auntie:

"This is a pity. Think about it. You are leaving your Motherland. Let them go if they want to, but you can stay with me and my "Powersyata". Don't you see that our, the people's power, is taking over. It will establish a just order. I have been a revolutionary since 1905 and nobody is going to harm me. On the contrary, we, Bolsheviks, shall be particularly honoured; we have earned it. You and my wards will be with me, and you have nothing to fear. Think about it before it's too late. "

I did not want to upset Galya but told her that I could not desert my parents, brothers and sisters. I remember her parting words:

"You will come to regret your decision. After all, I managed to talk your grandmother into staying and your father has been unable to talk her out of it ".

In early autumn we left for Korea in our ice- breaking launch "Prizrak". Our grandmother stayed behind on the estate with the overseer Ivan Mark. She managed to last there for three years at the end of which time she found out, purely by chance, that the new masters were planning to arrest her. Having faked an illness requiring an operation, she got in touch with some Korean friends, left for Vladivostok and entered the hospital of her acquaintance, Dr. Blumenfeld. Under the cover of the night she fled it in a Korean junk. One fine morning in 1925 we met her on board of that vessel in the port of Seisin.

Grandma lived with us for seven years and ran the household with the assistance of our former Japanese nanny Osada-san. She constantly wrote to her Bolshevik daughter who assured her that all was well.

We buried grandma in 1932 in the Korean cemetery adjacent to our new estate "Novina" which by that time already had a few Russian graves.

In 1936 we buried our mother, followed in 1937 by dear Osada-san who lived with us for twenty-six years.

In 1937 came the news that Galya and Victor Piotrovsky and their step- daughter Lucy were expelled from the Maritime Provinces and sent to the Naryn Region (located in Kyrgyzstan) as "special settlers". Later on they somehow managed to get to Feodosiya, in the Crimea, from where Lucy managed to escape to the United States.

When I was able to visit San Francisco half a century later, Lucy and her American husband Tim lived on the East Coast. We had a long telephone conversation during which she gave me a detailed account of the hardships her aunt and uncle endured in the village of Kolpachevo, located in the lower reaches of the Ob River. They were persecuted for having relatives abroad. The Bolshevik auntie's services to the revolution were of no help at all.

My uncle Victor Junior told me that she hanged herself in Feodosiya.

It would have been indeed "splendid" if I had listened to her advice. I have no doubt at all that I would have been declared "an enemy of the people" long before I was dragged off to Gulag. At least I managed to survive for twenty-five years as an émigré before that event.

Powers Senior and Galya's charges also met with a dreadful fate. And little wonder: her nephews' father was an American, never mind if it was two generations ago! He vanished without trace. One of his sons Basil ("Vassili" in Russian) came with us to Korea and later went to Shanghai. The other -- Phillip-- became a communist. After service in the Red Army he was sent to Korea in 1938 by the NKVD (a precursor to the KGB) in the guise of a fugitive from the regime, to spy on the Yankovskys. However, he was arrested and sentenced immediately after the Reds occupied Korea, the reason given being "a failure to carry out instructions".

Basil prospered in Shanghai, got married had a son, a good job, a solid bank account...But despite all this he fell victim to the propaganda of the patriotically- inclined so-called "Vozvrashentsy" (from the Russian word for "Return", former White Russians who were duped into believing in the goodwill of the Communists). He would not listen to his wife and in 1947, full of fervour to serve The Motherland, boarded the ship "Dostoyevsky" which took him to the port of Nakhodka, near Vladivostok. He and his fellow passengers subsequently earned well-deserved nicknames of "Dostoyevsky's Idiots" (after Dostoyevsky's novel "The Idiot"). They had been promised a welcome, which was to include bouquets of flowers, and a pipe band...The reality was somewhat different: "welcoming" submachine guns. Many of the "Idiots" ended their lives in the concentration camps of the Gulag or in the torture chambers of the NKVD.

Chapter 5. GULAG MEMORIES

......I was thawing out sitting on the lower bunk of a barrack in the Arctic mine of "Krasnoarmeysky" (named after the Red Army : "Krasny" - "red" in Russian), having just finished a ten- hour shift in a dreadfully cold snow- covered field. We were digging holes by hand, preparing the area for the blasting of the overburden. On the Chukotka Peninsula the sun does not rise at all in winter. A constant darkness reigns...All day long all I could think of was the warmth of the barracks. And all of a sudden a messenger from the camp supervisor appears on the scene:

"Get up! 'Godfather' wants you. Hurry! On the double!"

The rosy - cheeked corpulent camp supervisor sits behind a desk in a well-lit office wearing a uniform complete with shoulder stripes. On his feet are white felt boots with leather soles. Papers and photographs are scattered on the desk, a cigarette of the popular brand "Kazbek" is smoking in an ashtray (I can smell the brand from a distance).

I stand to attention on the threshold, and report in accordance with regulations: "Zek (abbreviated Russian name for "prisoner") Yankovsky, sentence in accordance with Articles 58/4, 58/11, 58/14 to 25 years imprisonment, here in accordance with your summons ".

He stirs lazily:

"Come closer to the table. Look. Do you recognise him?"

He points his finger at a photograph lying on the table... Cousin Basil' s face is staring at me from a small picture. "Oh God! Poor Vaska! How the hell did you get here?"

An emaciated inmate, dressed in a threadbare sailor's jumper, a man who has already sampled a large dose of the prison horror... And quite unexpectedly my memory delivers a different picture...

Shanghai, February 1941: Basil's wedding, with the newlyweds at the head of the table, with unending rows of plates, platters and bottles. Basil and I wear dinner suits and dazzlingly white shirts...The ladies are wearing evening gowns....

...In the mirror on the wall of the prison office I see my reflection...I see a dirty- grey worn jacket and my head which every ten days is shaved with a blunt razor by the camp barber when I am having my oblations. A scab from a frostbite is adorning my cheek...The vision from the past is a far-away impossible dream!

"This is my cousin Basil Powers".

"When did you see him last? Who was he working for?"

"I last saw him in Shanghai in 1941. He was managing a dog track. Dog races, you know." "What dog races? These are dogs' tales! He was a Japanese spy!"

"Quite the reverse, citizen supervisor! I heard that when he decided to return to the Motherland, the Japanese Secret Service suspected him of being a Soviet spy. I also heard that they arrested and even tortured him."

"Yeah, yeah, that's when they recruited him and sent him here. They thought that we were fools! Never mind, your cousin will get what he deserves...Anyway, enough of this! Go and have a rest."

This condescending "Have a rest" used by the prison authorities always struck me as a mockingly - benevolent request to "Go and kick the bucket"....

For the past thirty years my works have been published in various magazines, and during all that time many people whom I barely knew, approached editorial boards to enquire about me and wrote me letters, as soon as they became aware of my existence. However, I heard nothing from my cousins whom my auntie was hoping to raise as patriotic Bolsheviks. I enquired about them from the Gulag Central Administration Office and, at long last, received the following communication: "Phillip, son of Basil, Powers. Born in 1907. Died in a camp in the Irkutsk Region of heart failure in November of 1949. No information is available about Basil, son of Basil, Powers."

I fear that in the horrendous mincer of the so- called "repressions" (this "politically correct" euphemism is used by the present Russian regime instead of the accurate expression, "murder by the State") which took place in the notorious year of 1937, followed by equally terrifying forties and fifties, Basil and Phillip Powers lost their innocent naive shaggy-haired heads. They became the minced meat of Stalin's blood-sodden terror.

Chapter 6. POTPOURRI OF THE FAMILY HISTORY

My grandfather published quite a few articles in the "Transactions of the Society for The Exploration of The Amur Region". Here are their titles:

"The Askold Island"

"Tigers, leopards and deer "

"Horse- breeding in the South -Ussuri Region "

"The Discovery of Remnants of Ancient Sculleries on the Shores of The Amur Bay"

The shell mounds left behind by the original inhabitants of the area now known as "The Maritime Provinces" and discovered by my grandfather are referred to by present-day archaeologists as "The Yankovsky Culture".

Michael Yankovsky was a member of the Society mentioned above and made donations towards a fund established for the building of its offices. That building exists to this day.

The names of thirteen of the Society's members have been entered on its Board of Honour, which bears the inscription: "Their names are an undying component of the history of the Far East". His name occupies the seventh place, after the names of such luminaries as Admiral Makarov, Arsenyev, Boussier and Margaritov.

Yankovsky was awarded the Gold Orders of Stanislaus -- First and Second Class-- and St.Anne's Order, Second Class. He was the recipient of many gold and silver medals. Amongst them were the medals of the "Honourable Moscow Society of Agriculture "and "The Chief Directorate of State Horse breeding". Two military medals were awarded to him for "The Chinese Campaign" and for the participation in the Russo-Japanese War of 1904-1905.

Seventeen subspecies of butterflies first described by Yankovsky bear his name, as well as several species of caterpillars and birds. For example, he discovered the "Yankovsky Bunting" which inhabits a tiny area around Posyet where the borders between China, Korea and Russia meet. Botany knows the name of "Yankovsky's Sedge". He also helped our grandmother Olga to put together a valuable herbarium, which she donated to the local museum.

Grandma made an enormous contribution to our Sedemi estate. She was agile like quicksilver and completely tireless to boot. I still remember her in her dark skirt, with a bonnet on her greying hair, always with a bunch of rattling keys on the belt. She was in charge of all storerooms and all the numerous servants. But I never remember her utter a single swearword. I shall have more to say about her later.

As far as grandpa was concerned, he contracted a severe form of pneumonia following his many travels, including one to China (Manchuria) in pursuit of the Hung Hu Tse bandits. Doctors advised him to spend some time in a drier, continental climate. He left his eldest son (my father Yuri) and wife in charge of the estate and paid several visits to Moscow, finally building himself a house in Semipalatinsk (in present- day Kazakhstan) and settling there. In the last years of his life he would only visit the Sedemi Peninsula during warm autumn months. Michael Ivanovich Yankovsky died in the town of Sochi (Crimea) and was buried there in 1912.

His children's life paths were all different.

The eldest son Alexander, a dreamer and adventurer, asked his father for his share of the value in the estate at the end of the century and used it to seek a fortune in America. He took part in the construction of the Suez Canal and prospected for gold in Alaska. Having become a gambler he lost the gold and returned home where he married and worked as an architect in the town of Nikolayevsk-on -The Amur. With the aid of our mother, Alexander designed our home (which was known as "The Castle") at Sedemi. Many homes and the church in Novina (Korea) were also designed by him. My uncle designed and supervised the construction of a unique suspension bridge in Novina. The structure spanned the local river Ompo, with its supports located on each of the shores of the stream.

Towards the end of his life in Korea Alexander Michailovich ("son of Michael") was engaged in preparing entomological collections for distribution in Germany and America. He liked to spend some time in the winter months hunting on his own. During one of these trips in the winter of 1944, he caught a severe cold and was forced to stop in a remote hamlet called Nonsandon. Having heard of his illness, my brother Arseny rushed to Alexander's side, and uncle died in his arms.

Yuri (my father) and Yan married two sisters, called Margaret and Angelina who were the daughters of a prominent Vladivostok merchant, Michael Grigoryevich ("son of Gregory") Shevelev.

Yan, just like his sister Anna ("Comrade Galya "), graduated from an Anglo - French College in Yokohama. He was also a graduate of the Vladivostok Marine School. He was a tall and handsome man and a very kind and warm-hearted person. Having obtained his share of the family fortune from his father, he organised a deer - breeding co-operative on the Gamov Promontory, near the Korean border. There he built a beautiful home, which looked like a castle. The business was very successful, but a disaster soon followed: in January 1925 he caught a heavy cold which turned into what was then known as "The Spanish Influenza". He was only 35 when he died leaving behind a widow and two daughters: Geliana and Marianna.

Uncle Yan's abandoned home still exists in the "Vityaz" ("The Knight's") Bay. Aunt Angelina married soon after his death. Her husband, Captain Kichigin, turned out to be a ne'er do well drunk. Together they fled to Korea where Kichigin's daughter, Joanna, was born. From Korea the family moved to Shanghai. There the daughter of a prosperous merchant and a former lady of the manor, became a professional masseuse and used her newly- acquired skills to support her family for many years.

The youngest of Michael's sons, Paul, a short powerfully- built lad also studied in Japan. During the First World War he volunteered for military service. He was awarded the St. George's Cross for bravery. In 1916 he was sent to France as a member of an Auxiliary Force which was dispatched there to assist Russia's ally. He refused to accept the Russian Revolution and joined the French armed forces, returning to his native Vladivostok after the Allied victory.

He married a refugee from Petrograd (now St Petersburg) Natalia Nikolayevna ("Daughter of Nicholas") Romasheva who at that time was our music teacher at Sedemi. (The Romashevs were members of the professional Naval officers' class. Nataly's uncle Serge was an officer of The Far Eastern Fleet).

They fled to Korea with us, where Natalia gave birth to a daughter in 1923 whom they called Tatiana (Tanya for short). Their son Michael(1936-1952) was born some years later, when they moved to Shanghai.

Pavel Michailovich spoke five languages, among them Japanese and Chinese. Having held an officer's rank in the French Army, in the late thirties he was granted a senior commission in the French Police Force which existed at that time on the French Concession in Shanghai. My uncle was a very honest and just man who enjoyed great popularity, particularly among young people. Pavel served in the French Police for ten years. His life was ended by a terrorist bullet.

My father Yuri Michailovich studied at the Vladivostok Boys' High School. As I already mentioned, having turned twenty he sailed to America where he studied agriculture at the St Louis, Mississippi, Agricultural College which he attended as a "miscellaneous" student, i.e. without proceeding to a formal degree. He worked on the cowboy ranches of Texas acquiring the skills of that occupation. On the trip home in 1902 Yuri bought four thoroughbred stallions whose offspring formed the basis of high-class trots and horse- races in Vladivostok. He took part in many races as a jockey and a rider, having won many prizes.

Having taken over his father's enterprise, he showed great enthusiasm in the development of horse - breeding and deer farming and in the expansion of his father's ginseng farm. Yuri established professional fisheries and conducted rice-growing experiments. He built horse stables in the vicinity of the Vladivostok racecourse where every summer season he housed several dozen of his racing and trotting horses.

On the southern shore of the "Taboonnaya" ("Horse Herd") Bay he built two "dachas" (summer-houses) for the use by the family, friends and relatives. Twice he enlarged his father's fortress-like house.

Yuri took over his father's duties as head of the Anti - Hung Hu Tse Organisation of the Posyet Region. These activities earned him decorations from the leadership of the city and local government authorities. A well - equipped "Druzhina" (voluntary fighting detachment) was the result of his efforts. On many occasions he led his men in gun battles against the bandits. A bandit's bullet left a hole in the crown of his hat after one of these encounters.

He was an alderman on the City Council and a member of the Executive Committee of the "Society for the Development of Horse breeding". Yuri often spoke at the Society's meetings held in the city of Khabarovsk, and was awarded a silver medal for his efforts in agriculture.

The horses of the Yankovsky family won a large number of trophies in numerous equestrian events. Amongst them were dozens of gold and silver medals, glass holders vases, silver cutlery, as well as a large assortment of silver goblets inlaid with semi-precious stones from the Ural Mountains. Particularly valuable was a huge silver bowl, with engravings of horses on its handles, which was the trophy awarded in commemoration of the three-hundredth anniversary of the Royal House of Romanoffs. There were also three bucket-sized goblets, each weighing between five and six kilograms.

The first children's horse races in Vladivostok were held in 1919. My sister Muza won the first prize in the Senior Group. The second prize was won by another sister, the future poetess Victoria. I won the Junior Race on a fast grey mare called "Myshka" ("Little Mouse"). I kept the medal I received for that event for many years. It depicted a rider inside the engraving of a stirrup and had the following inscription: "Children's Races, P.O.P.K. ("Society for the Development of Horse-breeding in the Maritime Provinces"), First Prize, 1918". That golden medal was one of the heirlooms stolen by the first members of the Soviet military who visited our "Tiger Hamlet" where I lived with my young wife Irma in 1945. She trustingly left it in our bedroom when going into the kitchen to make some tea for our guests.

The most interesting outcome of the races was the victory of my brother Arseny on a fat pie-bald pony called "Pupsik" ("Dolly") because he was just five! I think that was some sort of a record, even though we were being taught horse riding, shooting and swimming from a very early age.

Returning to the story of my parents I must say that whereas our grandmother was the "commanding officer" of the Sedemi estate, our mother, Margarita Michailovna ("daughter of Michael") was the heart of its intellectual life. She loved literature, was a bit of a poetess and thespian, producing plays on a stage and in the open (in the forest). Mother selected talented actors among the young people. She was the first one to notice the talent of her cousin, Katerina Ivanovna Kornakova, who later married the famous actor Alexei Dikoy and became the favourite pupil of the immortal producer Stanislavsky.

Mother was a marvellous story-teller. This endeared her to authors Balmont and Arsenyev who used to be our guests on the Peninsula. The Japanese philosopher Moichi Yamaguchi was another one of her friends, as were many prominent actors. She passed on her love for the theatre, poetry and literature to the young people who surrounded her. It was therefore natural that it was with an enormous heartache that she was forced to abandon our castle- like house, which had been designed by her.

Chapter 7. KOREA. GETTING ON OUR FEET.

The history of life of the Yankovskys in Korea is most unusual. Being a self - confessed optimist and fatalist, Yuri Michailovich took too long to prepare for emigration. His biggest mistake was his belief that things would turn out, as he wanted them to. That was the time when many well-to-do people in The Maritime Provinces started to make plans to leave the motherland two or three years ahead of the impending disaster. They began to sell their properties and shift their capital into foreign banks. Many laid the groundwork for a new life in Japan, Manchuria or China.

However, Yuri kept waiting for a change in the military situation in favour of the White Armies. He had every chance to sell off about five hundred horses, a few hundred pairs of precious soft deer antlers ("pantui") and thousands of roots of ginseng. He could have acquired substantial holdings of land in Korea in good time. By the way, the laws of Japan, which at the time was in charge of Korea, did not prohibit such transactions, with foreigners being allowed to hold valid land titles.

There was nothing to stop my father from transporting one or two hundred spotted deer to such land holdings in his barges and motor boats. The plantation of ginseng would have been particularly easy to transport by loading the plants into moss-filled boxes.

Instead, alas, the evacuation in the autumn of 1922 started late and had to be carried out in a hurry. The "Willis" motor boat and the Ford motor car were abandoned in Vladivostok. The caged deer stayed on the shores of the Peninsula. When we arrived in Korea our total property holdings consisted of a small block of land on a hillside in a small port city of Seisin (now called Chongjin) which contained two huts, and a small area on a sandy vacant lot on the outskirts of the town which was to be used for horse stables. There were a total of sixty voluntary human exiles and sixty thoroughbred racehorses, which father spirited over the border with the help of the guards from the Peninsula, because he was incapable of abandoning his beloved mounts.

That crowd made short work of all the food and money which were collected in the Maritime Provinces at the very last moment.

The horses were lost. Father's "trusted comrades-in-arms" were accompanying them to a sale in Tientsin (in China) but sold them "on the side" instead, and disappeared with the money. The people who came with us had to be allowed to go to China or Manchuria, depending upon individual wishes, and had to be given fares and some money to start a new life. Those who decided to stay and the members of our family experienced the full brunt of the émigré life.

During the first year of our stay in Korea, the children (my sibs and I) attended a Japanese school, at the same time studying the curriculum of the Russian "Gymnasia" (high-class school), since there were many good teachers among the refugees. We thus learned Japanese and European languages. The Korean language was picked up as a by-product of playing with the local kids.

Work and study were combined. The family was making "Pirozhki" (Russian pies) and sold them in our mixed business, which included hardware sold on consignment from a German firm with headquarters in Tientsin. We sold boxed containers of kerosene from a cart, which we dragged around the city. Salted and smoked herring and "Ivasi" (a Japanese fish) were sent to the City of Harbin. Some of us were working as builders' labourers. Others were catching butterflies and preparing them for export to Germany. No longer having any horses, we children (both boys and girls) worked as paid professional jockeys at the races organised by the Japanese.

We weren't exactly starving, but the food rations were very meagre and had little variety: fish, rice, and potatoes. We lived in terribly congested Korean huts, which was very hard to take. Gradually we started to make money from hunting, although during the first years of our life in Korea, father was the only real provider. He was strict and demanding, but it must be said that he was an indestructible human being, who carried in him an inexhaustible supply of energy and initiative.

It was he who organised hunting expeditions for foreign hunters who paid for that privilege. My brother Arseny and I were employed as huntsmen. During the first decade of our life in Korea we shepherded dozens of hunters' groups from America, Canada, Sweden, Spain and England.

The first foreign visitors came from the residents of the capital, Seoul, but later, due to advertising, the catchment area was extended to Shanghai, Harbin, Tientsin and finally-- Europe. On several occasions requests for a safari were addressed to "Yankovsky, Korea".

Starting with our grandfather, hunting was the favourite pastime of our family (not in the role of paid huntsmen, of course). Nevertheless, a considerable part of my and my two brothers' youths were spent in just that role. When I was 16 and brother Arseny just 13, we were employed as staff "Legionnaires" in a "Tiger Safari" organised for the representative of the Los Angeles Museum. Mr Reid (that was the man's name) was a former cowboy and a powerfully built individual. Our monthly wage was 105 Japanese yen each, whereas the monthly wage of a casual labourer was 40 to 50 yen and an unskilled female worker was paid 30 sen (cents) for eight hours of a hard day's toil.

The expedition lasted for almost two months during which time we travelled in a large circle over the hills and through the forests of North Eastern Korea but unfortunately did not manage to hunt down a tiger. Tigers were becoming scarce. On one occasion, with the assistance of 22 hounds brought to Korea by Mr Reid, we pursued a tiger all the way to the Tumangan River, which forms the border with Manchuria. Our customer told us that his hounds used to accompany him on Lion Safaris. He and my father pursuit the unfortunate beast on horseback, with the rest of us "trotting" behind them under our own steam. The old cowboy was beside himself. He galloped through the "taiga" (native forest) like a man possessed, all the while encouraging his hounds with the screams of "Lion! Lion!!" But the tiger escaped unscathed into Manchuria.

My father wounded a large male lynx and sent me in pursuit of its blood - spattered trail, although this was a very dangerous task. I found the huge cat but must confess that I broke out in cold sweat when behind a snow-covered bush I saw staring at me a grey head, complete with bushy black- tipped ears. Luckily the animal was dead, having turned into a frozen mummy. It took us twenty-four hours to catch up with the rest of the expedition, which was resting in a God-forsaken village. A Korean porter was lugging our trophy on his back as we followed the other hunters' trail, having had to scale a huge mountain pass on our way.

As we were standing in the yard of their hut, we overheard a funny dialogue. Our young uncle Victor was asking Mr Reid to let him listen to some of his records. He was saying :

"Mr Reid, record player, please!" Reid was jokingly replying through his secretary - interpreter count Michael Olsoofyev whom he engaged in Harbin: "Michael, please tell Victor that my record player can only work when it is lubricated with lynx oil".

I shouted: "Open the door! The lynx is here!".... The boss was extremely pleased.

Later we had visits from Swedes, Spaniards and Englishmen. The famous Swedish author and traveller Stan Bergman arrived with an assistant and a Japanese cook and established himself in one of our "dachas" (summer-houses) which was equipped with central heating. I accompanied him on a hunting expedition during which we killed several wild boars. He devoted a whole chapter in his book "In the wilds of Korea" to our exploits, giving high praise to my and brother Arseny's hunting talents.

...Our family always aimed to please a guest. Father frequently remembered the time when he pleased the Governor of The Maritime Provinces. A group of beaters ("battue") was organised to drive some deer towards an ambush where the honoured guest was waiting for them. All of a sudden a handsome male with large horns appeared in front of the Governor who clumsily missed his prey. My father who was standing nearby immediately dispatched the noble beast by a shot from his powerful rifle. Whilst running towards the fallen stag with the unlucky marksman, he conceived a way to please him. Turning over the fallen carcass and pointing to the large exit hole left by his own bullet, he exclaimed to the out-of- breath head of the Province: "Here you are, Your Eminence! This is the hole made by your large calibre gun!" This made the day for the mug shooter...

Bergman, I and his Korean valet who was carrying his clumsy camera, spare shoes and socks, had been pursuing a herd of wild boars over steep hills from the early morning. The animals left their lairs after midday and I realised that they were very close to us. Very carefully I started leading our guest towards them. I peered from behind a dimly illuminated mountain ridge and saw a large boar on the adjacent slope standing tense and motionless in a dark hollow, to the north of my position. It was foraging in the deep snow and kept covering itself with it, which made it look uncannily like a fallen log. Only a slight trace of steam rising from one end of that "log" indicated the presence of a living thing.

Bergman was standing almost next to me but unfortunately was unable to see anything except the dense forest. Sensing that our quarry was about to bolt and disappear out of sight, I lifted my rifle and took aim. "For God's sake", rasped the Swede, and all of a sudden saw the wild pig. And then, curse it, he made another three steps forward and rested his rifle on the branch of a young oak tree...He was obviously too excited to fire his weapon without support! I was convinced that all was lost but the stupid animal was still waiting for something. It heard a noise but could not see us.... Bergman kept taking aim. Finally ---- bang! It looked like he slightly wounded the boar and it raced ahead like a torpedo. It would have most probably escaped, but I caught its dark brown body in the sights of my rifle. A shot, and the pig rolled over. I even managed to kill another animal while all this was going on.

I am sure the Swede understood full well who killed the boar but I managed to persuade him that the pig was his trophy. We moved both carcasses and put them side by side. I explained to our Korean porter how to aim and fire the camera and, perhaps, for the first and last time in his life he successfully took such a photo. That photograph appeared in Mr. Bergman's book, in the chapter describing a wild pig hunt in the Korean mountains.

Late one night our Novina received a visitor in the person of a member of The House of Lords who, accompanied by his wife, arrived directly from London. He was a swarthy stockily built gentleman. His wife was a tall skinny redhead who was four months pregnant, which was obvious from her rounded tummy.

The couple planned to stay for two weeks and asked us to organise a hunt for large beasts. In accordance with our tradition of taking turns, this time it was Arseny who was the organiser of the hunt. I took the hunting party, their luggage and guns to a remote village on the Tumangan River, called Nonsandon, and returned home. There was no snow in November of that year which augured badly for the success of a safari. Even though almost all the leaves had fallen and the ground was frozen, it was practically impossible to see the animal tracks. But our guests turned out to be very difficult and demanding.

From the very start of the hunt Arseny was killing deer, with the Chinese cook turning them into stews and soups, but there was no sign of large game. The peer became very nervous: "Your deer are not what I want! We are not really interested in their little hides and tiny horns! What we want are dead bears or wild boars. It is about time, Arseny, for you to show whether you are any good as a hunter!"

My brother spoke good English but instead of replying in kind, he was obliged to be polite to his employer. He looked the Englishman straight in the eye: "All right, sir, even though the absence of snow is making my job very difficult, I am going to show you what sort of a hunter I am!"

On the following day he assigned a Korean tracker to the guests and went hunting on his own. Without hindrance from the "helpers" who stymied his efforts through their chatter and noisy progress through fallen leaves, my brother made a silent approach to a large boar who was foraging in an oak grove. Having killed the animal, Arseny returned to the hut while it was still light to enlist the help of its owner. The Korean farmer harnessed a bull and the slaughtered beast was brought to the camp at the same time as the "helpers" returned from their daily trip. His lordship apologised for his short temper conceding that the earlier outburst was uncalled for...

Shortly after that episode Arseny discovered a water-filled hole in the ground which, judging from the surrounding tracks, was frequently visited by a huge boar. He announced his discovery to the customers during the evening meal adding that the beast was not visiting its "bath" every night and that in any case it would be difficult to kill it because the nights were moonless at the time of the expedition. All of a sudden her ladyship made a request "I want to go there tomorrow! Show me the way and I'll take my warm clothing so that I can watch out for the boar throughout the night and till dawn, if necessary. I absolutely must leave The Land of the Morning Mist with a worthwhile trophy! "

Nobody was able to convince her that the cold and dark conditions made the success of her undertaking practically impossible. That daughter of Albion was unshakeable in her resolve. The following night Arseny and a Korean guide escorted her ladyship to the boar's "bath", organised a place for an ambush and returned to the hut, secretly amused by the conduct of the "half-witted pregnant English woman". After dinner they spread out on the warm "kans" (hard beds built over flue pipes taking the hot air from the stove of a hut to the chimney), ready for a night's rest. His lordship climbed into his eiderdown sleeping bag, staying, as always outside, because he could not stand the smells of a native dwelling.

At the crack of dawn there was an almighty noise in the yard. A flushed peeress bounded in, screaming: "Get up! I shot him! I shot him! ". It was unbelievable but true. She did kill the defenceless animal, and took with her to London its lower jaw which was hacked out for her out of its head, complete with beautiful tusks, polished through long use. The boar's rough bristly hide joined the tusks on the way to London. This confirms an old Russian saying: "A determined woman can even force the Devil himself to laugh".

Our family of hunters had what amounted to a cult of weaponry, particularly rifled guns. Army rifles of various makes: so-called "three-liners" as well as Arisaks, Mowsers, Springfields, and, of course, Enfills were subject to modifications. The fore-ends of the rifle stocks were partly removed so as to make them lighter; the pyramid-like foresights were converted to spheres mounted on long thin necks. The spheres were adjusted to give a range of 200 metres, after which the supporting frames were securely fastened to avoid any chance of shifting when scraping past tree branches. In summer the front sights were painted white using an enamel, and in winter they were blackened with the flame from a match. White horse hairs were installed in the slits of the gun sights, which helped to take accurate aim in poor light conditions. The front sights were protected with small horns or rings.

In winter a rifle had to be wrapped in a flannelette blanket before being taken indoors. This allowed it to thaw out slowly, which eliminated rusting. All guns were left to warm up during tea or dinner-time after which they were thoroughly cleaned. A rifle butt had a hollow section where every hunter kept small brushes made from hemp, to which were attached little lead sinkers. A sinker, in turn, was affixed to a rope, which contained a loop designed for the attachment of a piece of soft cloth. Two hunters sat opposite each other, each in turn drawing the brushes through the barrel of a gun, thus cleaning it. We never went to bed without first cleaning our guns.

With the passage of years we were starting to catch up with our father, making more money when hunting on our own than when escorting paying hunters. We were also helped by our very capable kid brother Yuri who was rapidly growing up. Guests were becoming a burden. However, father considered it rude to refuse his services to old clients, and therefore when a Seoul resident Doctor Butts, a Canadian missionary, asked father to organise a safari for him and his friends, dad agreed, albeit very reluctantly.

The missionary arrived on the evening of the day he received the okay. His party was equipped with modern rifled guns, the only exception being an American youngster by the name of Roy who sported a smooth- barrelled gun of the twelfth calibre.

We started from a railway station called Chumpeeong from which we travelled in sleighs over a winding track, crossing a steep snow- covered mountain pass, to the hut of our old friend nick-named "Makar" . His real name was Yu Min. He was lame and had a long moustache, which made him look like a gangster.

Our companion on that and all other trips undertaken in those years was our cook Ivan Tchon Chan Gynn. He deserves a special aside...

...Ivan was a living legend. He ran away from his home in Korea when he was just a boy to live in Vladivostok and in later years proudly remembered serving as a navigator on the motor boat "Rynda" which belonged to our relatives, the Brynner family. He piloted "Rynda" to the Brynners' silver and tin mines in the Bay of Tetyukhe, combining that employment with the position of a secret agent of the Police Chief in Vladivostok. Ivan would press his finger against his large "Mephistopheles" nose flare his nostrils to imitate the appearance of a bloodhound and say: "My nose, same thing like dog nose. Who go where, who what do --I everything understand. Master police boss, he always says: ' Ivan, you champion!'" . He chattered in a pidgin, which was easily understood by the inhabitants of the Far East but was absolutely incomprehensible to former residents of Central Russia.

Being a loveable rogue, cynic, womaniser and jester, a veritable life of a party, that illiterate man was a talented practical joker. On one occasion our guest Mr. Butts made a fuss over the fact that Ivan served a hot meal on a cold plate which resulted in a reprimand from my father. The following day when being served a meal on a plate, the good doctor let our an almighty scream and dropped it on the floor: "This goddamned barbarian has served me a meal on a red-hot plate!" he roared...Ivan, who was immediately summoned by my father asked his boss to touch the plate: "Take, Yuri Mikauchi! The plate, it is nice warm!". Dad touched the plate and commented: "Mr. Butts, the plate is really barely warm; sorry, I don't understand the problem".

Late that night, when father and the guests had retired, Ivan beckoned to Arseny and me from the kitchen: "Come, see how I teach American Face lesson!".... What this character did was to heat a small section of the plate over a powerful flame, having marked the spot with soot. The guest was handed that section, with my father testing the opposite side...

We organised a few large bateaus for Mr Butts, with beaters forming a human chain extending over ridges and glens, which surrounded the valley of the Tumangan River. The quarry was chased up the hill, with the guest shooters standing on the ridges. All they were able to kill in two days were two young roes. Unfortunately there was no sign of wild pigs.

By the third day father decided to change tactics. He concentrated on a flat height to which led a few ridges. The beaters started to ascend them in the direction of the plateau. Somehow I found myself separated from the rest of the party and was the first one to get to the top. Having barely caught my breath I noticed a black shadow lurking between the trees. This was a young boar heading in my direction. When he was about one hundred metres away, I yelled: "Cuckoo!". The poor fellow stopped, listening to the unfamiliar sound. The first bullet made him jump. He tried to escape by making small hops, but the second and third bullets stopped him in his tracks. His legs were jerking for a while as he lay mortally wounded on his side, but soon he became motionless. He died beside an oak tree felled by a recent storm...

I put my rucksack and binoculars on the trunk of that tree and leaned my rifle against it. Having cleared a small area of snow with my boots, I started a fire and began to disembowel my prey. Warmly clad human figures, attracted by the smoke, appeared in the sparse forest. Grey suede coats belonged to the organisers of the hunt, with the guests dressed in khaki army jackets.

Everybody congratulated me on my success. Another tree trunk was dragged to the fire, with the men making themselves comfortable in anticipation of a meal...I extracted the liver from the warm carcass, followed by the heart and kidneys. My companions cut them up, applying generous quantities of salt. The pieces were then pierced by skewers and placed over the embers of the burning oak. Somebody produced a few cloves of garlic kept for such an occasion and garnished the purple liver...Hot embers made it swell. The air was filled with the hissing noise of cooking flesh. Small craters of creaking meat were forming on its surface. The liver changed its colour from purple to yellow-brown. It exuded an appetising smell...We made tea from snow, which we thawed out in our billies. Chopped twigs of a Chinese "Lemon Plant" were used instead of the real thing. The meal was delicious...

When we finished, Roy, the young American, announced that he "wanted to join Valery" . It was obvious that he had come to the conclusion that luck would follow me today and for the rest of the safari. We felt obliged to accede to his request. Father held four sticks of different lengths in his mitten and asked the guests to draw lots. The shortest stick said "North", the next one "East", etc. Roy drew "West" and we took off in that direction. The road took us into a deep ravine after which we started to climb a long ridge leading to our camp. We were bypassing dense groves of young oaks and walnuts, which had not yet shed their brown leaves and were halfway up the hill when I noticed a wild pig. It looked black against the background of snow and was crossing the top of the ridge, which was too far removed from our position for an accurate shot. I was well experienced in estimating distances by eye and guessed that the quarry was about 400 metres away. Was it worth my while risking the waste of a few cartridges which were very scarce (we needed a special permission to import them twice a year from Shanghai, buying them there through the members of The Russian Volunteer Corps)?

However, my companion also noticed the boar. He pointed in the direction of the intended victim and rasped: "Shoot! Shoot!" I succumbed to his plea and, after taking a careful aim, fired three shots in rapid succession from my "Lee Enfield" rifle. The boar suddenly rolled over, slid down the hill and lay still after hitting a shrub. The American was beside himself with joy. He was jumping up and down and waving his arms....

At that very moment a tiny yearling piglet appeared as if from nowhere. He was running for his dear life down an incline, resembling a flea. There was no way I would have murdered the pathetic little creature but Roy screamed with renewed vigour: "Shoot him! Shoot him!". This made up my mind... I sat down resting my elbows on the knees and held my breath. The piglet suddenly stopped as if listening to a familiar sound...His right flank was turned towards me. The distance between us was about 600 metres. I corrected my aim to accommodate the distance, and -- WHAM!!!... My victim lay motionless...

The joy of my hunting mate was indescribable... "You killed these creatures at a distance of half a mile!", crowed he.

"Let's pace out the distance", I said.

We were half way through that exercise when a grey hare bounded out of the undergrowth and tried to escape by making huge leaps to the left and away from us. I whispered: "Roy, hit him!" simultaneously emitting a sharp whistling sound. The grey creature stopped in its tracks, only to be killed by the first shot from the youngster. The lad bounded towards his victim, grabbed him by the ears and raced back to me. I shook his hand, untied his rucksack and stuffed the warm body of the prey into it...

The distance from my shot to the boar turned out to be more than six hundred paces, with about eight hundred paces to the little one. We disembowelled them, placed them side by side on the ground, covering the carcasses with branches of oak and fresh snow. In order to keep away wolves and foxes, we provided the cover of heavy logs with a further snow cover, into which were driven twigs with spent cartridges mounted on them. At the same time I established that I practically missed the little fellow: I aimed at his flank but the bullet hit him in the eye!

It was getting dark. Having finished the task of securing the carcasses, we started walking towards the path leading to our friend Makar's hut. When we were nearly there, we heard a loud noise and saw a hazel-hen flying out of the snow and landing on the branch of a nearby tree. For some reason Roy became very nervous. Breathing heavily, he took aim for an incredibly long time, with the unsuspecting bird waiting to be slaughtered... It fell like a stone. I naturally praised the lad.

We got to the hut late and in total darkness because Roy was very tired and on several occasions I had to stop and wait for him. The rest of the group was waiting for us to join them for dinner. We stopped in front of the entrance door, which was decorated with paper stuck to its surface, and took the cartridges out of our guns making a lot of noise with the gun locks in the process. Somebody opened the squeaking door and gave us the woollen blankets into which we wrapped our weapons whilst still in the frosty air, before crossing the high threshold into the living area. No sooner did we appear inside than my beaming companion ripped the hat from his head screaming in a falsetto:

"Listen gentlemen! I have shot a hazel - hen and a hare today!". This drew a universal applause. Roy collapsed on a straw mat lying on top of the warm "khan" and added in a flat non-chalant tone: "Well, and Valery also managed to kill two wild pigs".

That statement sounded so childishly innocent that it brought the house down. The lad was blinking his eyes, obviously not comprehending the real reason for the merriment of his elders

Chapter 8. KOREA. THE TURNING POINT.

The turning point in our life in Korea was due to pure chance. Father sold the motor car we brought with us from Sedemi, a so - called "Humpmobile" to the owner of a holiday resort near the "Kaneta" hot springs in the vicinity of a railway station called "Shuotsu", forty kilometres from the port city with a Japanese name of Seisin (now known by its Korean name of Chongjin, located in present- day North Korea). The new owner of the car invited us to his property. We spent the night in a veritable eldorado consisting of small cottages covered in fragrant runners of flowering wisteria. Our chauffeur, Vissarion Ipatyevich ("Son of Ipatyi") Vorobey ("Sparrow"-surname) told us that there existed in the mountains further away from Kaneta another group of hot springs called "Ompo".

A bus service could have taken us there but because we were short of money for such a luxury, we decided to walk. After walking for about ten "versts" (Russian measure of distance, with one "versta" equal to about one kilometre) and passing a hamlet built in the vicinity of some hotsprings and containing two guest-houses, we found ourselves in a lovely deep valley surrounded by tall mountains. In it was a small settlement consisting of two Korean huts with thatched roofs. We made arrangements with their owners to rent a couple of rooms for summer and moved in a few days later. We had to bring some tents to our new abode because the small huts could not accommodate our numerous family.

These were the first steps towards the creation of our future "Novina" . As I already mentioned, the word "Novina" means "a short dagger" in Old-Polish, and that dagger is depicted at the centre of our family crest. Having established a Russian settlement and health resort, we gave it the ancient name of our family, and "Novina" became a very popular holiday destination with the Russian émigrés who resided in Korea, Manchuria, China and Japan. It was also very popular with many overseas visitors who praised that "Jewel of The Land of The Morning Mist"

"Novina" was the brainchild of my parents. Father managed to raise the necessary capital for its creation from Harbin banks and from our distant relatives --the brothers Brynner. He gradually paid off the loans and became the owner of large tracts of farming land, orchards and forest. However, it was Mother who was, without any shadow of a doubt, the soul of that haven for exiled Russians. Their children (my siblings and I) also made a major contribution to the future prosperity of Novina through their work and enthusiasm.

The summer of 1925 saw us living in tents and huts, and making the first modest purchase of a narrow sliver of land on the shores of the local river. But by 1926 we managed to build a few ill-equipped shanties covered with galvanised iron, followed by the first real house we called "The Catamaran" . And 1927 saw the appearance of a large house designed in the shape of a letter "T". It was built on a rock above the river and had high foundations made from river boulders. It had walls made from larch boards and a stainless steel roof. The combined drawing--room and bedroom boasted a huge bed and a large fireplace made from bush rock. The kitchen was adjacent to that room.

Uncle Paul Michailovich used adobe bricks to built a house for his family.

A two - storied tower was built for my parents, complete with a balcony and a flagpole. A sturdy but somewhat primitive suspension bridge spanned the river.

The summer of 1928 signalled the beginning of rapid growth of Novina. Well-to-do émigrés and overseas people started to buy 300 - "tsubo" (a "tsubo "is a Japanese measure of land equal to six - by - six feet or about two - by-two metres) blocks of land and to commission the construction of small and large holiday homes. The first homes were built with our labour, with the later ones built by hired tradesmen. The sale of land enabled my father to increase his land holdings.

We expanded our landholdings to the shores of the Pacific Ocean which were located 18km from Novina, near a railway station called "Ruyken ". There the railway line runs parallel to a long sandy beach, and father acquired substantial landholdings in that area, calling the estate "Lukomorye", after a poem by great Pushkin.

Holiday homes of lovers of seaside holidays soon followed his purchase.

Chapter 9. NOVINA AND LUKOMORYE ---VARIOUS EPISODES

1. BUTAMOCHI

Natalie Nikolayevna ("daughter of Nikolai") Chirkina, the wife of the former Russian Consul in Seoul, and I were travelling from the mountain resort of Novina to the seaside resort of Lukomorye. A bus took us to the Shuotsu station. The whistlestop station of Ruyken, Lukomorye's railway access, was the next one after Shuotsu. A neatly dressed Japanese lad was selling sweet Japanese cakes "Butamochi". They were made from white rice flower with a filling of sweet beans and were extremely popular with adults and children alike. The sweets were packed in rectangular boxes made from thin sheets of wood and sold for two "sen" (cents) each. That meant forty cents per box... Prices were unbelievably cheap in those faraway days...

As we were trying to make it for the four o'clock tea-time, I beckoned the lad who carried his merchandise in a large box supported on his neck by a wide soft leather belt. "How many, sir?"

"Two, please!"

He deftly wrapped the sweets in paper bearing the company's logo depicting a geyser with an inscription: "Ompo - Shuotsu Hot Springs" . Tying it with a piece of string, he handed it to me with both hands:

 "There you are, sir!"

The long distance train raced up to the station with its usual accuracy of half a minute. We entered the carriage and I placed my purchase on the luggage rack.

The trip to the whistle-stop of Ruyken takes between ten and twelve minutes. We were looking out the window at the rice fields majestically floating by, at the mountains, blue at close range and purple in the distance, at a calm river with its sandy shores, which our train crossed over a noisy bridge. We chatted in anticipation of our arrival at the station, which was adjacent to Lukomorye. Our train braked for barely a minute, we jumped onto the platform and started walking towards a clump of "dachas" (summer-houses) we could see in the pine forest. When the last carriage disappeared from sight, I suddenly realised that our sweets were travelling south!

My companion was disappointed: "What a pity!", she said. And, naturally, I was the culprit...

"Let' s go back to the station, and I'll ask the station master to ring ahead to see if our parcel can be recovered. Japanese railways expect to give such a service."

"This is crazy ! Who is going to bother staff over such nonsense? ! You are idealising these colonialists!"

Nevertheless, I had my way. We returned to a tiny railway hut situated under a steep hillock covered in mixed growth. I told the station master, a short man wearing a cap with a red band, of our problem and added with studied nonchalance, trying to play on his patriotism:

"This Russian lady tells me that nothing ever gets lost on Japanese railways".

The flattered Japanese flashed the golden crowns adorning his teeth, saluted and explained that our express was going to stop only after passing six stops ; a train going in the opposite direction was going to reach that stop in one hour and was due at our station at half past five.

"I am going to contact your train at once. Make a note of the time of expected arrival. Come here as soon as you see the train bearing your parcel leaves the tunnel. I hope that all will be OK...."

I translated the conversation to Mrs Chirkina. The tall well- proportioned dark-haired daughter of the Don Cossacks glanced at me with her Persian eyes :

"I don't trust his malarkey ! This is just idle chatter !"

We followed a sunlit sandy path through a grove exuding a fragrant smell of pine tar and finished up on the beach. That magnificent beach, covered in golden sand, stretched for several "versts" (kilometres) along the shores of the immense blue ocean. A happy crowd was sitting on the sand in the shade of colourful beach umbrellas. Some of the holidaymakers were playing cards, others were sunbaking or surfing. No sooner did we sit down than the expansive Cossack beauty made an announcement laced with heavy irony :

"Ladies and gentlemen, would you believe that we bought some cakes for afternoon tea ---what do you call them ? ah --' butamochi ' --anyway, they have taken a long trip ! It is certainly a great pity but this patriot of local customs assures me that they will be returned with the next train ! Can you just imagine it ?!"

The holidaymakers appreciated the joke and smilingly shook their heads. Herr Lange, a German businessman from Shanghai, who was sitting in the centre of the crowd and had a reputation for being the life of any party, snorted with disdain :

"Well, everybody knows of our German devotion to duty, but even our railwaymen will not look for somebody's forgotten sweets ! I bet you that this is just a bluff! Let's bet a case of beer!"

Quite naturally, there is no way I could be absolutely certain that my Japanese friend was going to keep his word, but Lange got under my skin.

"All right ! You are on ! Let's go and meet the train! If the sweets are not delivered, I'll buy the beer. The tea can wait for a while.."

"I am sorry for you, Valery", said the German, triumphantly eyeing off the crowd, "but I am not going to let you off the hook".

The time of arrival for the train from the south imperceptibly crept upon us while we were exchanging this lively banter, and almost everybody decided to meet it. Lange would not let up :

"I do feel sorry for you, Yankovsky! You are such a hothead !"

At long last the party made a move. Halfway to the station we heard the whistle of the train, which emerged at great speed from the tunnel issuing a plume of smoke and overtaking our crowd. It paused momentarily at the station, blew its horn and hurried north. The red-cheeked solid German was unabashedly jubilant :

"Here you are ! Nobody left the train! Let's go to a bottle shop after we see the result! We'll have tea with beer instead of cakes ! Ho- Ho- Ho !!!"

I was disappointed but still hoped that the parcel was handed over from the train to somebody in the tiny hut of the stationmaster. This made me sheepishly suggest that we continue to the station.

To our huge amazement, we saw the smart little figure of the smiling stationmaster, wearing the usual cap complete with its red band. Yes, there was no doubt at all : in his hands he held the forgotten large parcel ! The diligent railwayman was as pleased as punch at the successful completion of his mission and accompanied the handover ceremony with a bow and a short explanatory speech :

"I must sincerely apologise... You will notice a different wrapping on the box. You see, it is very hot today, and the master of the remote station was afraid that the 'Butamochi' would dry out..... Therefore, he allowed your sweets to be sold to the passengers and used the money to buy a fresh lot... Our firm produces 'Butamochi' on all major stations, but, sorry, each station has its own logo..."

He concluded his speech with a long hissing sound of air being drawn into the gullet through clenched teeth, in accordance with the proper etiquette peculiar to his nation...

It gave me great pleasure to translate the speech, which had been made with great pride. My supporters greeted the translation with thunderous applause. Herr Lange's colour changed from red to crimson... I turned to him and jokingly suggested :

"Herr Lange, let us now go to the village to drink to your loss!"

The German was a born gentleman and a good loser. He bowed silently and took the wallet out of his coat pocket....

Half an hour later a delivery boy brought twenty four bottles of what was then the best Japanese beer, ---"Kirin Biru"--, to the dining room of the resort....

2. THE HISTORY OF LUKOMORYE.

I feel that the history of Lukomorye deserves a special mention. Few bays on the Korean shores of the Sea of Japan have such magnificent beaches. The Lukomorye beach consists of six kilometres of fine, velvet-soft golden sand. It starts from the Ruyken Station where it is adjacent to tall Korean mountains, covered in a clean pine forest, which extends all the way to the breakers.

My father bought a large freehold block of land in that area in the nineteen thirties. The deeds consisted of an impressive document adorned by a large seal of The Lands Department. Japanese law allowed the sale of land to all foreigners, including Russian émigrés. This was of great help to the Russian refugees, most of whom were in difficult financial circumstances.

We built a large "dacha" (summer-house) in the forest, which had a kitchen, dining room and a drawing room. Separate living quarters consisting of small self-contained dwellings were built adjacent to the main building to provide accommodation for holiday-makers from Manchuria.

3. CHINA AND JAPAN.

My sister Victoria had been the main hostess of Lukomorye for a number of years. Victoria looked very colourful. Her facial features were quaintly attractive and her body strong and sun-tanned (it reminded me of a sturdy Mongolian filly). She usually wore a light dress but changed into a bikini in very hot weather. "Ora's" (her nickname) unruly short hair was held in place by a wide ribbon, and between her lips she always had a menthol cigarette in a green, red or orange holder.

Ora was very energetic and resourceful, never losing her cool. If the kitchen hand was not around at the time when the cook was getting ready to prepare pancakes for the afternoon tea, she would walk to the Ruyken Station accompanied by little girls who adored her, and bring back on her shoulder a twenty-two kilo bag of white American flour. The coloured cigarette holder would never leave her on such trips. She liked wild game hunting and loved travelling.

Victoria was very popular with men. She was always surrounded by visiting poets, actors or ordinary admirers.

Picture the following scene...A colourful group of people is sitting on the sand next to the surf...Among them - Val, a poet from Shanghai, and Nikolai Kulesh, an employee of the Shanghai Municipal Council.

Val is a ladies' man, an intellectual and a cultured soul with an unimposing appearance. He is stooped, with long dirty nails, bad teeth and a mop of black and always greasy black hair. In contrast to Val, Kulesh is a blond smart fellow with a perfect figure of an Apollo, even though somebody has unkindly given him the nickname of "Apollo-Dooraksis" ("Doorak" means "Fool" in Russian). He is always bodily clean, cleanly shaven and dressed in accordance with the latest fashion. It is true that he is somewhat primitive and common but at the same time he is a self- confident snob who likes to impress.

Both are trying to impress the hostess of Lukomorye. One can see that with a naked eye.

Val is reading his poems and the crowd is listening attentively. This is annoying Kulesh. All of a sudden a gust of wind ruffles Val's hair who, as always, has no comb and says :

"Lend me your comb, Nick !".

Nick reluctantly pulls a small white comb from the back pocket of his fashionable shorts and hands it to Val who carefully combs his hair for what seems like eternity and dreamily returns it to its owner. Nikolai accepts the comb with two fingers, examines it at arm's length, and silently throws it into the surf....

In the battle of pretenders the score is fifteen --love in favour of Kulesh...

We three brothers used every excuse to escape to Lukomorye from the harsh rules and control of our father. We would drive the holidaymakers there from the Ompo Hot Springs, park the car in a cool spot and race to the surf.

On fine days the indigo - blue sea merged with the sky of the same colour on the far-away horizon. Somewhere near it, perhaps one or two versts (one "versta"--Russian measure of distance --is about 1 km) away, greyish sails of the fishermen's boats could barely be seen. Some of them let down their sails and bobbed up and down on the swell drying their fishing nets. We had a good rowing boat which could have taken us to the fishing boats but found it very exciting to swim to them instead.

We would organise a group of strong swimmers, always complete with two or three brave girls who put cigarettes, matches and sweets under their swimming caps before setting out with the men for the fishing boats. "The Oldies" would wave their arms and loudly tell us off, threatening to complain to higher authorities about our dangerous conduct, but the gang took no notice and kept leisurely swimming ever further through the waves into the open sea. It was not unusual for a one way swim to take a whole hour.

But what a pleasure it was to finally climb over the side of a large wooden contraption and to help the girls to join us! We would offer cigarettes to the hospitable fishermen and spread out on the sun-drenched clean deck, which had been washed by the rain and the sea.

Ahead of us, as far as the eye could see, is The Sea of Japan and behind---the green hills of Korea and the yellow strip of sand with barely visible figures, more accurately, dots, of white beach hats and large and small beach towels. We inhale the scent of the sea and the pervasive aroma of drying fish....The heavy barge rolls rhythmically, making one sleepy....And after a blissful rest, hot from the sun's rays, --back into the water for a return swim to the shore, to join our sister, the mistress of Lukomorye....

I must again say that she was very successful in her role. She was bossing around the Chinese cook and the Korean maids, keeping the resort spotlessly clean, attractive and orderly...Wild flowers always adorned the table of the dining room. Walks were organised by day followed by dances in the evening... These were followed by huge bonfires on the shores of the Ocean. They lasted late into the night and consumed large quantities of dried seaweed and flotsam.

4. "PUSSYCAT"

Our family was forever involved in domesticating wild animals. When we lived on the Sedemi Peninsula near Vladivostok, we would bring up young deer caught in the forest on cow's milk and they would grow up quite tame. At different times, we kept a small tiger, a baby jaguar and a bear cub as pets. In grandma's garden behind our house in Sedemi for many years lived racoons. They would come running when called and allowed to be hand fed.

Our first pet in Korea was a wolf cub. Upon reaching the age of eight months he quite unexpectedly attacked and bit a Korean child, ran into the forest and did not return.

"Pussycat", a lynx cub, was another such acquisition. Father brought home a wicker basket...A cute little grey- brown spotted head with yellow eyes and black-whiskered ears was protruding from a hole in the top. My sisters poured some milk into a saucer and called out : "Puss-Puss - Puss !" The youngster jumped out of the basket, raced towards the saucer and, to the girls' delight, started to lap up the milk with his little pink tongue. He was immediately christened "Pussycat" . He not only responded to his name but also very quickly befriended all humans and animals with whom he came into contact. He would sit on people's knees, was very fond of being stroked behind his ears and went for walks with the dogs. Whenever anybody would cross their legs when sitting down, Pussycat would run into the outstretched foot and hit it with his head as an invitation for some fun....He was very friendly with my hunting dog, a pointer called "Maika" . The pair would forever jostle, wrestle and push each other around, without causing any injuries whatsoever.

Some photographs taken in that period which escaped destruction show me sitting on a sofa in our "Catamaran" (the family home) with Pussycat and Maika sitting by my side and resting their heads on my knees. That photograph was published in a Journal called "Rubezh" ("The Border" in Russian) which was being produced in the Manchurian city of Harbin, a haven for thousands of anti-Communist Russian expatriates. My relative Volodya (short for "Vladimir") Vakhovich told me how one of the readers reacted to it.

The man was sitting in a tram and examining the picture I just described. : "Just look at it! Isn't it pathetic how some hunters will tell barefaced lies ! This character puts a stuffed animal on his lap and expects the reader to believe that it is a live lynx!"

With the passage of years Pussycat turned into a large imposing male who could understand many words. When he heard : "Pussycat, swimming time !" he would literally fly down the path leading to the river and hide in the bushes in order to ambush the passers- by. He would let all grown-ups and boys go past and waited for the girls. When they approached, he would jump out, grab their pigtails and fell them to the ground. But he would never bite or scratch any of his targets, licking their necks or cheeks instead and running with them to the beach. He would gingerly enter the water trying to catch small fish disturbed by his arrival. Then, to everybody's delight, he would plunge into the current and confidently swim, with his mutton chops floating on the surface of the water !

On one occasion my younger brother Yuri was walking young hunting dogs in the company of our mother past a sorghum field when a brood of pheasants took off from it. Yurka (short for Yuri) shot down a cock, which fell into the tall grass, pursued by the dogs and the lynx. Mother and son started debating which of the dogs was going to be the first to fetch the prey, when all of a sudden Pussycat appeared from the thicket with the pheasant between his teeth. The lynx carefully handed the dead bird to his mistress...

Mother was his favourite. When she lay terminally ill, he no longer had a favourite. And then he vanished...

On one fine day in August he accompanied a crowd of holidaymakers to the beach, swam across the river, spent a bit of time sunning himself but instead of swimming back, started the return trip by walking over the suspension bridge which spanned the river. This was not unusual --he had done it before...But this time it was Sunday and in the middle of the bridge he encountered a group of unknown tourists. They were Korean women in colourful blouses who, upon sighting a "wild animal", began to scream and wave their umbrellas, obviously frightening our Pussycat. The lynx raced back and found himself in the forest, in a spot where nobody took him before. He must have experienced a sudden sense of being in his natural environment!

He returned in the evening and, as usual, joined the dogs in eating the evening meal consisting of a thick soup. Somebody called him but realising that it was not his beloved owner, he again escaped into the mountains. We all thought that was his last visit.

Two months went by... Late one November evening Arseny and I returned to Novina after a hunting trip. The nights were getting cold, and my brother decided to empty the car radiator to prevent it being damaged by a frost. I picked up my gun and rucksack, repaired towards the house and was about to enter the veranda when a shot behind my back disturbed the quiet...Racing in the direction of the sound, I recognised Arseny's figure near the chicken coop...In his hand he held a rifle...

"What did you shoot ?"

"You see, some sort of an animal had attacked the chooks, and they started rushing about and making noises.. I saw a shadow with a pair of eyes sparkling in the dark and, well, took a pot shot..."

Timothy Magai, the Korean manager of the deer farm, came running when he heard the shot, carrying a torch we called "The Bat".

"An animal" -- he said -- "don't know what animal, he go-go near deer house. Deer, they whistle, whistle very loud..."

We entered the hen-house... Two savaged white chickens lay dead on the floor. Alongside ---the figure of a prostrate animal. Our first impression was that of a wolf, but when "The Bat" illuminated its face, we recognised Pussycat ! The tell-tale mark was a front tooth, which he damaged at the time when, as a kitten, he played with a rag attached to a piece of string. During the game he made an awkward jump and the tooth got caught in the rag. The damaged tooth always protruded beyond his lip, giving the appearance of a perpetual grin...Now Pussycat's dead head was smiling at us...

We concealed the unfortunate wild cat's tragic end from our dying mother, telling her instead that Pussycat decided to escape into the forest....

5. THE BUTTERFLIES.

During Novina 's early years, entomology was an important source of our income. My father Yuri (George) Michailovich had a lot of practical knowledge in that area, having learned about it at his father's knee. He got in touch with "Messrs Staundinger and Bunghaas", a large German firm with headquarters in Hamburg, who gave him orders, based on magnificent catalogues displaying full- sized coloured pictures of bugs and butterflies.

We used to trap the bugs (mostly belonging to the species known as "Deer", "Carabusses" and "Captolabrusses") in the forest. The traps consisted of petrol or kerosene cans cut in half and buried flush with the surface of barely noticeable paths used by these creatures. The tins were concealed among the grass and fallen leaves with the bugs falling into the traps when taking their nightly strolls along the paths. All a duty "entomologist" had to do was to pluck them out of the traps the following morning. Bugs, which had no commercial value, were set free, but handsome specimens whose glistening backs displayed all colours of the rainbow, were taken home for dispatch to Germany.

The situation with the butterflies was far more complex. The daylight specimens were not generally in high demand, presumably because there were a lot of them on offer from various sources. However, some varieties of "monarch butterflies" were sought after, among them "Papilio Maaki", and "Papilio Radde" . The former appeared in May-June and the latter --in August. They were jet black with a greeny--gold sheen, and were often seen fluttering above forest meadows. There were also orange specimens with black stripes. However, our parent company was particularly interested in a species called "Parnassius" whose members are giant beige butterflies covered in large variegated red and black spots, and which were highly prized by collectors. Like mountain goats, we chased the "Parnassiuses" over hills and dales, brandishing our butterfly nets among the flowers and tall grass. The best specimens were packed in special envelopes. Generally speaking, that part of our business was relatively straightforward.

The most popular butterflies belonged to the nocturnal variety. They had to be caught in the dark of the night with the aid of a torch. Being very fragile, it was extremely difficult to catch a "clean" butterfly, i. e. one whose scales coverings its wings were intact. The way out of the problem was to grow them. But the question was, how?

Novina is surrounded by mountains covered in numerous specimens of Far - Eastern flora which forms the nutritional basis for all of its bugs and butterflies. The difficult part was to find the particular plant used by a specific caterpillar, which was the host of the butterfly we tried to grow. The recognition and nurture of that caterpillar presented an additional problem.

To that end, in a valley surrounded by the mountains, we would install a small white tent, shaped like a pencil case, equipped with a powerful carbide- fuelled light suspended in its interior. We took turns in spending a night in such a tent. Attracted by the flame of the torch, night butterflies of fantastic shapes, colours and sizes, of the kind one never saw by day, would glide from the mountain slopes and, with a characteristic rustle of wings, fly into the tent. An experienced operator had to recognise the wanted subspecies and to catch (this was absolutely essential !) a <u>female</u> butterfly which had to be carefully tied with a piece of string to the exterior of the tent and left there till daybreak. It is usual for such a female to drop her eggs onto the surface of the tent during her imprisonment.

The eggs were removed in the morning and placed on the leaves of the tree, which was the customary source of nourishment for a particular species. The leaves were then transferred into a hessian bag, which contained a whole branch of the appropriate tree, e.g. oak, hornbeam, elm, ash, linden, Manchurian nut or marigold. Dozens of such bags were used because we were growing dozens of subspecies of butterflies. The bags had to be checked almost daily since growing caterpillars become very voracious and can perish if the whole family of these creatures is not transferred onto a new branch from the primitive incubator, thus ruining weeks of painstaking effort.

Tiny caterpillars rapidly grow to the size of a man's finger and change their colour from green to red, brown or even black. They stop eating once they reach maturity and fall to the bottom of the bag.

When that happens, they are transferred into specially prepared soil --filled boxes. The boxes are protected by thin sheets of tin (to stop mice from eating the chrysalises) and have covers made from metallic mesh. The caterpillars burrow into the soil and are transformed into chrysalises. They hibernate till spring when the observation begins anew. The net covers on the boxes located in a cellar or an apiary are lifted every morning. And, finally, a wonderful picture greets the observer : a beautiful butterfly with trembling wings sitting under the cover! The butterfly is immediately poisoned with cyanide and handed over to Yankovsky senior who expertly mounts this latest specimen inside a glass - covered box with a cork bottom. The lucky butterfly will adorn a museum or a private collection in far away Europe or America...

Among the butterflies we sent to all corners of the world were quite a few of the seventeen subspecies discovered by my grandfather on the Askold Island near Vladivostok and bearing the name of Yankovsky...

Chapter 10. THE STORY OF THE SHEVELEV FAMILY

I think it appropriate to tell the story of a family, which is inextricably linked with the Yankovskys: the forebears of my mother whose surname is Shevelev...

Shevelevs belonged to the class of hereditary Russian merchants who are mentioned in a book by M. A. Belokrys entitled: "Our ancient friend: The Written Word" (published in Ulan-Ude, capital of the Buryat Autonomous Republic, Siberia in 1980). I am going to quote some facts from a chapter of this book called: "The friends of the Decembrists (i) in the town of Verkhneudinsk (ii)" . (Notes: {i} "Decembrists" were members of the officer corps who staged a political uprising in St Petersburg on the twenty fifth of December 1825. They were severely punished by the authorities, with some of them being sentenced to penal servitude in Siberia. {ii} Verkhneudinsk --present day Ulan - Ude).

Documentary evidence shows that a Verkhneudinsk merchant of the top guild by the name of Alexander Shevelev "was arrested as a result of an accusation of having verbally insulted His Imperial Majesty Paul Petrovich (Tsar Paul The First of Russia) which, if proven, constituted a political crime." Alexander Shevelev was taken to the town of Irkutsk (Siberia) for a preliminary investigation and was subsequently reported to the Governing Senate of The Empire. He spent many months in detention and was shackled hand and foot. That accusation was dropped after The Emperor's death.

A magazine called "The Lyceum" which was published in St Petersburg, carried an article entitled: ' A Verkhneudinsk merchant by the name of Alexander Shevelev donated his timber home with all accessories having a total value of 2 225 roubles to the local school. In recognition of that generous act, His Imperial Majesty graciously awarded him a golden medal, which the aforementioned is allowed to wear around his neck '.

The same magazine wrote about Alexander's son George: "In August 1832 the Governor - General of Eastern Siberia Lavinsky received a request from the Chief of The Gendarmerie (Secret Police) Benkendorf to question G. A. Shevelev about the information received from secret agents that Shevelev was helping the exiled Decembrists to send unauthorised correspondence to their supporters." Shevelev was summoned to Irkutsk and subjected to brutal questioning the minutes of which are still in existence.

Shevelev denied all allegations. He admitted having met the Decembrists during the time when they were being transferred from a prison in Chita (Siberia, about 800 km East of Irkutsk) to the "Peter The Great Factory" (in the same area). He further stated that the Decembrists' wives----Mmes Muravyova, Volkonskaya, Naryshkina, Fonvisina, Rosen and Youshnevskaya stayed in his estate overnight.

Even though the authorities were unable to prove Shevelev's guilt, they nevertheless "rewarded" him with their attention. They cancelled a variety of building contracts he had with the Government which sent him broke. <... Original text interrupted here by V. Yankovsky, as not being relevant to his story. >.

In 1847 George Shevelev was forced to sell his large house in Verkhneudinsk (now Ulan - Ude) and to move to Kyakhta (another town in Siberia, approx. 300 km south of Verkhneudinsk) where Gregory Alexandrovich (son of Alexander started a stage coach business and even personally drove "troikas" (a Russian horse - driven carriage pulled by three horses). He was killed during one of his business trips when frightened horses wrecked his troika."

His son Michael Grigoryevich (my maternal grandfather) was born in 1844. He showed an aptitude for languages and completed a Chinese-- Russian interpreters' course in Kyakhta. In March 1861 he and five other young men who distinguished themselves in the study of Chinese accompanied a Russian trading mission on its trip to China. He spent many years in China working for a tea exporting company in the towns of Tientsin and Hankow and succeeded in forming a partnership with a well-known merchant by the name of Tokmakov. During his life abroad he befriended Lee Hun Chan, a well-known Chinese statesman.

Michael married Alexandra Dimitriyevna Sinitsin, the daughter of Dimitri Sinitsin, a Kyakhta merchant. She was the granddaughter of Nikita Filippovich Sabashnikov who was a senior official of the "Russo-American Company of Kyakhta".

After his marriage my grandfather went to live in Vladivostok where he became a ship owner. His other achievement was an honorary position as an interpreter of the District Court. He was also a member of The Society for the Study of the Amur Region.

Michael was known for his charitable works, having, for example, donated one thousand roubles towards the construction of a museum. He had a huge Chinese library and enjoyed reading books written in Chinese. He died of cancer in 1903.

Michael Georgiyevich and Alexandra Dimitriyevna (we called her "Boosya Alya"— "Boosya" being the abbreviation of the Russian word "Baboosya"-- "Grandma") had three children: Son Vladimir who was born in 1879 and daughters Margarita (my mother) born in 1884 and Angelina (1893).

Uncle Volodya (Vladimir) married a Ukrainian girl by the name of Xenia Germanovna (daughter of Hermann) Zayaz who bore him three sons: Igor, Oleg and Gleb. The boys spent every winter in the city moving to their grandfather's estate on the Shevelev Peninsula, in the Gulf of Ussuri, in summer. We frequently visited each other.

However, a tragedy struck...During one of his visits to the Yankovsky's estate at Sedemi Volodya fell in love with our teacher Mary Alexeevna Patrina whose nickname was "Nayada" ("Nymph") and divorced Aunt Oxana (Xenia). After the divorce he joined a deer-breeding co-operative organised by my other uncle, Yan and built a large house on the Gamov promontory where he installed his Nymph.

Unfortunately, our former teacher had a very fickle and short temper which prompted old ladies who sponged on our Boosya Alya to compose a nasty ditty: "Our Volodya wanted to get himself a nymph but the Devil said: 'Here you are --have some poison instead ' ". (The Russian word for Nymph –'Nayada'-- sounds like 'na yadu' – 'have some poison').

The eldest son of Uncle Vladimir, Igor, moved to Sedemi from Vladivostok. Oleg, his second son, moved between the Gamov Peninsula and his mother's house in Vladivostok, whereas Gleb, the youngest, studied in an English School in the Chinese town of Tientsin.

Igor joined us on the trip to Korea and later migrated to Europe. Some years later Oleg graduated from a Commercial school in Vladivostok after which he was given permission to join his mother and brother Gleb in Shanghai.

Soon after his arrival in Shanghai Oleg was sent to Korea where our family took him under its wing. He was a first class sportsman who excelled as a professional boxer, having become a middleweight champion of China. He married Mura Vasilieva, a girl from the city of Harbin, who owned a "dacha" (holiday home) in Lukomorye.

Oleg's and Mura's son, Svyet, is currently living near his mother in the American state of Arizona. Oleg died in San Francisco but wrote a book about his and his parents' lives shortly before his death. The title of the book (written in Russian) is: "Childhood and youth of Oleg Shevelev and stories of some experiences in Shanghai". {San Francisco, 1988}.

Gleb worked in a firm called "Brynner & Co." During that period he married Anna (Nyusya) Ganina, the daughter of a well-known Russian merchant with businesses in Manchuria . Gleb and Nyusya had two children: Marina and Vladimir (Vova). After Mao's victory in China all our relatives fled to the USA.

Vova married the granddaughter of General Horvat, Irene (Note: General Horvat was the General Manager Of the Far Eastern Railway built by the Russians at the turn of the 20th century. The railway passed through Manchuria.). Vova and Irene have a son by the name of Nikolo and a daughter called Natasha. The family is living in California. Vova inherited the best qualities of his forebears: he is an honest businessman and a remarkably understanding person. Just like the famous merchants Shevelev, he is full of kindness and attention to his relatives and friends. This includes my family. The genes of the Russian merchants of the First Guild, who always generously helped those near and dear to them, are alive and well in Vova Shevelev.

In conclusion, I must narrate the sad demise of Vova Shevelev's grandfather, my uncle Volodya, who married "The Nymph" Nayada...

Uncle Volodya escaped from the Reds and came with us to Korea. Unfortunately, he succumbed to Nayada's plea to return to Russia. He went back to The Maritime Provinces but was arrested soon afterwards and ended his life in the Gulag, having died in 1937 in the NKVD (forerunner of the KGB) concentration camp near Vladivostok in a district called "Vtoraya Rechka" ("Second River"). As for Nayada, she collected all his valuables and returned safely to the Far Eastern town of Blagoveshchensk...

Chapter 11. DEER FARMING IN NOVINA.

Yuri (George) Michailovich had a long-standing dream of establishing a deer farm in Novina. Therefore when he heard that some very capable Korean trackers caught a few spotted deer, with their bare hands, in the vicinity of an old fortress Puryon which was now a railway station, we immediately went there. Father took with us a Korean interpreter by the name of Chkhon Chan Gyunn who was the man who delivered the news of the capture. The journey to the station took a few hours, and soon we were following a beaten cart track high into the mountains having waded across many mountain streams on our way. Father was concerned that the story about the deer was another of many disappointing "yarns", but luckily he need not have worried...

By nightfall we reached the hut of a well-known local hunter by the name of Kim Chung Bong and immediately saw four reddish- brown deer (two stags, one grown female and a young doe) which were confined in a small yard behind a makeshift fence made of vertical poles. They were very timid and rushed about their enclosure at the mere sight of an approaching human being.

Our host turned out to be a middle-aged man with a sparse greying moustache and an old-fashioned hairdo--a bun on the top of his head. He invited us inside, sat us on some straw mats and asked us to join him for dinner during which he explained the method used in capturing wild deer...

During the early spring the deer are quite weak because there is no more winter fodder and the new grass is far too short. This is the time when the incredibly sharp-sighted pathfinders follow an animal's tracks over wet ground through the day and through moonlit nights. The pursuit continues until the exhausted animal lies down, unable to move any further. It is quite unbelievable but true: the hunters capture the fatigued prey with their bare hands!

We agreed on a price for the deer, placed them into cages, made up on the spot and loaded on two-wheeled carts drawn by painfully slow bullocks. The priceless cargo was delivered to our Novina, more than one hundred versts (one versta is approx. 1 km) away.

Those four deer formed the basis of the future prosperity of Novina.

With the passage of years the deer herd grew bigger and the tender deer antlers (known by the name "pantui", grown by deer stags in spring and normally discarded in autumn), as well as the progenitors' offspring, became the main source of our family's income.

Well-to-do Koreans paid a deposit in spring and joined a queue of other customers. At an appointed day a pantui - carrying stag was forced into a restraining lock where he was firmly held by the handlers while his antlers were being cut off with a small saw. Greyish- pink young and tender antlers were full of health - giving blood.

During this procedure the customer would sit patiently on his haunches waiting for the antlers to be separated from the deer's head.

At long last, the antlers are off, and are quickly passed by hand to operators standing outside the cage. The two wounds on the stag's head are bleeding profusely, with fountains of blood spurting out of them, dousing the faces and white coats of the operators. The chief operator issues a command: "Drink!" and the ecstatic "bloodsucker", shaking like a leaf, starts to gorge himself on the blood, sucking each stump of an antler in turn. His eyes are closed, he is choking on blood but continues to convulsively suck the salty elixir of youth. On many occasions a "bloodsucker" would be overwhelmed with ecstasy and had to be dragged away from the head of the injured animal.

After the main "bloodsucker" had his fill, other customers, who paid a smaller fee, used to join the sucking ritual. When everyone was finished, a bucket of ice-cold water from a nearby well would be thrown over the stag's head, the doors of the lock would be opened and with a giant leap the unfortunate animal would escape from his tormentors into the yard next to the torture chamber!

I remember one obstinate stag nicknamed "Hare Lip" always refusing to enter the lock. Every year he had to be caught, felled to the ground and manually held prostrate during the whole procedure. The accomplishment of this feat was left to the most foolhardy lads who always included myself and my brother Arseny.

This resulted in a veritable "corrida" which attracted a host of onlookers, including quite a number of belles, and every participant of the "show" did his best to impress them. Quite naturally, our ardour often resulted in personal injury.

We built a cow shed and an apiary alongside the deer enclosure.

Timothy Magai, the Korean manager of the dairy, and his family moved into the nearby "fanza" (hut) which used to belong to the owner of the land which was now part of our farm.

Timothy fled The Russian Maritime Provinces as a result of "de- kulakking" and general persecution of Koreans in that area.(Note : The Communist doctrine in Russia aimed at destroying "the 'kulaks{so-called wealthy farmers, as defined by the authorities }' as a class". This meant, in practice, that millions of farmers were "de- kulakked", i. e. dispossessed by the State and subsequently imprisoned in various concentration camps of the Gulag).

Sidemy in Russia

"Tower of the Ancestors" in Novina, north Korea.

Arriving as refugees in Seisin, Korea.

Photographs

Novina in the Ompo River Valley, Korea.

Novina's first common house is built.

Keeping bees for Honey.

The suspension bridge.

Photographs

The Chapel in Novina.

Winter and summer christenings.

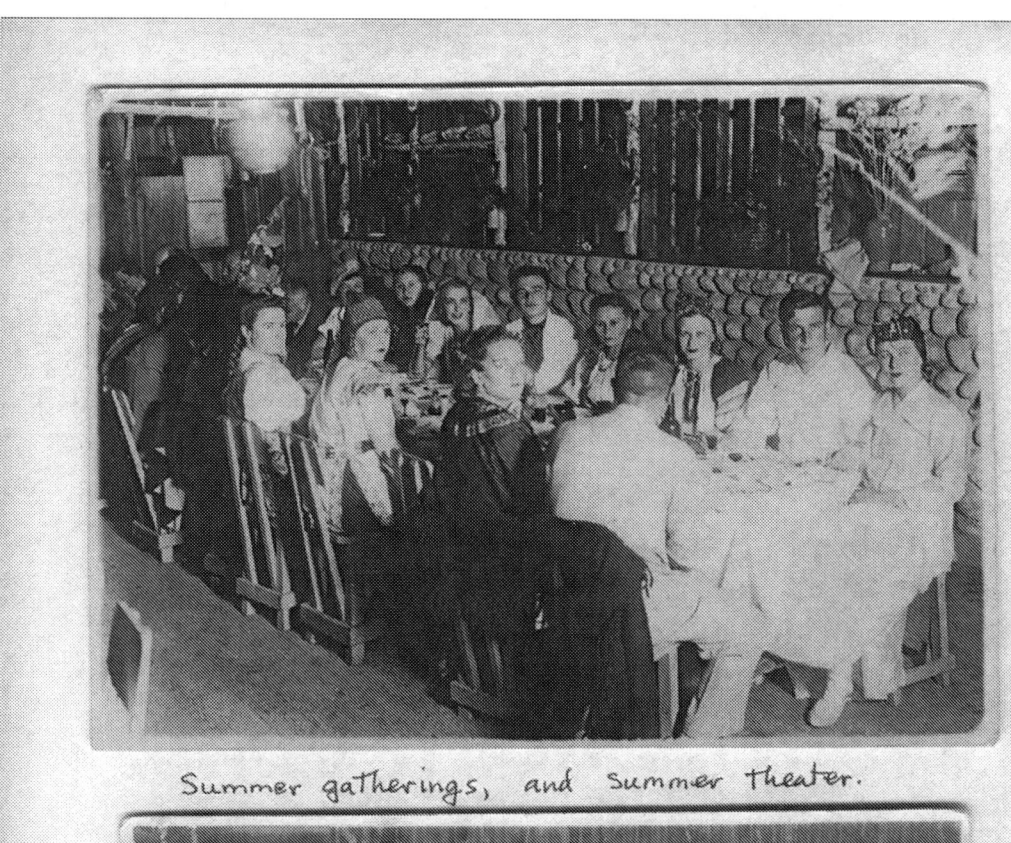

Summer gatherings, and summer theater.

Summer Theater.

PHOTOGRAPHS

Children's Summer Theater - 1934

The waterfalls and "chalices" above Norina.

Mermaids in Korea?!

Photographs

63

The logging train, to and from the mountain.

Novina vs. Lukomorie.

Photographs

Raising deer herds in Novina.

Anastasia, Valentin, Irma, and Valery.
Sokolovsky Valkov Meyer Yankovsky

Extended Yankovsky family and friends, in the 1940s.

Victoria "Ora" Yankovsky

"Daisy's Lynx."

Margarita "Daisy" Yankovsky and her lynx.

Yankovsky hunters in Korea.

Arseny, Yuri the father, Yuri Jr., and Valery Yankovsky.

Huge and dangerous wild boar. Yuri with lynx.

Photographs

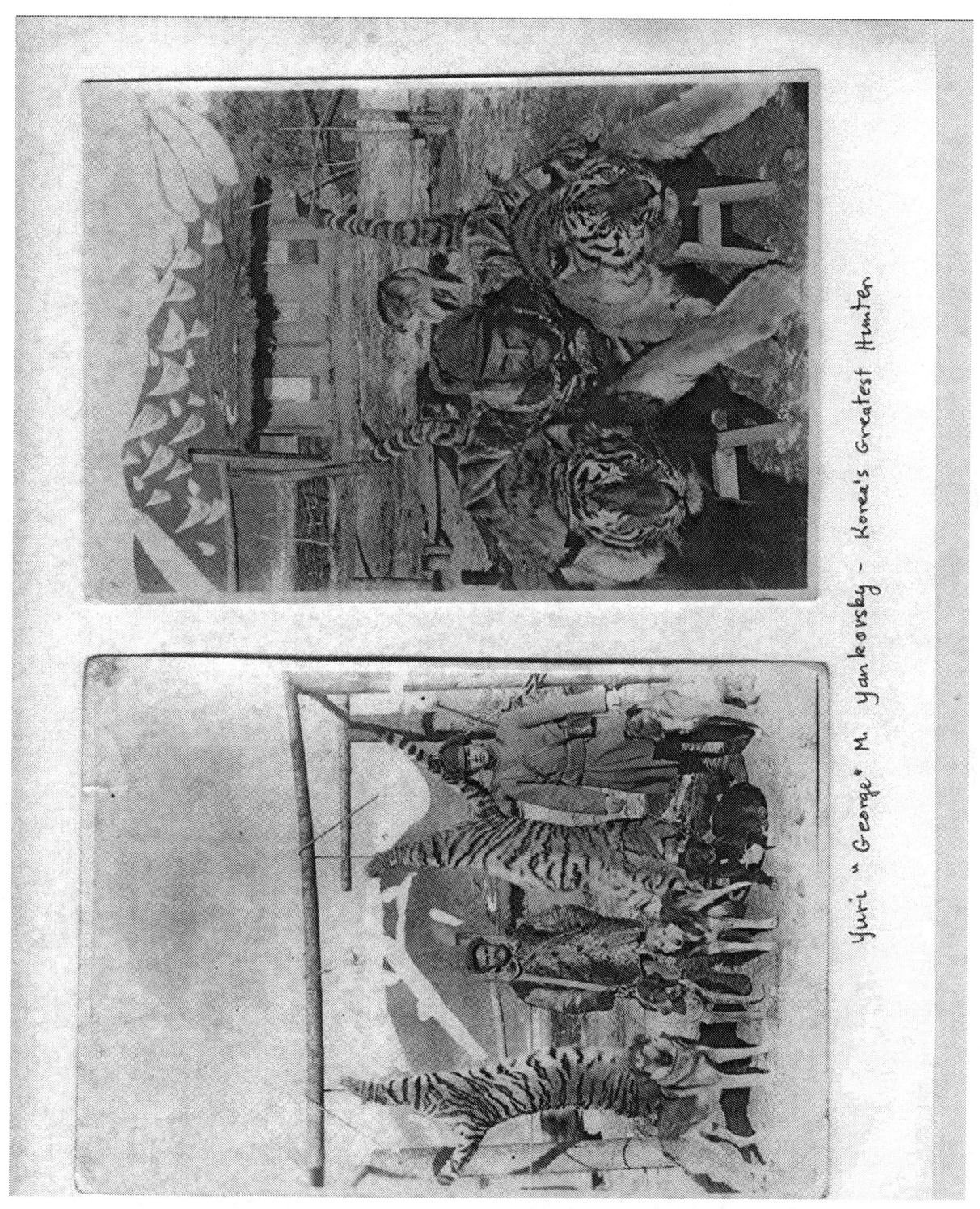

Yuri "George" M. Yankovsky – Korea's Greatest Hunter

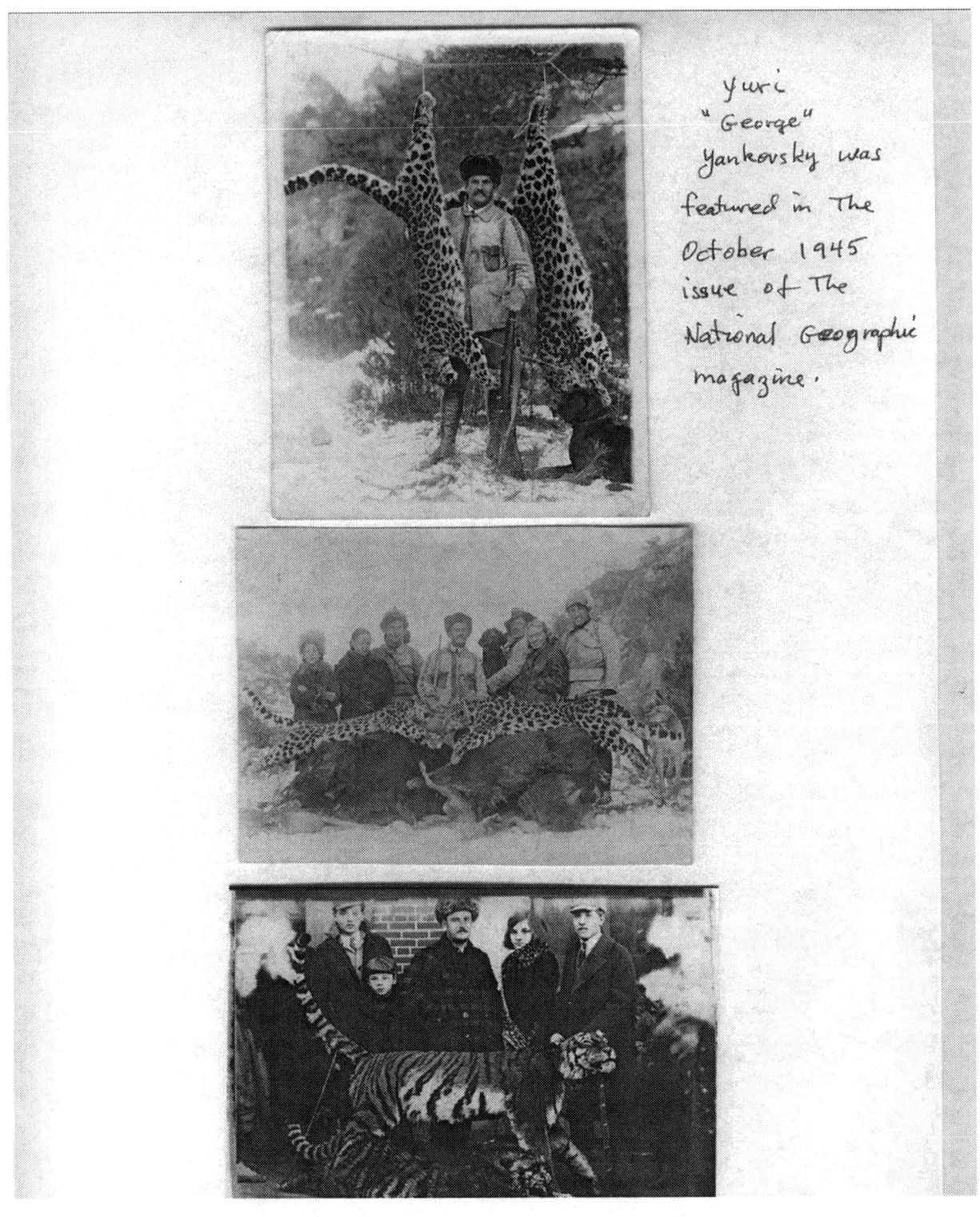

Yuri "George" Yankovsky was featured in the October 1945 issue of The National Geographic magazine.

Chapter 12. IVAN KUZMICH RESNYANSKY AND DAIRY FARMING WITH A DIFFERENCE.

Our holiday resort business grew bigger bringing with it long - awaited prosperity. We bought one and, shortly after, a second motor car and built a garage to house them. On the rise of a picturesque hill a small chapel- like church was lovingly created out of river boulders.

The influx of house guests increased the demand for milk but it was extremely difficult to bolster the size of our modest dairy farm because our Korean farm-hands came from a background where dairy cattle were used only as beasts of burden and had no idea how to organise milk production. The problem was a formidable one.

We got in touch with recent refugees from The Maritime Provinces, two "de--kulakked" farmers of our acquaintance by the name of Resnyansky and Patyukov, who lived in nearby Manchuria

They told us that two "pantui" would get us a good milch cow. Being father's right hand man at that time, I was the obvious choice for carrying out that task.

The fast train ride to the Manchurian border took only a few hours. The Manchurian town of Tumangan lies across the border river of Tumyn. By that time (my story relates to the year 1934) Japan was in full control of Manchuria having created the state of Manchukuo. It was the base of their famous Guangdong Army. For that reason Tumyn acquired the Japanese name of "Tomon".

Customs police entered our carriage, quickly checked our travel documents and the train continued on its way towards the heart of Manchuria. By the next morning it arrived in the ancient city of Kirin located in the upper reaches of the mighty Sungari River, where I spent some time admiring Chinese pagodas and granite - encased bridges.

The Chinese "fanza" (hut), a temporary abode of our friends, the latest refugees from the Soviet Union, was located on the outskirts of town and took some finding. One of them was Ivan Kuzmich Resnyansky, a tall man with a greying cuneiform beard, and the other -- Michael Michailovich Patyukov, a solidly built thick-set cleanly shaven round-faced individual. Patyukov's wife had a very raspy voice which caused Kuzmich to refer to her as a "Blunt Saw " (Note: It is a Russian custom, particularly among the farmers, to often refer to a person by his or her patronymic omitting the first name. Hence, the abbreviated "Kuzmich" instead of "Ivan Kuzmich").

"Why a 'Blunt Saw ' ?", I asked him when we were alone in the back yard. Kuzmich scratched the back of his head with his palm and grinned baring two rows of gold teeth under his greying moustache :

"Ho-Ho ! You see, a sharp saw cuts quickly : whoosh ! and the job is done ! But this woman --heaven forbid --keeps nagging like a blunt saw : rasp --rasp --rasp ! There is no end to her displeasure! No, my friend, a sharp saw is far better than a blunt one!..."

These two remarkable characters deserve a special aside.....

......The two former Russian farmers, who later became gold prospectors, were brought together by fate in the town of Ussuriysk in The Russian Far East. Ivan Kuzmich satrted his gold prospecting career in a gold mine on the river Zeya (in The Russian Far East, a tributary of the Amur River) belonging to a Russian industrialist by the name of Adrianov. "He was a good boss", Kuzmich used to say, "he never used to maltreat his workers". Resnyansky remembered his boss standing on a balcony of a hilltop mansion overlooking his open cast mine. Even though the mine owner spent a lot of time in Paris, the mine was very well managed. The workers were well provided for and received large bonuses.

When the Bolsheviks came to power, Kuzmich set out for the Kolyma Range (in The Russian Far East). He joined a group of freelancing wandering prospectors who, using pack horses, found their way to an area located seven hundred kilometres north of the Bay of Nagayev (the present-day location of Magadan, a Stalinist slave labour area, not in existence at the time).

They discovered large deposits of gold and panned a lot of it making use of long summer days of the Far North. Life was primitive : a tent ; pancakes made from flower bought for the trip ; fish caught in the nearby stream. Partridge and grouse shot by the prospectors provided the only source of protein. Work was back-breaking, with little time left for sleep, and the diet was inadequate.

When a Soviet geological expedition appeared in their area, they realised that their days as free prospectors were over and scuttled to the four winds.

Ivan Kuzmich found his way to the seaside where he boarded a ship and made his escape. Behind his belt was a small pouch filled with golden nuggets and gold dust. The sea voyage took him to Vladivostok from where he went to an apiary located in the "taiga" (Siberian forest) near the town of Ussuriysk owned by an old friend.

There he met Patyukov who also had some gold panned elsewhere. Like Kuzmich, he was uncomfortable with the new regime. Both men understood each other well due to shared recent vivid memories of the fate of their dispossessed parents, and decided to flee to Manchuria. Without attracting anybody's attention they stocked up on foodstuffs and footwear and made for the border which lay beyond a nearby watershed and was marked by a poorly guarded forest cutting.

The sight of the border filled them with foreboding. "All right", they said, "so we'll cross the border but how about the gold ?" Both men were acquainted from early childhood with the behaviour of the "Hung Hu Tse" (Chinese bandits) as well as of the Chinese police. "These people will get hold of us as soon as we get to their territory, search us and rob us of the hard-won gold. This would be a lucky outcome...The more likely one is that they will murder us..."

They came to the conclusion that the safest way was to hide about one hundred grams of gold dust in each of their old quilted jackets and to bury the leather bags containing the bulk of their fortune on the Russian side of the border. The idea was to get to the town of Harbin in Manchuria where they could assess the situation and get ready for a return trip to retrieve their fortune.

This was quite simple in theory, but just imagine battling your way through impenetrable taiga and remembering the route you took ! Just try to walk through the forest, over the mountains and along barely visible paths to a station of The Far Eastern Railway in Manchuria and catching a train to the unknown town of Harbin! And as if this is not enough, retrace your steps to salvage your wealth! No, truly, only seasoned children of the Taiga could have the courage to accomplish such a task!

But these adventurers not only made their way to Harbin and sold a few grams of gold which allowed them to eat their way back to a good physical condition and to buy new clothing and foodstuffs for a return journey which they undertook almost immediately. They also found their trail which led them back to the ancient cedar beneath whose roots they secreted their treasure. They ran an enormous risk of being spotted by the Soviet border Guards and the Chinese Hung Hu Tse bandits. But they made it : thick layers of moss masking the hiding place were removed and the small but heavy leather bags full of precious metal again saw the light of day !

The two daredevils did not linger on and immediately started on the return journey which brought them to Harbin--the Russian town on Manchurian soil...

Both men invested in spotted deer famous for their health - giving horns - the "pantui".. Patyukov took up residence in the Manchurian town of Kirin and Resnyansky joined our family in Novina where we enjoyed his company for nigh on ten years. During his sojourn with us he related another touching story...

"Here I am in Harbin, just walking along the street.. A down- and - out guy is staggering towards me...As soon as we started passing each other I said to myself : 'Almighty God! This is none other than my old boss --Adrianov--the owner of the gold mines on the Zeya River!' And he recognised me too -- recognised his old worker...We embraced and started talking. Adrianov told me that the new regime in Russia destroyed him financially. He was lucky to have escaped with his life because he fled with the help of some good friends just as the Communists were about to arrest him. 'But see, Kuzmich', he said, 'I fled without a penny, just wearing these rags...'"

Kuzmich felt terribly sad and offered one hundred Japanese yen (at the time equivalent to the dollar) to the unfortunate former millionaire. Crying with joy, Adrianov took the money.

This was his salvation : it enabled him to buy some decent clothes and to join his old trusted friends in another town to start a new life.

In Novina Kuzmich looked after our apiary and tended his spotted deer in summer spending all winter hunting wild game in the taiga. Despite the fact that he only had a limited formal education (two senior years of a parish school, i. e. a total of about five years), he used to subscribe to several newspapers and was a superbly literate man with a distinctive Gothic-style handwriting. He asked us to send all mail addressed to him in winter to a remote hamlet. Kuzmich would leave his abode in the taiga once a fortnight to visit it in company of his dogs.

During winter he usually lived in a tent or a dugout where he kept a detailed diary of daily happenings which he would mail to us. Among the routine notes of daily life in the taiga and descriptions of the results of his hunting forays were also philosophical thoughts about world politics in which he was very interested. I still remember his prophetic thoughts about the Russo-German War : "I am very concerned for my Motherland and at the same time am consumed by the fearful thought : 'What will happen if the Hunns will conquer Europe?'"

Ivan Kuzmich Resnyansky ended his life in a way similar to the majority of terribly unfortunate White Russian émigrés. During the first days of occupation of North Korea he was arrested by the Soviet Security Forces, with many others who were declared "especially guilty persons"... It was many years after that event that I found out about his death...

In Moscow (after I was released from imprisonment), many years after Kuzmich was arrested, I met his eldest son Ivan Ivanovich ("Son of Ivan ") Resnyansky. He cried when he told me that his father was convicted and sent to a concentration camp in Vorkuta (located in Russia, approximately 500 km north of the Arctic Circle) from which he did not return...

Being a graduate of the Stalinist "University of Untold Millions", I feel with the pores of my skin that the hard - core criminal thugs, who were among the convicts, tracked down the old man, knocked out his teeth while he was still alive, only to murder him after their grisly deed was done..

Getting back to my original narrative, I managed to get a good price for the specially prepared deer horns ("pantui") which I brought with me to Kirin from Novina and bought a red --brown cow of the "Kholmogor" breed, whom I chose because of her large udders, a sign of a good milch cow. The beast was loaded on a train and sent to Novina accompanied by one of our workmen. The following day I boarded a train for the return journey to Korea, well satisfied with the result of my mission .

After two hours our train stopped at a large station called Doong Hwa, and I got out onto the platform hoping to buy a bottle of milk or mineral water. Unfortunately no refreshments were available but my attention was drawn by a large train standing on the next platform loaded with tarpaulin-covered trucks. I was very fond of motor vehicles, and to satisfy my curiosity walked along this and the next few platforms peering under the covers and trying to have a good look at the foreign--made blue trucks. Somebody's curious head poked out of our train but I took no notice of it.

After returning to my seat I was joined by a polite Japanese in a military uniform. He showed a great interest in my persona, enquiring into my background, the destination of and the reason for my trip. Having thus passed the time of the day he departed, with the train continuing to roll towards the Korean border.

The border town of Tomon at long last...I was sitting in the carriage waiting for the customs check, keeping my suitcase on an overhead shelf, and being quite certain that half an hour later our train would rattle across the Tumangan River bridge, which meant that home was very near....

My pleasant expectations were interrupted by the appearance of two uniformed members of the Japanese Gendarmerie (Military Police who were also responsible for some aspects of State Security). Their long sabres in steel scabbards rattled ominously... Approaching me they asked me to remove my suitcase from the shelf. I thought that they were going to examine it but the senior man barked an order:

"Take your things and follow us to the exit! Hurry!"

I decided that the customs search was going to be conducted in the station building but the Gendarmes bypassed the well- lit hall and made for the darkness of the night. I asked :

"Where are we heading? My train is leaving soon !"

The reply was curt :

"It doesn't matter ; we are going to the Gendarmerie Precinct !"-- and we continued our walk into the darkness....One hundred, two hundred, three hundred paces...The railway station had been left far behind but we were still walking over vacant lots and past dark Chinese huts...My foreboding increased with every step. "Hell, where are these characters taking me? What if they are Hung Hu Tse bandits in disguise ? They could have found out that I sold some "pantui" in Kirin and perhaps have been watching me all the time, this being their opportunity to ambush and rob me at the border." That suspicion became a conviction. "What an idiot !", thought I, "It looks like I let myself be fooled !"

Holding my suitcase in one hand, I used the other one to get hold of a small six--shooter 25--calibre Browning pistol which I kept in my trouser pocket. It was of no use to me in Korea where there were no bandits, but I quite legally always took it on my trips to Manchuria. It was not easy to obtain a permit to carry a rifled-barrelled pistol but father and I enjoyed special privileges and the ability to carry such a toy in my pocket was extremely appealing to my youthful vanity. I often used it, albeit for target practice.

My captors were walking a bit ahead of me and by now I had practically no doubt as to their identity. Seeing that they were bandits, I thought, they would most certainly murder me. The only way out was to kill them first and to make a run for the station. All I needed was some light from a nearby building, and---bang---bang, both would be gone. It was important not to make any unnecessary movements and to avoid any noises when removing the safety catch from the hand-gun. Luckily, all that is needed in this type of pistol is to depress a spring at the back of the handle and simultaneously pull the trigger.

Those moments were critical...The pair walking ahead of me never got to know how close they were from being obliterated. This of course also applied to me because I was about to kill real gendarmes which would have meant death by firing squad for me. Luckily for me, as the fateful moment drew nearer, a well-- lit window of a small single-storey building appeared in front of a dark Chinese hut. I realised that I was not being led into a dark field and took my hand off the pistol....

We entered a small office where an officer of the gendarmes was seated behind a table. He let my captors go and said fairly politely :

"Put down your suitcase and take a seat, please".....

And all of a sudden, his demeanour changed. He started shouting like a man possessed, with spittle flying out of his mouth :

"Are you armed ??!!... Drop the gun on the table !!!... "He pulled out a shining polished handgun and aimed it at my face : "What were you doing on the Doong Hwa Station??!!"...

"I was looking for some milk..."

"You are lying !!! Our people saw you studying and listing military hardware!!... Where is your notebook ?"

I showed him my small notebook which of course did not contain any military information.

He leafed through it and thrust it aside. "O. K. ---out with the truth !!!"

"The truth is that I was on my way home to Korea from Kirin where I bought a cow...My train is about to leave.."

"It does not matter how many trains come and go !! They are no longer for you, 'Soren No Sopai (Soviet spy)' !!. I am going to shoot you !!!" ...He banged the table with the handle of his Mowser pistol, all the while aiming it at me.

It was only then that I understood what I was being suspected of and what this man was trying to prove.

Many years later I found out that a similar if not greater spy-mania was rife in the Soviet Security Services, and, strange as it may seem, in an infinitely more civilised CIA, the only difference being that the Americans spent a long time studying their own and foreign suspects. Having justifiably or otherwise become convinced of the guilt (or lack of innocence) of a person suspected of disloyalty, they would jail or expel the former or sack the latter, ruining their careers but never taking their lives without a court--proven guilt.

However, neither the Japanese nor, alas, Soviet Counter-Intelligence were constrained by any such scruples, following, instead, Stalin's inhuman principle : "It is better to murder ten innocents than, heaven forbid, let go one possibly guilty person..."

In other words, when I finally realised the gravity of what this slanty-- eyed samurai who was about to plant a bullet in my innocent twenty-three - year -old scull was accusing me of, I understood that I had to present hefty arguments in favour of my innocence.

"Mr. Captain, Sir ! We are White Russians ! We fled the Reds twelve years ago ! Please ring the Gendarme Precinct in Seisin, Korea. They have known our family for a long time!"

"Don't tell me what to do ! Tell the truth or I'll shoot you."

I knew that his threat was not an idle one.. There was absolutely nothing to stop him from slaying me, an émigré who had no rights to speak of, and claiming later that the "Soviet Spy" attacked him in an attempt to escape from questioning. He sat pensively for a few moments, got up and said, glaring at me :

"Sit here and think things over. I'll be back soon...Don't leave this chair !"

He called a young soldier and told him to keep an eye on me.

Deeply depressed, I sat on the hard chair trying to imagine the outcome of my predicament when suddenly I heard the gendarme's voice coming from a few rooms away. He was on the phone to somebody. I heard him mention our surname and realised that he was speaking to his Seisin office. Even though he said "don't tell me what to do", he followed my advice. The conversation seemed to last an eternity, with me sitting motionless on the chair, awaiting my fate.

All of a sudden he was back, sat in his chair but did not reach for the pistol.. After lighting a cigarette, inhaling deeply and filling the room with smoke he growled :

"Yeah... Looks like it was a mistake...Sorry...But I am sure you understand that I had to follow up the report from my subordinates"...

He returned my Browning pistol and offered me a "Sikishima" cigarette (a popular brand at the time).

It is quite natural for an intelligence officer to dream of catching a spy and the samurai was disappointed but nevertheless conducted himself with dignity. He glanced at his watch and pronounced :

"Your train has left, of course. But I can offer you a soldier's rest-room. The young fellow will bring a couple of blankets and you can spread them over the "tatami" (straw mat floor covers) next door. Have a rest till dawn... I am really sorry that I had to detain you but this is all in a day's work...We are required to be vigilant in the service of the State...Anyway, the youngster will wake you up at four and will carry your suitcase to the station"..

He bowed stiffly and left. I spread the rough woollen blankets on the tatami and plunged into a deep sleep...

The sun was still below the horizon, turning the east a lemon green, when the "Blue Express" running between Changchun (the capital of Manchuria) and Seisin rattled across the bridge over the Tumangan River taking me home, to Korea. The events of the previous night seemed a faraway nightmare...

Chapter 13. NOVINA'S HAPPY DAYS. LARISSA.

Novina was becoming ever more popular with holiday-makers. Various, often very interesting people, mostly from Harbin and Shanghai, were visiting the resort, among them writers, artists, and politicians. Harbin was a part- Russian city and Shanghai - an international one.

Well- known actors spent the holiday season in Novina and Lukomorye, for example Tomsky from Harbin, Dalevich and Vera Panova from Shanghai.

Another well known personality was the editor of a number of papers and the magazine "Rubezh" ("The Border") Yevgeny Samoilovich Kaufman with his wife and sister in law Agnya Alexandrovna (nicknamed "Gutya") Bibinova. Gutya's husband was the editor of "Rubezh".

The following literati come readily to mind :

A writer by the name of Michael Sherbakov.

A poet with a pseudonym "Val".

Two well known artists : Mr. Kichigin who always came with his wife, and a Mr.Adrianov.

A well known botanist and entomologist Numa Avgustovich Desuslavi.

A bitingly funny anti communist female cartoonist with the pen name of "Vita" who cheated the Gulag by migrating to America before World War II.

Poetesses Larissa Andersen and my sister Victoria Yankovsky.

As I mentioned before, my sister was the permanent hostess of the seaside resort of Lukomorye.

Another celebrity was the stepmother of the future Hollywood star Yul Brynner who was also my distant aunt. In her younger days, when she was known by her maiden name of Katerina Kornakova, she had been one of the favourite pupils of the famous Russian producer Stanislavsky.

Katerina married Yul's father Boris Brynner and spent every summer in the luxurious family "dacha" (holiday home) in Novina. One of her house-guests one year was Natalya Ilyina, a writer who became well known in the Soviet Union after returning there from Shanghai in the 1950's.

The holiday season was full of fun, thanks to my mother Margaret Michailovna and Natalie Nilkolayevna, the wife of uncle Paul (my father's brother).Mother was a great producer and Natalie, talented musician that she was, looked after the orchestral side of plays, musicals, concerts and, of course, dances. Another exciting event was the election of "Miss Novina".

Outdoor sporting activities were interesting and plentiful. They included "gorodki" (a vigorous Russian version of lawn bowls), volleyball and tennis.

We used to organise excursions to the source of the River Ompo flowing through Novina which took us to a picturesque high mountain ridge located about 100 kilometres from Novina and named "Lyusuye Gory" ("Bald Mountains") by us.

Another popular spot was "Mertvoye Ozero" ("The Dead Lake"), a site of an extinct volcano, about 50 km from Novina. The all-day excursion involved a train trip.

A much shorter distance away were "Tri Chashi" ("The Three Chalices"), a series of spectacular waterfalls gouged from rock by the Ompo River, about 20km upstream from Novina. Keen walkers made the return trip in one day, but it was more convenient to catch a small train used for carrying timber, running along a narrow gauge line into the mountains.

The seaside resort of Lukomorye offered a glorious beach, whereas the beaches on the River Ompo in Novina provided a combination of smooth rocks, polished over millenia by the fast-flowing crystal-clear stream, or the cosy soft sand of quiet lagoons....

1. LARISSA

The tractor is coming ! Quick! Get your things!"

The inhabitants of Novina and their guests who had been sitting on the benches, in the pergola and on the large open space between the theatre and the tennis court, quickly picked up their rucksacks and baskets and hurried to the highway along which ran the tracks of the narrow gauge railway. On their way the holidaymakers passed through the arches of the front gates, made of bush rock and adorned with huge ceramic vases full of profusely flowering nasturtiums.

The noise of the approaching train could be clearly heard from the direction of the Ompo Hot Springs, and all of a sudden it appeared from behind the nearest turn of the road. It was drawn by a tiny toy-like tractor emitting blue rings of exhaust gases and pulling about twenty open carriages used to transport timber. When the train drew alongside the theatre -cum-club which was barely visible from behind the clumps of flowering acacias, the driver braked sharply, waved to us and shouted in Japanese :

"Embark quickly ! I have very little time !"

This was merely meant to impress the travellers because he knew full well from the traffic controller, who contacted him the day before, that a group of Russian inhabitants of Novina was to be delivered to the timber company office located three "versts" (kilometres) from the legendary "Three Chalices".

When everybody was safely seated on the small square platforms, the driver revved, rapidly jerking the train into motion and continued ferrying the coupled carriages into the mountains. Very soon the train entered a narrow gorge winding its way between rocky mountains covered in thick forest, and a turbulent crystal - clear river flowing over a base of huge granite plates and rocks polished by the stream. Large waterfalls could be seen at every turn of the road.

When the valley widened one could see neatly tended fields of sorghum, corn, potatoes and soy beans surrounded by clean Korean "fanzas" (cottages), with their paper-covered doors and thatched roofs. Further down the road the rocky, pine and oak - covered mountains abutted the railway line.

The train belonged to a timber company. Its route started at the Shuotsu station and ran past the Ompo Hot Springs, past our Novina and ended in the heart of the Bald Mountains, the site of the timber concessions. Larch, fir and pine trees were being cut there. It made the return trip loaded with long logs which were invariably straddled by reckless passengers who were prepared to ignore frequent accidents.

This trip took us, the owners of the holiday resort of Novina and their guests, along part of the road, namely to the first transfer station. I sat on a carriage in the middle of the train, behind two female backs adorned by black bikini straps --the owners of which are my sister Victoria and her Harbin friend, the love of my young life, the poetess Larissa Andersen. Only now do I notice the striking difference between these two backs.... My sister is at least half a head shorter than her friend but her sunburnt shoulders and shoulder-blades seem to be at least fifty percent wider! Victoria, also known as "Ora", is a seasoned hiker, a hunter, and a strongly built lass.

By contrast, Larissa, a poetess and ballerina, is a shapely beauty. She has luxurious chestnut-coloured hair, eyebrows which look as if they had been painted on her face, violet-blue eyes, a slightly snubby nose and a bewitching smile. I called her "The Magnificent Lalla", a name given to one of his subjects by the great Russian poet Sergey Yesenin, and she accepted that nickname. Lalka was of course immensely popular. My brother Arseny and I fell over each other to teach her to drive our old motor car and to ride horses. We took turns to gallop with her in rain and shine on our two black horses. The horses used to get tired, refusing to gallop and walking side by side instead...

On one of our trips home from the railway station I handed the steering wheel over to Larissa. All went well until we reached a sharp bend of the road which had been recently covered with blue metal. The car started skidding and my pupil drove it into a ditch. The ditch was too deep for me to be able to drive the car out of it without some assistance. I went looking for a bullock with a Korean drover who told me that the beast needed a cart to be able to understand what was required of him. The cart having been attached after some delay, the ox understood that he had to exert an effort. That he did, and dragged the car out of the ditch showing his enormous, locomotive-like strength.

The poetess was deeply distressed standing to the side, with the hands clutching her throat. She appeared to be convinced that this was the end of her driving career. However, I decided to restore her confidence and opening the car door pointed to the steering wheel :

"Go ahead !"

She glanced at me with surprise. Lifting her eyebrows she smiled out of the corner of her mouth and took the wheel. The trip to another danger spot, at the entrance to a rocky grotto where I was expected to take over, went without incident. As I found later, this earned me some brownie points...

In the evening we went to the First Waterfall. The full moon was in the sky, the waterfall made mysterious sounds and looked just like molten silver. We sat down on the huge granite plates, still warm from the rays of the sun....and she was the first one to kiss me!

I was elated at this development and gave her a few passionate kisses but was not game to go any further. Despite the fact that I had some experience in these matters, I treated Lalla differently. I felt as if I was holding a priceless crystal vase in my hands which I was afraid to break. This attitude came from my father. When I turned fifteen, he spoke to me in terms which made a life-long impression. The gist of his communication was as follows : "You will meet many women during your earthly journey, Valery. But remember this : You have no responsibility for those of them who had already been married ; however -- and make this the most important principle of your life -- you can only touch an innocent young maiden if you have resolved to marry her. The world is full of predators, rogues and liars but my son cannot be amongst them --remember this for the rest of your days!"

He did not ask me to make a solemn promise but I have followed his advice throughout my long life. It is not up to me to say whether this was the right decision...

But I digress....Where was I ?

Ah yes, our little train finally made it to the intermediate station and having collected our belongings we proceeded to wait for our porters. In the meantime, the girls were amusing themselves with a rather dangerous game. They would climb onto a huge pile of logs, stacked ready for shipment, and shout : "Catch!" . This meant that one of them was about to take a dive as if into a swimming pool. We would catch the "diver" in full flight, seize her firmly and make a full turn to break the fall. The daredevil was then placed on the ground, with some lads effecting a soft landing, with the others producing a more spectacular finale to the dive.

At long last we were joined by our constant assistants in these ventures, two Korean youths by the name of Lee Pok Teggee and An Yun Choree who brought with them a tiny pack cow (<u>Note</u> : Koreans use bovines as beasts of burden) which they hired from the nearby village. We loaded the provisions and tents on the cow keeping our personal belongings in the rucksacks. The excursion starts with a walk through the forest along a narrow mountain path leading to the legendary Three Chalices.

We are dealing here with a unique wonder of nature. It is the creation of the turbulent southern tributary of the Ompo River which over many centuries carved out of granite a wondrous ensemble of three water holes with almost vertical walls. The clear mountain stream fills the upper waterhole with greenish - blue water which swirls as if it were on the boil ; the turbulent liquid finds an exit towards the second "chalice" and rushes into it over a natural sluice. The "boiling" action is enhanced in the second reservoir, accompanied by the creation of whirlpools. The water continues to move and falls over the edge of that reservoir into the third chalice, creating a ten--sazjen (a "sazjen "is a Russian measure of length equal to seven feet or about 2.1 metres) waterfall with spectacular edges which look like liquid lace. It is impossible to keep one's gaze away from this wild splendour !

The winding path took us along a steep mountainside past many waterfalls, and whereas it continued on towards the peaks of The Bald Mountains, the object of our trip that day was a spot opposite the Second Chalice where we went about establishing a camp on a large clearing used for that purpose for many years. The holidaymakers crossed the Ompo River over a rickety narrow bridge spanning its banks and pitched their tents on the clearing among the remnants of many old camp- fires. The tents were delivered without incident by the tiny brown pack cow which avoided the dangerous bridge crossing by using a shallow ford upstream from the First Chalice.

At long last the tents are pitched and diligent ladies with their Korean helpers are beavering away at the camp- fires. The crockery and foodstuffs are being laid out. Out come bread, rice, vegetables as well as smoked legs of wild pig ham and pieces of wild pig bacon, the latter two being the results of our winter hunting expeditions. They were superbly prepared by our catering manager, Anton Pavlovich Kozak, a former member of the Czech Brigade. That Brigade took part in the Civil War in Siberia in the 1920's on the side of the White Armies.

Our ultimate goal is to use the camp as a base for a trek to the lower treeless reaches of The Bald Mountains in search of ginseng but the immediate aim is to have a swim. We slide into the ice -cold water of the upper chalice over the warm smooth rocks and continue an old argument whilst swimming in small circles : is it possible to slide into the second chalice over the natural sluice connecting both reservoirs? It is quite awe - inspiring, because even though the surface of the sluice is very smooth, it is extremely narrow, resembling a polished bamboo rod, and the current is very strong. Of course, a few scratches are not something to be afraid of, but the main question is whether it is possible to surface in the second chalice without being sucked under its surface by a bottomless whirlpool. Nobody has yet risked such an adventure....

We are debating this question at great length, but all of a sudden Kolya Gusakovsky, a short but thick -set and powerfully built lad with shining myopic eyes, shouts out :

"Enough ! I am going ! Watch!"

He swims towards the edge of the sluice and stretches out his arms. The powerful current picks him up and drags him bodily into the open pipe. There he is, careering with his head thrust forward in the fast stream, resembling a powerful trout !.. He makes it to the second chalice but then disappears out of sight!...There is no sign of him in the boiling water ---he has vanished...

The girls are screaming their heads off...We are all terribly tense...But after what seems like eternity we see a blond head covered in matted hair bobbing up and down in the water. There he is, blinking his eyes to the roar of the enthusiastic crowd : "Bravo, Kolka!"

We realise that the feat is not death - defying after all, and form a queue to repeat his brave stunt. However, nobody ever risked a dive into the third chalice, because the last and main waterfall was perfectly vertical, ending in a black lagoon full of shiny polished trees with powerful roots, which were dumped there by the stream after being gouged out of the soil of distant mountain ranges by powerful storms. We only admired and, of course, photographed this last "Niagara" fall, with its unbelievably beautiful chalice, from the safety of nearby rocks.

Both Larissa and I loved the mountains but my love for them included hunting whereas Lalla was disgusted by "murder". I did teach her to shoot but only at artificial targets. There was one occasion when I talked her into shooting at a bird sitting on a rock thinking that she would miss it. Lalla fired and the white seagull fell like a stone from the top of a white rock !

My "Diana, the hunting goddess" was inconsolable and unforgiving.

We also quarrelled on the trip to the Three Chalices, although I do not remember why. All I remember is that she vanished into the forest. I spent a lot of time looking for her travelling in ever diminishing circles all over the place when I suddenly heard an enchanting sound of a song. It was Larissa --of that there was no doubt --but where was she ? The voice appeared to be coming from heaven. And there she was --on the top of a huge tree -- looking for all the world like a large bird listening to its own song!

"What are you up to ? Get down ! Come on, get down or you'll fall and injure yourself ! And be careful ! Don't panic : I'll catch you if you slip !..."

There was no reply but she finished her song, slid into my arms and we made our way back to the clearing and the tents. And again we were arguing about some nonsense. I was insanely and stupidly jealous of her admiration for the famous American movie actor Garry Cooper. The more she worshipped him, the more jealous I got. My vengeance consisted of getting hold of a portrait of Cooper in one of the newspapers and shooting at it. It was terribly childish but it is no use pretending that it didn't happen.

I attached the full-sized coloured portrait of this very handsome manly actor to the trunk of a large oak, pulled out my 32 - calibre Browning pistol, my constant companion on such trips, out of its holster and ---one - two - three--- planted three bullets in his forehead, cheek and a cleanly shaven chin. Larissa stood to the side observing my antics and, in her usual manner, not uttering a sound. But she couldn't completely control herself and burst into tears after the third shot. I thought that she felt sorry for her hero and was about to start indignantly accusing me of stupid conduct, but what I heard was utterly unexpected :

"Shoot me, shoot me ! It is so incredibly beautiful here ! I don't want to go back to the dusty city full of brick houses! It is better to die here and now amongst this magnificent nature ! Shoot me, shoot me !"

She clutched her tiny fists to her throat, with large transparent tears streaming from her violet eyes...I was taken aback by her violent reaction and barely managed to console Larissa. Frankly, I did not believe her at the time, thinking that she was sorry for that guy Cooper and was simply pulling my leg. Only very much later did I realise that she was sincere... Her artistic nature was overwhelmed by the phenomenal beauty surrounding us and it was painful for her to part with it. Perhaps I should have embraced her and said : "Don't leave ! Stay with me here forever..."But something stopped me, even though I came very close to uttering those words...

Strange though it may seem, I was driven by conservative feelings which are so rare in a youngster. I followed the precepts instilled in me by the parents : "You are too young to take on the responsibility for another human being, even though she is very dear to you." This sounds quite paradoxical : What sort of a Romeo was that ? Nevertheless, I am convinced that I was constrained by the realisation of the fact that I was too green to undertake any serious steps...

In the meantime, fleet-footed souls among the campers decided to set out in search of wild ginseng. Each searcher was provided with a stick cut from a local tree for the purpose of pushing aside shrubbery, grass and spider webs as well as for general support. We formed a human chain and started roaming the steep slopes of nearby mountains. We stumbled and fell, sustaining numerous minor sprains and strains for our trouble but found absolutely nothing. This despite the fact that local Korean professionals often dug out decent--sized roots which they used to bring to Novina in baskets made from pine bark. My brother Arseny used some of these roots to establish a small hidden plantation in a rocky spot on our estate.

At the crack of dawn of the next day the hardiest members of the expedition set out for the summit of the Bald Mountains. This was a very long and arduous trek which started with a walk along a narrow poorly defined mountain path winding its way along the slopes of a rich subtropical forest. On its upward way the path meanders across the banks of a small rocky brook. The hiker is confronted with such rare species of vegetation as yew, Karelian birch, magnolia and thick shoots of wild grape, actinidia and wild lemon. Gradually the brook gets smaller and vanishes completely, and the forest is replaced by stunted birch and larch followed by fields of rhododendron. Higher still are bare rocks with occasional fields of bilberries.

When the traveller reaches the top of the mighty Korean Ridge of Seryon, he is confronted with a grandiose panorama of endless grey, green and blue ridges and peaks which stretch as far as the eye can see. And far in the misty east one catches a glimpse of a corner of the blue sea - the sight of our resort of Lukomorye.

We lay down to have a rest and found ourselves among a large field of matt-- blue bilberries which we proceeded to devour. We crawled on our stomachs filling our mouths with handfuls of the delicious fruit. All of a sudden somebody sang out :

"Look ! The dogs are grazing too !"

This was a sight to behold : our four hunting laika dogs were emulating their human masters, crawling on their bellies, enthusiastically clicking their teeth and chewing the bilberries which were turning their tongues blue.

Our group accomplished the ascent in record time of a single day. The return, downhill, trip was accomplished at almost a running pace. The weather was getting worse towards the evening with the first heavy rain drops beginning to fall while we were still on our way. No sooner did we rush into our tents than the torrential downpour struck with all its force.

The rain was like a wall of water, falling for a night, day and another night. There was no talk of a fire. Some of us slept, others told fairy tales, still others were chewing what was left of dried bread. The water rises quickly in the mountains. On the second morning we were shocked by the grandiose sight of huge waves of a brown torrent racing along the entire width of the stream. Had our tents been pitched even a little bit lower, the camp and the hikers would have been swept into oblivion leaving behind an empty space. Majestic though the picture was, it was very frightening and our position critical. To add to our discomfort, we had just enough provisions for the planned length of the expedition. Starvation rations had to be introduced. At the same time we were cut off from the rest of the world not even being able to get to the track which brought us here.

But here we were blessed by a completely unforeseen event : our pack cow gave birth to a calf ! Nobody had the slightest idea that she was expecting. Truth be known, though, her calf lived only for one day, having been devoured by the hungry hikers who cooked him in a pot on the second day. Luckily the soup kept us going for another two days...Some bright soul realised that the young mother could be milked, although it never happened to her before, because the Koreans never used any milk in those days.

...... As a matter of interest, once, in a candid moment during my childhood, I told my playmate Kim Chung Byagi, who was the same age as I, that Asians always smelt of garlic, to which he replied that all Europeans had an intolerable odour of sour milk, particularly noticeable when they stood on the windward side...

At long last, the skies cleared, the sun appeared and the trees and grass acquired bright fresh colours. And, as is always the case in the mountains, the water level started dropping rapidly. But we were hungry and did not want to spend a single extra hour as prisoners of the elements. As our group had a few strong lads, a decision was made to build a bridge. We cut down a mighty larch which was dragged to the stream and thrown across its banks in a narrow spot, resting on each side on some rocks. A second, thinner trunk was thrown across the stream alongside the first, allowing for a safe transfer to the other bank of the members of the group requiring assistance. Tents and the rest of the belongings followed suit. And only then did we remember the pack cow tethered in the forest clearing ! It waded across the stream on the way down, but what were we to do now? There was no question of a foot crossing because the terrifying yellow stream would immediately drag her into the waterfall which, of course, meant instant death...

The only way was to get her to swim across the torrent assisted by a rope. It was undoubtedly risky but it was the only way. A strong rope was tied around the beast's trunk, around its shoulder blades and neck. Having checked the knots, we stood on one bank holding the long end of the rope, ready for a signal from the other side...The Koreans kicked and pushed the unfortunate desperately resisting animal into the boiling torrent and shouted: "Drag !!!"

The cow was naturally immediately dragged away by the mad current. Its head was bobbing up and down, occasionally completely disappearing from sight. The pitiful thing was out of its mind with fright, with fountains of water issuing out of its nostrils, but the humans were tugging strongly and in unison, and after a minute or two it made it to the other side, shaking violently... Water was coming out of the cow as if it was a barrel with holes in its sides. I am sure that if animals have memories, this pathetic creature remembered that swim for the rest of her miserable days...

When we got to the railway, we found out that the narrow gauge railway was also damaged in some parts of its length. It was being quickly repaired and the first train was expected any day. The majority of my companions dispersed in various directions having decided to wait, but I noticed an overturned carriage which had already been repaired. Having been given permission by the station manager, I put it on the rails with his assistance. The manager handed me a primitive brake consisting of a lever-cum-stick which is placed in the corner of the carriage. One of its ends is held by the "driver", with the other one being applied to the wheel to control the speed of motion. Of course, such a mode of speed control takes some getting used to.

Everything is ready at last. I call my sister and, of course, the blue-eyed poetess plus only one other person because the small platform can only take four people. We push the carriage and jump into it. The motion is slow at first, accelerating gradually to a point where bushes lining the road flick past like in a real train. I let go of the brake when the road straightens out and brake before a turn to make sure that the track ahead is not damaged. Once a dangerous section is passed, I give the carriage the gun. The feeling is indescribable : there is no sound of a motor or smell of diesel, only a slight noise from the cast iron wheels when they meet the joints between the rails. The general impression is of an air flight. The wind presses against my face, tousles my hair and huns in my ears. And the air is filled with the fragrance of grass and invisible flowers drying after the recent storms!

All of a sudden the fields and huts of the Korean farmers disappear from sight to be replaced by the River Ompo boiling in its bed of granite alongside the rail track. Another analogy comes to mind : a mad gallop on a full-blooded stallion when the wayward wind pushes the rider's ears flat against the head... We pass the seventh, sixth, fifth and, at long last, the first waterfall, round the last bend --- and here they are---the large and tiny dachas (holiday homes) flashing past us on both sides of the road, together with the poplars and acacias on the main alley of our Novina. The faces of our friends and acquaintances greet us...Everybody is waving and smiling. Many of them thought that we had fallen victim to the wild nature..

We see The Theatre and the stone pillars of the entrance gates through which we started this dangerous adventure only a few days ago....

Fate dispersed us throughout the world. Larissa married a well - to - do Frenchman and visited Africa, India and Tahiti, the island in the warm waters of the Pacific Ocean. I was at the opposite end of the same Ocean, in the ice wastes of Chukotka.

At long last, everybody is at home :

Lalla is in France, Victoria in America, and I in Russia....

It is so hard to imagine that in Korea, The Land of Morning Fragrance, the waterfalls are still just as full of noise and brilliance....

But, this time, without us, without our youth...

Chapter 14. THE CLOUDS ARE GATHERING BUT LIFE GOES ON.

The Japanese administration demanded a meticulous registration of all arrivals to Novina because the police were weary of infiltration by spies, particularly from Russia. However, their attitude to our family was generally quite friendly because the authorities encouraged the development of farming everywhere in Korea and Manchuria. In addition, Novina was frequently visited by military personnel and civilian tourists who were taking a cure at the nearby Ompo Hot Springs.

As a rule, the Japanese visitors would admire the deer through wide cracks in the surrounding fence and pay reverential visits to our church accompanying them with deep bows. It was also generally regarded as a must to be photographed on the suspension bridge designed by my uncle Alexander.

We had visits from high officials from the regional city of Ranan, from the Korean capital of Seoul and from the state of Manchukuo (the name given by the Japanese to Manchuria after 1932). These visitors included members of the Military and even the governor-general of Korea himself, general Koiso. He was very fond of fishing and would spend hours standing barefoot with his fishing rod on the warm stones of the banks of the Ompo River. During his visits he would generally take tea or drink beer in the "Ancestors' Tower" on our estate.

Some Japanese writers, poets and journalists became our close friends. But it was with the Koreans that we formed genuinely close friendships. They were usually not city dwellers, merchants or professional transport drivers but villagers, and first and foremost--hunters. We spent many a night with a lot of them in thatched- roofed huts or even in the open; in winter and summer we found ourselves sharing a tent and breaking "bread". There is, however, no bread in the Korean diet. They eat boiled sorghum, corn, oats or even rice, accompanied by spicy soy bean soups, dried fish and boiled potatoes. Their meals were garnished with the hottest imaginable condiments, such as red pepper, white radish and specially prepared cabbage.

The owners of huts scattered in the mountains and seasoned pathfinders of tne taiga (native forest) became as close to us as brothers. Few remarkable characters will remain in my memory for the rest of my days. I call them "The Korean Dersu-Usala", after the hero of Arsenyev' s novel by the same name (<u>Note </u>: Vladimir. K. Arsenyev was an explorer and author who lived in the Russian Far East in the first third of the 20th Century), and one day am going to write a separate novel about these people.

Here are the names of some of the people with whom my brothers and I went through "hell and high water" :

Huang Bong from a plateau above the clouds ; Hang Te Djung from the shores of the Tumangan River ; Kim Chung Bong, the one who lived near the ancient fortress Puryon...

They were unassuming and brave dwellers of the timeless taiga, true patriots, most of them. Despite the seemingly unshakeable hold of the Japanese authorities on Korea, with the majority of the population resigned to the status quo, they never lost hope that sooner or later their country would regain its independence. It was impossible not to share their hopes even though such subjects could only be discussed during quiet times, sitting by the camp fire in some remote corner of the taiga.

We lost our mother in 1936. Much too early, at the age of 52, she was taken by the dreaded cancer. We buried her next to our grandmother amongst scraggy pine trees in an old Korean cemetery in Novina. Our grief was profound, of course, but life went on...

1. A TRIP TO HARBIN

Harbin..... Every human, particularly a young one, sees reality from his own point of view. The perception of life by young Russian émigrés in Manchuria was no exception...

For example, Natalya Ilyina (a former Russian émigré who returned to Russia from Shanghai after World War II and became a popular writer) describes her life in Harbin in dark, morbid terms. This may well be understandable because even when she was an adult she had to share a pitiful existence in a single room with her mother (who was a teacher) and sister. Despite the fact that she was always a welcome guest in the home of our uncle, Boris Brynner and his wife, our auntie, Katerina Karnakova, Natalya always suffered from an inferiority complex and resented being dependent on their generosity even though she spent a few summer holidays with the couple in their dacha (holiday- home) in our Lukomorye. Hurt pride produced resentment...

It has to be said that having occupied Manchuria the Japanese showed an ambivalent attitude towards the White Russian émigrés. There were cases of oppression, of arrests by the Gendarmerie (Secret Service) and even torture of people suspected of anti-Japanese activities. There was also the compulsory service by young people in special military units called "Asano". This having said, there was free trade and free enterprise and a law which allowed freehold titles over land, coupled with a favourable treatment of people who wanted to engage in farming.

There will always be disgruntled individuals complaining about the powers that be and that period was no exception, with complaints about "oppression" by the Japanese "samurai" (a derogatory nickname based on the Japanese word for "warrior ").However, legitimate or not, such complaints pale into insignificance before the horrors visited upon the unfortunate natives of Russia living in The Far East after the arrival of their long-awaited compatriots who brought with them such delights as the Soviet NKVD ("People's Commissariat of

Internal Affairs", renamed "KGB" in later years), SMERSH ("Death To The Spies") and MGB ("Ministry of State Security")...

Looking back, all of those who hated the representatives of the Kwangtung Army (the name of the Japanese occupation forces), and particularly those who went through the hell of Stalin's Gulag, regard the years of life in Manchukuo as heaven on earth. Thousands of former White Russian émigrés remember their sojourn in that foreign land with genuine love, despite the fact that they lived there as guests, first of the Chinese and then of the Japanese.

This can be seen not only from my writings but also from the writings of former citizens of Harbin who have found asylum in Australia, Europe and America. Quite recently I read with great interest and empathy a book by Elizabeth Rachinskaya entitled "The Kaleidoscope of Life", published in Paris in 1990. There are many such books, although, quite naturally, any human life is full of dramatic and frequently tragic events. Our life in Korea and Manchuria contained such episodes. Refer, for example, to my story about how I was suspected of being a Soviet spy, related in Chapter 12 of this book.

I was only eleven when we fled to Korea but I remember the town of Vladivostok very well. This is why when father and I were visiting Harbin, I could have sworn that I was back in Russia. There were Russian signs on shops, cafes, chemists and educational establishments. Friendly Russian faces abounded, the street crowds were well dressed. The traffic kept to the left and the taxi drivers were Russian. One could hail a passing taxi anywhere by merely signalling the driver. The taxi would stop and ask: "Churin (a well known Department Store)?...Modiagou (a suburb populated by many Russians) ?...Old City (another suburb with a large Russian population)?..."The fares were 10--15--20---kopeks (cents)...The passengers were discharged upon arrival at their precise destination...

Taxi drivers drove Fords, Chevrolets and Dodges and were patiently waiting at a taxi rank near the Harbin Central Railway Station, lowering the hoods of their convertibles in summer. The rank was shared with horse driven carts, with Russian and Chinese carriers. Everybody was polite and attentive...

The shop assistants were fawning upon their customers, which was a carry-over from the customer-- seller relations of pre--revolutionary days, a legacy of the old merchant traditions.

In the Jewish shops on the Mostovaya Street (a street in the "Docks" district of Harbin, near the Sungari River, the equivalent of the CBD of a modern city) one heard, as if one was in Odessa (a city in the present -- day Ukraine with a polyglot population and a large Jewish merchant community before The Russian Revolution) :

"You only try this on! This is really something very special !"

If you told the shop assistant that you were staying in a hotel (father and I were staying in the "Modern Hotel"), you need have had no further worries about your purchase. When you returned to your hotel in the evening, you found all your purchases in your room, neatly packed and tied with twine, complete with a comfortable handle, which ensured that the twine did not cut your finger....

In the morning of our arrival in Harbin I left our hotel through a gently groaning revolving door and was flabbergasted to see cohorts of beauties walking along the main thoroughfare --the "Kitayskaya ('Chinese') Street". I shall remember that stunned feeling for the rest of my days ! Truth be known, their numbers appeared to have dwindled by day two, with a further reduction with the efflux of time, but nevertheless, the majority of women in that part of town were beautiful and well dressed. The impression was extremely colourful, particularly from the point of view of a savage --a hunter from the faraway exotic Korea !

Father introduced me to his old and new friends :

The dignified grey-haired former Governor--General of the Amur Region (adjacent to Manchuria) Nikolai Lvovich ("Son of Leo") Gondatti.

A Mr. Melgunov, who had been Gondatti's aide-de-camp.

An also grey-haired well known writer Nikolai Appolonovich Baikov who had been a member of the team of the original builders of The Chinese Eastern Railway passing through Manchuria. Being a passionate hunter, Baikov questioned us with great interest about hunting in Korea.

When father and I were alone in our hotel room that evening, he told me that Baikov wrote entertaining stories but often gilded the lily when describing his hunting exploits. Later in life, when I acquired a lot of experience in these matters, I realised that father had a point.

We also made the acquaintance of the charming publisher of the magazine "Rubezh" ("The Border") Eugene Samoilovich ("Son of Samuel") Kaufman and its editor a Mr. Rokotov (that was his professional nom de plume, the real surname being Bibinov).

A visit was made to our distant relatives, the brothers Leonid and Boris Brynner. Boris was the father of the famous actor Yul Brynner. Both of them bought blocks of land from us and each built two dachas (holiday homes), one in Novina and the other one in Lukomorye. As already mentioned, they and their families spent their summer holidays in these dachas.

We also paid a visit to the manager of the Harbin Plywood Factory Michael Alexandrovich ("Son of Alexander ") Hintze, his lovely wife Natalia Borisovna ("Daughter of Boris") and three youngsters ---Misha (Michael) , Viva (Vladimir) and Dima (Dimitry) . Misha is living in Australia at present and he and I have been in regular correspondence over many years. Mr. and Mrs. Hintze built a dacha in Novina before their children were born.

Two more dacha owners visited by us were a Harbin boxer by the name of Mr. Yuzefovich and Kostya (Konstantin) and Moorochka Vasiliev (a brother and sister) who built a dacha in Lukomorye . Mura (Note :"Moorochka", is the "tender" form of "Mura") has remained my lifelong friend .

My second visit to Harbin took place in 1935 . It coincided with the sale by the Russian Government of The Chinese Eastern Railway to Japan, accompanied by a mass repatriation of the Russian employees of the undertaking. That was the time of a boom in the fortunes of the Harbin merchants, because the discharged employees had been paid in gold currency.

These well provided for people bought literally everything : dress materials, furs, jewellery, and musical instruments -- in other words anything of value. They knew that such merchandise was unobtainable in Russia. What they did not know about was the reception which awaited them "at home". Thousands of these innocent former employees of the Railway very soon found themselves in concentration camps of the Gulag, and many others ---in the dungeons of the regime, with bullet holes in their skulls.

Be as it may, I witnessed a rare sight of empty shelves in some of the largest stores. That temporary shortage was soon overcome and Harbin was back to being its bubbly self. Theatres and restaurants were full. Balls and dance parties were held. Famous actors, such as Henkin from Russia and Shalyapin from Paris, visited the city.

Summer was the time when people made their customary pilgrimage to the islands on left bank of the Sungari River (the city was located on its right bank) and to the popular beach suburb called "Zaton" ("Boat Yard"). Zaton was famous for its volleyball and tennis courts, its swimming, walks and boating.

On the city side of the Sungari, at the point where Kitayskaya ("Chinese") Street meets the river, stood the two - storied Yacht Club. Large and small private launches and numerous passenger rowing boats used for the transportation of passengers were moored at the jetty. The Chinese rowing boat owners would shout : "Madama, siree, let's go!"

Towards the evening white -sailed yachts would glide in all directions over the surface of the calm river. The youth of Harbin were happy and carefree --unaware of the gathering clouds --having no premonition of their terrible fate---the same tragic fate which befell the innocent employees of The Chinese Eastern Railway.....

2. BACK TO NOVINA

In retrospect, the Russian exiles ("émigrés"), both in Novina and Lukomorye, lived, as the Russian saying goes, "as if under Christ's shirt" (meaning "under Christ's protection"), like in paradise.

Violet and pink azaleas flowered in April on the mountains. May brought the flowering of the "sakura" (Japanese plum) in the nearby hamlet of Ompo which had a large Japanese population. Small lamps which were lit at night were installed in the tops of the flowering trees. This produced a fairy-tale-like picture of pinkish-white tree crowns. A faint aroma of the flowering plum enhanced the charming effect.

Apricots, pears and apple trees followed suit.

White sweet smelling acacias started flowering profusely from June onwards. They grew in great abundance along most paths and roads.

Later still came the turn of orange and red lilies (we called them "sarankas") and wild flowers known as "the Maltese cross", as well as of purple and violet irises and flowering jasmine.

The mooing of cows returning from the pastures to the farm and the whistling of farm deer could be heard in the evening

Ivan Kuzmich Resnyansky, a kind-hearted soul, could be seen beavering near the apiary made of bush rock.

Our energetic house manager Anton Pavlovich Kozak would make sweet purple - coloured wine out of crushed ripe wild grapes. He was a great expert at turning the carcasses of wild boars, bears and deer into delicious ham and bacon.

A rich harvest of apples, pears, apricots and plums used to be collected in Novina in September of each year....

Chapter 15. THE FIRST CLAPS OF THUNDER -BUT LIFE GOES ON.

1. A CLASH OF RIVAL ARMIES

In the middle of 1938 a border incident took place on the common border between Korea, Manchukuo and Russia. The subject of the dispute was a hill called Zaozernaya ("Beyond the Lake"). The sound of rifle fire mingled with the crackle of machine guns and the boom of cannons. This was the beginning of a short local war which became known in history as "The battle in the vicinity of Lake Khasan".

The Japanese authorities in Korea declared a state of emergency. Reservists were called up in the cities, and the police station in the Ompo Hot Springs, next door to our holiday resort of Novina, became the theatre of playacting involving the hostilities. I was summoned to it as a representative of the Russians living in Novina.

The officer in charge of the station, a middle-aged bald Japanese, by the name of Mr.Osavabucho, sat next to a telephone at a table in the centre of a large room. He wore a military - style cap and had the facial expression of at least a commander of a whole army engaged in military action. His two Korean assistants called "The Big Pak" and "The Little Pak" sat at two small separate tables. Official -- looking papers were strewn all over Osavabucho's table. The table lamp was obscured with a piece of black paper to produce a blackout. Representatives of the citizenry of the Ompo Hamlet occupied several chairs placed against the station's walls.

They included :

The owners of local guest houses ; a Mr. Sato, the owner of the local shop ; the manager of the bus station ; the postmaster, and, last but not least, the elders of the nearby villages. Mr.Osavabucho pointed to the chair designated for me and solemnly continued his speech which he was delivering in Japanese :

"Sakai jihen! Kokunai no chui!" ("This is a border conflict ! The country demands vigilance!") He continued : "Everybody must be prepared !...Of course, our glorious armed forces will win but we cannot exclude the possibility of enemy air attacks, and for that reason a total blackout has to be observed at night. Anybody guilty of ignoring this order will be punished in accordance with the emergency laws !"

The skirmishes grew ever more violent, with reinforcements being moved to the Zaozernaya Hill by both sides. That hill, all of 155 metres high and lying close to the nearby sea, changed hands several times. Luckily, nature intervened in a decisive way through an exceptionally strong cyclone which started in the Russian Maritime Provinces and came down onto North Eastern Korea. Torrential rain lasting several days flooded trenches, washed away roads and stopped the military hardware in its tracks. Things got to a stage where even tanks and self-propelling cannons were stuck in the mud. That cataclysmic event cooled down the ardour of the warriors who started negotiating a peaceful resolution of the incident.

2. THE CYCLONE AND A GOOD SAMARITAN.

The usually crystal clear and clean River Ompo running through our estate turned a murky yellow colour and broke its banks. The foaming torrent was carrying timber bridges and whole trees washed away somewhere upstream. The water kept rising, and in the raging stream started appearing carcasses of drowned cows owned by the Korean farmers and, what was quite astonishing, even of wild pigs. The bus service between the hamlet of Ompo and the railway station was interrupted which gave rise to rumours that the trains were about to stop.

Panic set in amongst our holidaymakers. One couple--a Harbin actor Vassili Ivanovich ("Son of Ivan") Tomsky and his spouse--asked my father to take them to a train leaving for the North--to Manchuria.

Our family had two fairly old sedans driven, in turn, by my brother Arseny, uncle Victor and me. On the day in question, the 18th of August 1938, I was the duty chauffeur.

The corpulent powerfully built actor sat in the back nursing his suitcases, with Madam Tomsky occupying a seat next to me in the front. The farewelling well-wishers shook their heads pointing to the steam-like foam rising from the river and urging the Tomskys to postpone the journey. However, nothing could shake the resolve of the stubborn couple. The ageing Ford spluttered into action, and we were off.

No sooner did we pass the Ompo Hot Springs than I realised that the situation was very dangerous...The buses had stopped running and my driver mates were indicating with urgent gestures that the road was impassable. And indeed, the Ompo which would normally murmur peacefully far away in the valley, was now spread right across it, with its reddish - brown waves loudly pounding against the granite-encased sides of the highway, which was winding its way along the mountains. Usually tiny brooks running down the mountains, turned into powerful turbid water-falls which were undermining the road surface.

In order to check the depth of these cross currents I stopped at the most powerful one of them and tested the depth of the ditch with my foot. We had to cross it one way or another because the way back was cut off.

I grabbed the steering wheel and steered the trusty old Ford into the torrent. The car sunk almost to the bonnet in the water and was labouring valiantly... At this very moment the actor's wife let out a scream and thrust her arms around my neck :

"No! No! No! We are going to drown !"She yelled, hanging on like a mad cat..

THE FIRST CLAPS OF THUNDER - BUT LIFE GOES ON

My exquisite manners of a young squire notwithstanding, I was forced to shove an elbow into her side and to use some harsh words which quietened her down. In the meantime the magnificent machine roared its way across the torrent and raced towards the railway station.

However, another obstacle lay ahead of us : we found ourselves hemmed between the sheer cliffs on the left and a raging river on the right which was ready to devour us. In some spots the water was splashing over the road, noisily hitting the car. Large stones were rolling down the hillside, accompanied by mud slides. Should any of these objects have made the road impassable, we would have been doomed. Worse still, there was no way we could even turn around to go back. It was obvious that our car was the last one to make this trip as there were no vehicles travelling in the opposite direction.

We were heading for a blind corner. The immediate question was : what's behind it? The trouble was that we were facing at least one kilometre of such twists. I inwardly blessed myself and muttered a prayer : "Lord, save us !"

He did...We got through, my back wet with perspiration... A low-lying valley lay ahead, still shielded by an unbroken dam. We passed the holiday resort of Kaneta, protected by the same dam, and raced towards the station. The steam train was about to leave, with white mist billowing out of its engines. Tomsky and I barely had time to throw our suitcases into a carriage and to unceremoniously push his corpulent wife up her rump into the train. No sooner did we accomplish this than the train took off...This was the last train north, towards the town of Seisin (now Chongjin) and the Manchurian border.

No trains were heading south. The panic stricken locals were shouting on top of their voices that further towards the mouth of the river, three rivers had formed a single torrent which had demolished a telephone line and was washing away the highway and part of the rail line. Screaming women were running through the railway settlement, dragging their children behind them. Kids and women were bawling out their eyes. Men were dragging bicycles and carts loaded with personal belongings.

"Moori--ya, Moori --ya", went the chant : "A flood! A deluge!" They were bellowing that water was engulfing the station from all sides...

What am I to do ? I park the car in the corner of a large garage of the by now deserted local service station, which has a concrete floor, and race outside.

To my astonishment, three familiar figures are walking towards me, all three of them from our seaside holiday resort of Lukomorye. They were: the petite wife of my cousin Oleg Shevelev, Mura ; an energetic young mother of three little boys Natasha (Natalie) Hintze and my old hunting buddy Valentin Valkov. The trio made an uneventful train trip in the morning to do some shopping and got caught up in the disaster. They were at a loss as to what to do next. Even though the rain had stopped, the water kept rising threatening to flood the station, trapping the prospective passengers. The mothers were quite naturally in a panic. Mura whispered :

"Valerchik (a "tender" form of "Valery"), I have a little son in our dacha (summer house) in Lukomorye. "

Natasha joined her :

"I have three of them ! What am I to do?"

Both women look pleadingly at me...

I think for a moment and decide that we should try to reach Lukomorye on foot by walking across the railway bridge. But the time is of the essence even though the bridge has solid piers made of rock...

I run towards a Korean corner shop where I buy two bundles of rope, which is as thick as my finger, from its panic-stricken owners. Back to the bridge! On the double!

We climb the embankment and quickly assess the situation. We are surrounded by a sea of yellow water with huge waves rolling over its surface. The bridge is holding but it is vibrating and emitting a buzzing noise. It is impossible to see either the other end of the bridge or the opposite shore because both are covered in haze. Upstream and to the right of us we see the familiar vehicular bridge, which we use on the Novina --Lukomorye run, still holding its own against the flood. As we look at it, the old blackened structure, undermined by now by the torrent, rises into the air and with an almighty roar crashes into the water! The mad stream begins to drag its pieces in our direction, hitting them against the supports of the railway structure and pushing and twisting them right beneath our feet, where the clearance from the water surface is by now less than a metre.

As a precaution, we tie the rope around the waists of our female companions. There is not a soul on the bridge except our small group... The ladies turn pale and start to squeal something but this is not the time for listening, as the fate of the vehicular bridge can any minute befall its rail counterpart. I hold one end of the rope, with my mate Valkov holding the other one, at the end of our column. I shout to the accompaniment of the infernal din :

"Move forward! Sing!", and start shouting the words of a military song :

"Hey, you falcons, soar like eagles !

Hey, you Cossacks of the Baikal Sea!

Ataman * Semyonov's with us,

Leading us to victory !" "

(*Note : "Ataman"---leader of the Cossacks)

The rest of the group is enthusiastically following my vocal example, and we walk along narrow boards laid between the rails on top of the sleepers of the bridge...Through the water spray we are marching into the unknown. Because of the spray we still can't see the other end of the bridge. What if there no longer is the other end?...

After the ordeal was over, Natasha confessed that she forced herself to look only at my rubber boots flashing in front of her, refusing to think and keeping up the rhythm of the walk. Truth be known, I cannot remember what I was thinking of at the time.

At long last, we catch a glimpse of the other side of the bridge and our salvation--the opposite shore of the river. By now we are almost running towards it, but as we set foot on the other side, the embankment gives way to the water which had been undermining it, and slides into the abyss, leaving us without a foothold ! The rails and the sleepers are hanging in mid-air..

"Let's crawl!", bellow I an order..

We crouch on all fours and, crawling like "plastuns" (lower ranks in the Cossack infantry), reach the other shore. We step on terra firma and embrace each other. There are no more serious obstacles ahead of us... We move swiftly, with bravado accompanied by nervous laughter.

Presently, Lukomorye appears in our sights. The sun is fierce and the sandy soil has absorbed the moisture from the downpour. There are no signs of a flood...On walking past the luxurious dacha of my uncle Boris Yulyevich Brynner, we see uncle Borya (short for "Boris") standing on the veranda with his usual charming smile :

"Come in for a tick! How did you get through, heroes all of you? We have been told that all bridges have been washed away!"

Both young mums decline his invitation and race to meet their offspring, but Valentin and I join him on the veranda. The sight of the peaceful pines and the gently murmuring sea makes a startling contrast with the awesome beginning of this frightening day which culminated in our crossing of a precipice.

With a slight stutter which usually indicated a state of nervousness, uncle Borya told us how astonished he was to see the rain coming down in an unbroken wall of water, when he stepped on the veranda the previous night!. He said that even though he was widely travelled, he had never seen anything like it before in his life.

Later that evening we all sat on the open terrace of a dacha rented by Natasha Hintze enjoying the onset of a warm peaceful night, the gradual appearance of the glimmering stars and the deep murmur of the nearby ocean. Our brave and by now very chirpy lady companions were vying with each other in the description of our adventurous morning.

Somebody started to sing in a low voice with the rest of us joining in. Following that pleasant interlude, I was asked to whistle two romantic tunes which I used to perform quite well those days : "A Cigarette's Blue Haze" and "The Fragrant Flowers of The White Acacia"...

.....It is well after midnight and I am walking Natasha's girlfriends, Mura Sheveleva and Mila Bocharova, to their homes, well, actually --dachas. Silently and noiselessly we follow a moonlit path.

I am in the centre, with a girl on each side.

Quite unexpectedly, Milka (another version of the name "Mila") whispers seductively : "Put your arm around me, Valery!"

Mila is on my left...It is, frankly, quite embarrassing to put one's arm just around her, and I put my arm around Moorka's waist as well...Mura peels off at her dacha which is halfway between Natasha's and Mila's abodes, with Mila and me continuing our journey...

To my great astonishment I suddenly hear an urgent whisper : "Embrace me stronger, much stronger!....."

To be perfectly honest, I always fancied the well-proportioned blond Militsa Georgiyevna ("daughter of George") , Mila for short. There were, however, two difficulties : the first one was that she had a fiancée, and the second--that my then friend with a nickname of "Vera Belaya " ("Vera The Blonde") hated her guts. That feeling was reciprocated, with both women being sworn enemies. As a result of this feud, my relations with Mila had been cool right up to that night.

Can you imagine my astonishment when all of a sudden that beauty started to mutter incoherently, putting her arms around my neck, clinging to me and whispering :

"You are so strong, so brave you are so...oh....so...!"

All I could think of was that my performance the previous day made her regard me as a hero ; and it is a well known fact that women worship heroes, even those who only conquer nature. The seductress was truly ravishingly beautiful, as beautiful as that night, as the Lombardy poplars surrounding us, as the stars and the ocean!

I feel like confessing my feelings for her but an unkind thought is gnawing at me and knocking at my subconscious mind : "Don't trust her ! It's all a game! She wants to seduce you and then boast of her conquest to her rival, belittling you at the same time!"

My soul is torn between virtue and sin. I mutter :

"You are enchanting but I have no right to kiss you!"

Undaunted, she responds as if having read my thoughts :

"I know what is stopping you ! But never mind, we can wait...Listen, let's go to my dacha, but there is a danger that the landlady will hear us... I'll go in and pick up a pillow and a quilt...We can go to the seashore and stay there the whole night..."

My soul was in a turmoil, I was overwhelmed..Luckily, reason prevails. I decide not to be seduced and to show that wonderful bird of paradise that she is not all-powerful...

I pour cold water on her passion :

"No, Mila, I am going !"

Mila catches her breath, draws away from me and stands upright. Her eyes, as beautiful as the sky before a thunderstorm, darken and flash ominously, reflecting the light of the moon.

"Well, what can I do ? It is a pity..But I can assure you that you will often remember this night with regret..."

She turned and went into her dacha without giving me another glance.

"What a hero!", thought I. "Imagine being able to withstand such an onslaught!"

But the feeling of pride at my strength was mixed with the annoyance at having missed such an opportunity. Had my Verka known of my loyalty, she would have surely worshipped me for it. But none of them ever found out how often I remembered that moonlit night and whispered :

"You fool! You damned fool!"

3. VERA BELAYA ("VERA THE BLONDE ")

Early next morning quite a few of us walked back to Novina. There was no longer any road at the spot through which I made it with the Tomskys only the day before. Half of it was completely washed away, with the other half being covered with huge boulders, clay and fallen trees. We had to bypass dangerous sections of the road, climbing along mountainous goat tracks and wading across flooded creeks.

The flood interrupted the vehicular traffic for more than a month. However, this was nothing compared with the depressing and gloomy sight which greeted me upon arrival in Novina.

Our "Catamaran" (the name of a combined lounge--dining area, built with great love out of bush rock, with my and my siblings' help, when we were still children), the kitchen, the adobe dwelling of Uncle Paul, the two timber dachas (summer houses) and the suspension bridge ---all these structures were turned by the storm into a wasteland consisting of stone and sand mounds. It was impossible to comprehend that things which appeared indestructible, having survived several previous floods, were literally turned to dust...They were gone, never to return..

However, a much more serious problem was awaiting me personally --that of my relationship with a woman with whom I had been very close....

...Two figures appeared among the scene of devastation : "My" Vera and an English businessman --my friend from Shanghai . They came to meet us, with Vera Petrovna ("daughter of Peter") being quite irate with me. Indeed, what an impertinence to cause her so much anxiety! She was apprehensive and jealous at the same time. She was incapable of controlling her emotions, and her feelings were being betrayed by her facial expression and the look in her eyes. I compared her eyes which were discoloured by rage with the divine colour of Mila's eyes, with my lady-friend coming off second best . If women knew how dreadfully ugly they appear when they are unable to conceal their dark emotions, they would perhaps be more careful in displaying them....

Three cheers to those of them who are able to preserve their dignity under all circumstances....

....Vera Petrovna Burundin, nee Lazareva, first came to Novina from Shanghai as a holidaymaker. Being a startling-looking blonde, she very quickly acquired the nickname of

"Vera Belaya " ("Vera the Blonde"), as opposed to her friend Vera Nichols who became known as "Vera Chernaya" ("Vera the Black"). Both were Russian exiles and both were married to well-to-do foreigners. Vera Nichols' husband was a Greek with a British passport, and "my" Vera was married to a Swede. These beauties were the first ladies of Novina during three successive seasons. They were surrounded by admirers and had been elected Beauty Queens of the resort.

Vera Petrovna was full of conceit on account of her many male admirers. She had been to Sweden to visit her in-laws who treated her as their own daughter. Her husband had a good job in Shanghai which enabled them to have a comfortable life-style. Despite all of that, she filed for divorce from her husband so as to be able to marry me.

That sophisticated woman of the world added a lot to my life of a semi-savage. She introduced me to her aristocratic airs and graces, to the English language, popular magazines, the games of mah-jong and poker, expensive drinks and cigarettes, and modern dances...

One year Vera brought her ne'er-do-well brother Kostya, a lout, to spend the summer with her. I spent a fair bit of time nursing that drunk, to the point of bringing a doctor in the middle of the night to our house to attend to his liver poisoned by alcohol (and that in a 25-year old oaf !). The upshot of it was that I threatened to bash him up and threw him out. After that my beau refrained from inviting him ever again.

She often used to make short business trips to Shanghai and returned any time she felt like it. Vera would even accompany us on our hunting trips in the taiga (Dense virgin forest in the Far East and Siberia). Despite all this, her husband kept refusing her a divorce...

The first year or two of our life together were like a fairy-tale but as time went on, her dominant personality, combined with insane jealousy, came to the fore. Ugly scenes became more frequent, even if I, for example, danced two times in a row with the same person. I warned her several times that I could not stand such conduct, particularly in front of others. My suffering lasted for a long time, perhaps even too long, because when one is in love one does not lose hope of being correctly understood.

Finally my patience was at an end...Following a by now customary ugly scene at a party, I silently took her by the arm and brought her home. We passed the veranda and entered the drawing room where I lit a large kerosene lamp with a green shade. (There was no electricity in Novina at the time). Vera would not calm down, stamping her feet and screaming that I was behaving indecently, "chasing every skirt". That was most unjust as I had not been unfaithful to her right up to that night.Cutting a long story short, the cup of my patience overflowed and I decided to teach her a lesson..

I went to the bedroom and took off the wall a riding whip made of leather, which was hanging alongside the rifle. My companion gave me a challenging look : "Just you dare!" But it was too late..I stepped towards her, grabbed her by her blond locks, bent her over and delivered three blows along her back, as if she were a recalcitrant horse..Actually, the blows fell at an angle--from the shoulder to the buttocks...Having accomplished this deed, I threw away the whip and settled down under the green lamp pretending to read a magazine. Vera stormed into the bedroom and burst into tears.The pages of the magazine danced in front of my eyes --I did not understand a word... Her screams behind the locked door were unsettling me...I can't remember how long the performance lasted, but all of a sudden the bedroom door burst open and she walked into the room wearing a terry towelling bath robe... Turning her back to me, Vera threw off the robe :

"Look at what you have done!"

Swollen purple scars, with a reddish-blue hue, were covering her back from the shoulder to the waist!.She stood sideaways,obviously expecting an apology.. But I got up and said overcoming my pity for her :

"You got what you deserved", and walked into the study, with Vera returning to the bedroom, proudly holding her head...

I was certain that spelt the end of our relationship but resolved not to apologise under any circumstances.

Much to my surprise, that proud woman acknowledged the following day that she had been wrong, even apologised and, what was most astonishing, confessed that she did not really resent the "caveman's lesson" because no man had ever assaulted her before. And true to her resolution, her conduct became impeccable for a while...

Neither before nor after that shameful night did I raise my hand at a woman. I decided that she was cured from the attacks of possessiveness, which, regrettably, was not the case.Barely a month later there was another explosion which made me realise that the whip was no cure-all and that under no circumstances should it become part of our relationship. I saw many unfortunate examples of violence in other marriages, with the resultant bruises and "shiners". Vera's condition was obviously incurable...

Following yet another ugly scene, this time on the volleyball courts, I took my love home and, having silently picked up a tooth brush and a towel, repaired for a vacant room in one of our dachas (holiday homes). Walking along a clear path, beneath a star-studded night sky and looking at the poplars and acacias, I realised that a three-year long enslavement was over at last, and, believe me, felt wings starting to grow on my back!

A few days later I went to Manchuria on business and sent a telegram containing just one word : "FAREWELL".

Vera returned to Shanghai from where she wrote that she had a nervous disorder which caused her irrational conduct, for which she apologised, asking me to start afresh.

Luckily, by that time I had calmed down and lost my feelings for her. Accordingly, my reply was a firm "No".

Some time afterwards Vera Petrovna married an English colonel with whom she left for India.

Her last few tender and friendly letters came from Delhi.One of them was accompanied by a farewell photograph of her feeding white swans on the shores of a magnificent lake...Sic transit...

4. NOVINA RECOVERS

As I already wrote,the frightening floods of 1938 washed away the adobe house of my uncle Pavel Michailovich, the building we called "The Catamaran", the resort kitchen and the Suspension Bridge. All that was left of those five buildings were mounds of sand....However, our business was so prosperous that we were able to restore the damaged structures, making them even stronger. But in accordance with our decision, the buildings were rebuilt away from the flood zone.

A tall theatre building sporting a balcony was erected in a large elevated square next to the highway, adjacent to the tennis court. A large dining room, with a stage at the back were located inside it. Behind the stage were an office and the resort kitchen joined to the office by a passageway. Large shelves were built along the walls of the dining room.

Silver trophies won by the Yankovskys' racing and trotting horses were displayed on some shelves. A few other shelves displayed a collection of skulls of animals killed during our hunting expeditions. They ranged from the small skulls of a weasel and ermine, followed by larger ones of a wild cat, a fox, a grey and a red wolf, a leopard and a few bears. The crowning glory of the collection was the skull of a giant tiger with its powerful yellow tusks. A whole shelf was devoted to a collection of upper and lower tusks of wild pigs. Yet another one held a range of horns of roes, wild mountain goats, deer and elk.

Our house guests and visiting tourists spent hours studying these rare specimens.

The main function of the theatre was realised during performances which could accommodate up to one hundred patrons.

Across the highway from the theatre we built a winter residence in the shape of a rich Korean "fanza" (hut). It had about ten rooms, including a dining room, a kitchen and an office.

And so went our life : holidaymakers, deer, the farm and hunting..At long last we were able to give up the paying safari-- hunters who became an unnecessary burden. We three brothers --Valery (yours truly), Arseny and Yury caught up with their farther in hunting skills.

The numbers of Hung Hu Tse (bandits) in Manchuria dropped sharply as a result of measures taken by the Japanese. Hunting in Manchuria always yielded better results than in Korea. For that reason our family started to concentrate on its north-eastern corner which was adjacent to Korea.

The results were very encouraging. Each hunting season yielded valuable trophies such as hundreds of does, many dozen wild pigs, deer,some with expensive pantui (soft horns), elk and bears. In addition to that, we killed a lot of predators such as leopards and tigers. In those days tigers used to terrorise the population of the taiga (virgin forest) regions and adjacent timber felling operations. There were times when tigers, having tasted human flesh, would kill one lumberjack after another, and even invade their barracks. The workers used to abandon their workplaces and flee from the taiga. Asians were panic stricken when confronted by a tiger and often asked Russian hunters to punish the rapacious beasts.Our family was one of those which received such requests.

In spring and autumn we used to hunt wild ducks and geese.For that purpose, we built a hunting lodge in a village called Yenchon, north of Seisin (now Chongjing).

In the beginning of November our family made hunting trips in search of pheasants.Photographs taken at the time show our old Chevrolet with scores of long-tailed cocks and speckled hens hanging from its sides.

The first snow saw us, in company of our experienced Korean assistants, take our dog pack, trained by my brother Yuri, into the taiga . Our family had a contract with the manager of the timber-felling crews on Handaokhedse Station (North Eastern Manchuria), Vassili Ivanovich Kojevnikov, for the supply of animal carcasses. However the best, the choicest carcasses were sent home to Novina to be smoked by our expert, Anton Pavlovich Kozak . The Kozaks (Anton and his wife Maria Ivanovna) spent many years in our employ.

Chapter 16. SHANGHAI IN 1941 - VARIOUS EPISODES.

1. I TRAVEL TO SHANGHAI.

On the sixth of August 1940 a hired Chinese assassin and terrorist shot and killed my uncle Pavel Michailovich Yankovsky who was the Head of the Investigation Branch of the French Police in the City of Shanghai . At the time of the assassination he had been in charge of the investigation into the murder of the Chairman of the Bureau of the Russian Emigres in that city. Pavel was rash enough to make a statement during a card game in the circle of his close friends to the effect that he had the case "in his pocket". It remains a mystery to this day as to whether the Soviet or the Japanese Secret Service organised the hit.

Pavel Michailovich was buried in Shanghai with suitable pomp and circumstance and his widow received a considerable payout. Uncle's widow asked me to come to Shanghai to help her with various fiscal matters. My trip was to take place in January 1941.

The majority of White Russians who had dachas (summer-houses) in Novina stayed in them only during summer, returning to their main abodes in Harbin, Seoul, Tientsin or Shanghai. There were, however, a few who stayed for the winter. An old friend of our family, Yevgeny (Eugene) Avgustovich ("son of Augustine") Ellers was one of them. Ellers was born in Vladivostok and emigrated to Shanghai. He bought a picturesque block of land on a steep slope of a hill on which he built a large and elegant dacha (summer house). His companion in that venture was Boris Krivosh.

Ellers used to make occasional business trips to Shanghai. A solidly built man who walked like a sailor, he bore a striking resemblance to the movie actor Banionis. A good story teller and a happy-go-lucky guy, my friend was usually the life of any party. He was famous for the rendition of a funny story of his own creation entitled "How an Englishman tried to send a small dog from Australia to Kobe". It was incredibly popular amongst the Russians in Shanghai and was frequently recited by various people at social gatherings.

This was the man with whom I decided to go to Shanghai. He and I ordered tickets for our sea voyage which was to start from Inchon, the port of Seoul.

The ship was scheduled to leave on Monday the thirteenth but superstitious Ellers categorically refused to board the vessel on that day. I had to go on my own with Eugene making a round trip via Seoul, Pusan, Modji and Nagasaki...

The port city of Inchon, which had been called "Chemulpo"in Korean, is known in history through the tragic loss in its vicinity during the Russo-Japanese War of 1904-1905 of our military vessels "Koreets" ("The Korean") and "Varyag" ("The Varangian").Standing in a solemn mood on the deck of a small Japanese ship "Chindo Maru", I was trying to imagine that distant tragic day... It seemed to me that at the far end of the misty bay I could see the smoke from the chimneys of the Japanese fleet, the flashes from its guns. I sensed the impact of the enemy shells exploding around me...

The two thousand tonnes "Chindo Maru" crossed the Yellow Sea in twenty four hours and made a short stop in the famous Chinese holiday destination --the port city of Qingdao, which was practically empty at that time of the year. A day later we entered the mouth of the Whampoa River on whose banks is situated the port of Shanghai. To the left of us we could see the smoking chimneys of the industrial suburb of Putung and to the right --the embankments of the port --the famous Bund.

Flag-bearing warships of many nations were moored midstream. We observed cruisers, frigates and mine sweepers belonging to England, France, Italy and The USA. The largest fleet was that of "The Land of The Rising Sun", because by that time Japan had been prosecuting a war against China for three years and was establishing its supremacy in that region.

The city of Shanghai consisted of the purely Chinese part, and foreign concessions, the main ones being the British, French and, of course, the strongly fortified Japanese Concession.The car taking me from the docks to the city stopped at the border of the Japanese Concession which was near the bridge crossing a canal. It was guarded by small of stature Japanese infantrymen who looked like mannequins with their rifles and bayonets on the ready. On the opposite side of the canal were the dashing figures of much more relaxed well built Indian soldiers wearing white turbans and British uniforms. They were carrying Enfield ten-shooter rifles with which I was familiar through my hunting expeditions.

That side of the canal astounded me with the swirling human sea consisting of Europeans of many hues, Chinese, Malays, Burmese and Filipinos. The mixture of garments, faces and languages was mind-boggling. This was a veritable "Far Eastern Babylon".

In my travels I visited various cities in Japan, Korea and Manchuria. I spent some time in Kirin, Mudanjiang, Tientsin and, of course, Harbin.However, none of them were remotely similar to this human ant heap. Take Shanghai's Nanking Road as an example: its peak hour traffic consisted of a never ending snake-like procession of cars travelling bumper to bumper at walking speed. It reminded me of a slow moving chameleon because of the diverse colours of its sedans and open vehicles...

2. AUNTIES GELYA AND TATA..

I had to visit an auntie --but this time not the widow of the slain Uncle Pavel (Paul) but an Angelina Michailovna Yankovsky--Kichigina. She was the younger sister of my late mother and a spoilt offspring of the Vladivostok merchant of The First Guild, Michael Grigoryevich Shevelev. The main characteristic of Aunt Angelina throughout her life was crass eccentricity.

In her early youth she defied the laws of the Russian Empire to go through a secret wedding ceremony in a remote village with my father's brother Yan (Ivan) Michailovich. When the time came for her to receive a handsome inheritance, Angelina embarked upon crazy adventures, for example, buying doomed "Kerensky Roubles" (the currency issued by The Provisional Government of Russia in March 1917. That government was overthrown by the Communists in October 1917). She bought that currency with gold-backed Japanese yen, simply because she received millions of the worthless paper money in return.

Another one of her crazy actions was to bring to Vladivostok a huge leopard which had been caught and partly tamed by her husband Jan. She named the unfortunate animal "Samson" and paraded it on a leash through the streets of the city. She was forced to abandon that exercise because one of its female residents passed out when confronted by the beast during one of its walks...

Despite all of these foibles, that spoilt grand lady showed a remarkable ability to overcome the difficulties of life in exile. She got hold of a weird high voltage contraption and became popular as a "high voltage masseuse". Her clients included Chinese millionaires and their numerous wives (polygamy was widely practised in China at the time).

The clients paid generous fees, and soon Auntie Gelya (short for "Angelina ") rented a two-storied cottage in a quiet street called "Rue Grouchi", almost in the centre of the French Concession. Life in the cottage became very busy. Various relatives either stayed or lived in the house. Visitors and inhabitants included friends and friends of friends, as well as actors, poets of both sexes, business people, boxers and, naturally, enlisted men from the Russian Regiment in Shanghai. All were welcome, and everybody ate, drank and slept whenever and wherever they wanted.

A twenty four hour service for the guests was provided by Chow Ing Choy, a Chinese cook who came with the family from Vladivostok, and a young Chinese man servant (referred to as "boy"in the colonial jargon).Eating, drinking and entertainment were left to individual tastes. The phone never stopped ringing, the record player was always going, and singing and dancing continued unabated on weekends and week days.

It is little wonder that the cottage very quickly acquired a semi- honorary and fully justified nickname of "The Madhouse". Aunt's second husband Fedor Kichigin was chasing every skirt and drinking with anybody who had even a few dollars, with his wife working from dawn to dusk.

I spent three days in that house and was completely overwhelmed. Despite howls of protest from Aunt Gelya, my female cousins (her daughters) and her bohemian entourage, I rented a room in a boarding house whose pleasant and attentive landlady nicknamed me "Tarzan". That did not stop me from paying frequent visits to the "Madhouse" which remained dear to my heart.

During the first few days of my stay in Shanghai I paid a visit to uncle Paul's widow, Auntie Tata (short for "Natalia"), her daughter, cousin Tanya, who, seemingly overnight, had turned into a seventeen-year-old stunning beauty, and her son, little cousin Misha . The meeting took place in their house, the house where Uncle Paul lost his life.From there we went to uncle's grave to pay respects to the dear departed. In the days that followed, I rendered all the necessary assistance to Auntie with her affairs...

But life went on, and I was not even thirty...

3. TARZAN IS BEING SHOWN THE SIGHTS.

Despite the fact that I was not quite thirty, I had a lot of friends and relatives in Shanghai, because every summer scores of Shanghai residents visited us in Korea, and it was my turn to be entertained by them.Quite naturally, I was inundated with invitations to parties, restaurants, dances, boxing, dog races and "Hai-Lai". At that time "Hai Lai"was a very popular game. It is similar to tennis, and was played by Spanish professionals, with the audience gambling on the outcome of the game and even the results of individual rallies.

Just imagine how I reacted to all those brilliant stimuli after months spent living in tents or snow - covered cabins during my hunting expeditions in the Manchurian taiga (virgin forest)! During that time I hardly ever took off my jacket or trousers sewn out of home-made chamois, and my constant companions were a rucksack, my binoculars and rifle. There were no comforts to be had in the harsh environment of snow and icy wind... Believe me, the change was quite incredible!

My long-time flame Larissa Andersen offered to take me to a concert given by Alexander Vertinsky (an actor and singer who was famous in the Russian emigre circles between 1917 and 1946, and who made a career as a film actor in Russia after returning there circa 1947).

Vertinsky had just arrived in Shanghai from Paris...

A grey-haired player sat at a black grand piano at the centre of the stage, with a tall gentleman dressed in a black tail coat and sporting a white tie standing at the front. Vertinsky gave the concert on his own. His singing with the "r's" pronounced in a French manner, was, as always, inimiatble. Unfortunately, I was less than impressed with the contrived gestures of his large white palms. As well, the abundance of powder on his face struck me as being somewhat unmanly...

During interval Larissa grabbed my hand and dragged me behind the stage.

"Come, come, let me introduce you to Alexander Nikolayevich ('Son of Nilkolai')!"

We entered a large dressing room whose floor the great actor was pacing from one corner to the next, having discarded his tail coat and donned a silver dressing gown. He was surrounded by a gaggle of women and young girls who were following him like a pack of devoted pooches, chattering incessantly and trying to catch his eye. They kept chirping :

"Alexander Nikolayevich! Alexander Nikolayevich! Alexander Nikolayevich!"

I felt sickened and wanted to leave immediately but Larissa firmly grasped my hand :

"Wait, do wait! I am going to introduce you!"

She raced towards the picturesque assembly and said in a loud voice :

"Alexander Nikolayevich! Allow me to introduce to you Valery Yankovsky from Korea!"

Vertinsky stopped pacing and gave me a condescending look :

"Ah ! Ah! Kowea, yes, yes! I wemember! Somebody awweady towd me! I think I met your fawwer and, I think, your sistow!"...

From the height of his greatness, Vertinsky proffered me two fingers...Truth be known, I could barely resist making a rude gesture with my thumb, and replying with the words of a well known rude joke :

"No, Your Eminence! Two fingers are far too many !

Please accept my one finger in return!"

However, I was toowell- mannered for such an outburst. Instead, I turned around and said to the poetess :

"Enough of this ! Let's go back to our seats!"

That was my one and only meeting with the great man.

The weeks I stayed in Shanghai passed with the speed of a hurricane. I was the talk of the town which was symptomatic of a society not fully absorbed in making ends meet. Such beauties as Mila Bocharova and Vera Nichols would ring me and pick me up in their cars. Mila had a blue Ford and Vera drove a twelve- cylinder Packard.

Each of them thought that she was the first one to call, which forced me to tell a pack of white lies.Both Mila and Vera took me to the French Club, the most popular in town.

It is indeed something to behold... The dining tables surround a recessed "lake"of the dance floor. Dancing couples walk to it down a few steps and gyrate on a surface which is glittering like new ice. The floor which was ordered from Paris is not only slippery but also bends like newly-formed ice, in synchronism with the movements of the dancers . It requires a special skill to stay on one's feet without falling over!

Another exciting treat was given me by my cousin on my mother's side, Oleg Shevelev. Known as "Baby Rousse", he was the recent middle-weight boxing champion of China.At the time of meeting him, Oleg was the boxing coach of the enlisted men of the Russian Regiment in Shanghai. He took me to see a boxing match bvetween the Russian lads and foreign boxers.

The prize was being contested by twelve couples, the finalists being a Russian boxer by the name of Viktor Tikhonov and the American boxing champion of the Far Eastern Fleet.

The first round was won by the American boxer. He aggressively pursued Tikhonov who was forced to adopt a defensive stance. Oleg was beside himself.

"You just wait", he said.

During the break Shevelev raced to Victor's corner and gave him whispered instructions.

The bell went and the boxers were at it again, with the handsome sailor rushing forward as in the first round. All of a sudden, there was a left hook from the south paw Tikhonov, which connected with his opponent! The American boxer hit the canvas with a thud, like a sawn down giant tree in the taiga (Siberian or Manchurian virgin Forest).

The umpire began the count but Tikhonov's opponent could not get up.

A thunderous applause greeted the winner !

Strangely enough, the English spectators were the most enthusiastic. They jumped up and shouted :

"Rousse, bravo! Rousse!"

Following my trip with Shevelev I got taken to the dog races by my cousin on the father's side Vassya (short for "Vassili") Powers. Vassya was the manager of that racecourse....

.....A grey hare appears in front of the stands and begins to race along the track pursued by a pack of Borzoi (pedigree) dogs.The dogs are numbered, the patrons are backing them through the Tote and the bookies. The roar and the screams of the crowd are deafening...

The winners celebrate with champagne...

4. A CLOSE CALL.

I used to be very friendly with a stunning beauty, a half-Armenian, half-Jewish girl by the name of Kiska Mit who often spent her summer holidays at the Ellers's dacha (summer house) in Novina.I looked her up in Shanghai, came to see her one day and took her to work in the bar of the largest cabaret and dancing establishment in town. Having had a few dances with Kiska I went home.

The phone rang early next morning :

"You were very lucky to have left when you did last night! You'll never guess what happened! Just after midnight, at the height of the evening, the front door burst open and about six men stormed into the hall pointing their guns at the crowd. ' Everybody under the table!' -- they bellowed -- ' put your wallets and purses on the tables ! We are going to search you and anyone trying to conceal their valuables will be shot!' They then blasted out all the lights in the hall... Just as well that you were not there! Knowing you I, doubt whether you would have crawled under the table! Not with your Browning pistol in your pocket!"

"Yeah, that must have been quite something ! But does anybody know who these characters were ?"

"They said they were Korean terrorists. The police are here now. But what chance do they have of finding them?"

5. WELL SUITED.

When I arrived in Shanghai, I brought with me two suits made in Harbin, which was absolutely inadequate for a man-about-town in that "Babylon". Luckily, there were plenty of excellent tailors who could make a first-class suit at practically a moment's notice. The war in Europe resulted in an exodus of many Jews to the Far East, with many skilled tailors among them.

Unfortunately, visitors to Shanghai were strictly limited in the amount of Japanese currency they were allowed to bring with them, the reason being that a Japanese yen was worth two and a half Chinese dollars. I managed to smuggle in a few large denomination notes in a tube of toothpaste but that was pure luck. Not everybody was able to get away with it as the following story shows...

...Many Russian emigres tried to transfer their assets from Manchuria but did not know how. The family in my story sold their house and used the money to buy diamonds. The eldest sister got a bright idea. She put the gems into a jar filled with crystallised honey and asked a friend to give the jar to her younger sister in Shanghai. When the ship docked in Shanghai the sister's friend was put out by the way the customs officers were rummaging through the passengers' belongings, checking even the smallest items, and decided to get rid of the jar, throwing it overboard into the muddy waters of the Whampoa River. "Honey is honey everywhere", he thought, "I'll buy a jar of it when I disembark".

No sooner did he get through customs than the younger sister rushed to him, greeting him like a long lost brother : "Hello! Am I glad to see you!! Where is my honey?"

The smartie laughed :

"Let's go into town at once ! I am going to buy you a jar of choicest honey in the first delicatessen we see!"

..........A dreadful pause follows this cheerful statement.....

...Pale as a ghost, the younger sister passes out on the floor of the Customs House!..

Getting back to my story, I borrowed the money for the tailor from my uncle Pavel's (Paul's) widow, Auntie Tata, and placed an order with a refugee from Germany for two heavy and two light lounge-suits as well as a dinner-suit and a fashionable overcoat. The Jewish craftsman, who had been financially ruined by Hitler, produced a work of art... He only needed one or two fittings to transform me into a dandy!

As a matter of interest, I was also recommended a Chinese tailor who was a real master of his trade . That man would not take any measurements but simply carefully study his customer asking him to turn, squat, etc. At the end of the session he would say : "Come the day after tomorrow". And ---would you believe it--the lounge or dinner suit fitted like a glove ! The only problem was that he charged double compared with the Jewish artisan.

6. EUGENE ("ZHENKA") ELLERS.

Shortly after my arrival in Shanghai I was joined by Zhenka (one of the diminutive forms of the name "Eugene") Ellers who, as I mentioned, took a circuitous route via Nagasaki to arrive at the same destination. It is difficult to describe what followed his arrival but I'll try...

Ellers teamed up with his friend Boris Krivosh whom I knew from Korea. Thick - set red-haired Krivosh had a wide red pock-marked face--- a classical visage of a banker from a detective film. He had two investment properties which supported his lavish lifestyle. Having become a Yugoslav citizen, he felt unassailable. Boris had a lot of real estate interests, buying and selling houses in Shanghai. He owned luxury motor cars and even had a comfortable cruiser. The cruiser was used for frequent hunting and boozing trips on the Whampoa River in company of his numerous friends.

He would organise dinner parties in his large apartment which culminated in a few select guests being taken to a cabaret in his luxury "Lincoln Zephyr". And not just one cabaret, mind you, but two, three or four...

A cabaret called "Argentina"comes to mind... Borya (one of the diminutive forms of the name "Boris") would buy a swag of tickets at the box office costing two dollars each. Each ticket could be used in exchange for a dance with a hostess. Having equitably split the tickets among his guests, he would lead them into the main hall which contained tables for customers. The dance hostesses sat along the walls between some potted palms.

These women constituted a fascinating mixture of racial types. There were Spanish beauties, Italians, Greeks, Russians, Chinese, Filipinas, Thais, and veritable "Tea Roses", the so-called "Portuguese", the offspring of Southern Chinese women and Miditerranean sailors. European ladies wore evening dresses, with the Asians in long silk chongsams with a slit along the leg reaching all the way up to the hip...

A band at the end of the hall was comprised of guitars, saxophones and trombones. Overhead lights were turned off every few minutes, to be replaced by flashing coloured lights whilst the band played tangos, fox trots, "Blues"and Charlestons. Each dance lasted for only two minutes, at the end of which the customer placed the ticket in his partner's palm. She was paid half of its face value by the establishment.

Customers were allowed to invite the girls to their tables. It has to be said that they were anything but vulgar types.

Drinks were served by a most impressive-looking waiter who was gliding between the tables as if on a skating rink. A flick of the fingers instantly brings the tray-bearing waiter to one's table.

"Yes, Sir ! Whisky ? Brandy? Gin?"

The guest silently indicates on his glass the level to which he wants it filled, and then tops it up with soda-water to his own taste from a container sitting on the table...This is a very clever system, because the soda water stops the patron from getting disgustingly drunk. Unfortunately for me, I woke up the following morning feeling the results of an "alcoholic overload". My landlady was aghast :

"How much did you drink last night, Tarzan? Just have a look in the mirror! You have a burst blood vessel in your eye !"

The phone rang later in the evening in the "Madhouse" which I was visiting that day. On the line was Regina, Krivosh's live-in girlfriend, who was as pretty as a little doll :

"Hello! Is that you, Valery? Listen, "he" and his mates have gone in his cruiser for a couple of days...Do you get my meaning? Is Zhenya with you? Hurry up and come for dinner. I am giving my servants the night off...Just me and my girlfriend...A cosy atmosphere..."

Ellers and I grab a taxi and fly over... The table in the familiar dining room is laden with exquisite food. Bottles with drinks of various kinds are on the table...Gentle music is playing...

We dance in the nearby dining room without heeding the time and it is well past midnight when we decide to turn in . A comfortable bedroom is next door to the dining room, with a huge bed occupying its centre..

"More than enough for the four of us! "

-- says Zhenka matter-of-factly --

"Let's pretend that we are separated by the astral body of a dead Chinaman..."

Savage that I am, I find the experience quite novel and hesitate for a few seconds, with the ladies smiling invitingly from beneath the bed sheets. It is hot in the house and we men have taken off our jackets a long time ago....

Ellers takes off his shoes and removes the trousers in a business-like manner, carefully hanging them on the bed-head...

Then---silence....Well, almost....

In the middle of the night there is a fight between Zhenka and his friend. He jumps up, gets dressed and walks out...

That meant that I had to walk home at dawn...

Even Shanghai is quite empty and silent just before dawn....

Two days after that episode Ellers came out with the following:

"I need your help with a very interesting project. You see, I bought some ships which had been sunk in the Yellow and East China Seas. The paper work is in perfect order. Among them there is a mine sweeper which got stuck in shallow waters between some reefs. It has a covering of first class alloy steel. The Japanese are very interested in this type of metal. It will naturally be very hard to raise the ship to the surface but this is not our problem. All we have to do is to sell the papers which make me its owner. Get it?

As a matter of fact, I already have two trustworthy prospective buyers. We'll have to enter into a contract with them and collect a deposit, and then they can go to hell. Are you prepared to help me?"

We spent two days conducting complicated negotiations. Meetings were held in offices and restaurants. As far as I was concerned, the documents were very rubbery, to say the least, having been issued by some sort of agency investigating disasters at sea. The agency established the location of various wrecks and supposedly had the right to salvage them. It seemed that the vessels had no rightful owners.

Twenty years in Korea, which was a Japanese Dominion at that time, taught me the methods of commercial negotiations and gave me a good knowledge of spoken Japanese. The present case involved proving that Ellers's papers had value, and that it was impossible to start salvage operations in their absence. It would have been obvious to any thinking person, though, that in the political climate prevailing at that time, the Japanese were indisputable masters of the Far Eastern waters. Their country was practically next door, and all the nearby ports had Japanese naval bases. In other words, they were in charge of the situation.

However, the negotiations also had a psychological dimension because the Japanese are great believers in official documents. That was the card I played.

Zhenka rummaged through his briefcase, extracting and brandishing a bundle of documents with their impressive-looking seals and signatures, with our clients trying to weigh up all the pros and cons of the situation. They sighed, groaned and puffed, whispering to each other and scratching their foreheads...

In the end they signed the contract which was worth many thousands of dollars and paid a handsome cash deposit. I could not help thinking that the whole deal was shonky but the deed was done. Eugene handed over some of the documents, issued a receipt for the deposit, and we departed after exchanging polite bows with the businessmen.

As soon as we were on our own, Ellers shook my hand and said:

"Good on you, Val! How much commission should I pay you? Let's go and have a drink and you can tell me what I owe you!"

"It's quite OK, Zhenka! Forget about the commission" (I really did not feel like getting paid by him). "If you want to reward me for my efforts, how about presenting me with the Belgian six-shooter Mowser rifle my cousin Vasska (a diminutive form of "Vassili") Powers has been offering for sale?"....

...........I took Zhenka's present to Korea and used it for the best part of five years, until it was confiscated in 1946 by the Russian Intelligence people (members of the so-called "SMERSH"---an acronym of the Russian name for 'Death To The Spies'---group)...

Anyway, we did go to a first class Chinese restaurant that day to celebrate our success. We were elated because for a while the deal seemed on the verge of falling through. We raised our glasses to our friends, to Korea, to our hunting expeditions and to the future occasions when we would get together to remember that day.

Ellers ordered a banquet consisting of eight dishes. We drank brandy with chasers of hot Chinese "beer" (actually, a potent spirit made from sorghum). The banquet lasted for three hours and quite naturally we did not notice a change in the weather thinking that it was simply getting dark.

However, Shanghai became quite unrecognisable during those few hours : the sky was overcast and it was snowing! The snow flakes were small and melted almost immediately, but it was snow nevertheless.It must have been falling throughout our meal because the melting snow started to cause local flooding. The overflowing gutters turned the streets into "the canals of Venice".The only thing that was lacking were the gondolas...

The pedestrians were panic-- stricken, much to the delight of numerous rickshaw coolies who ferried them across flooded streets in their man-driven carriages.Despite the fact that Zhenya and I were quite inebriated, we had enough sense to hire two rickshaws to take us across the street from where we wanted to walk to a nearby taxi rank.

The crossing went off without a hitch but when we started walking towards the rank, we immediately came across a wide muddy "river" which had been a wide street only a few hours before. On its "bank" we observed a hesitant group of well dressed Europeans who I thought were English. Ellers and I paused as well but Zhenya gave me a defiant look :

"Let's show these guys ! Start walking across!"

We had no inhibitions due to our inebriated state. Zhenya took off his shoes and socks and rolled up his carefully pressed trousers. Without a moment's hesitation, I followed suit...The English group looked aghast. One of them said pointedly loudly :

"Look, Russians, of course!!!"

The water was icy but we did not feel the cold and started blindly wading across the street. I still remember hoping that we would not step into a ditch.The taxi rank was by now clearly visible across the street. We scrambled onto a dry section of the footpath and raced barefoot to the rank.

A woman's face screwed up with contempt appeared from the office window. It was obvious that her first impression was that of dirty bare feet.

"What do you want ?"She asked in a mocking tone.

Zhenka pulled out a bundle of five dollar bills out of his pocket, smashing them against the window-sill and barked :

"Taxi at once!"

The contempt was instantly replaced with obsequiousness, the face changing from long to round:

"Yes, Sir!!!"

And true to the woman's promise, a new Ford appeared in front of us almost immediately. The driver opened the door and we jumped on the back seat. Ellers thrust the money at the cabbie and told him the address. The chauffeur threw a multicoloured woollen blanket over the back rest of the front seat.

"Rub your feet thoroughly, it's all been paid for!"

Our feet, the same colour red as a gander's, started rubbing the warm surface of the blanket, producing a series of dirty yellow stains...

We stormed into "The Madhouse" looking just as wild as after we started our water crossing, raced to the first floor and jumped into a large bath filled with hot water. Sitting opposite each other in the bath, we were laughing our heads off....

....Six years passed after that day....A war erupted in The Far East followed by sworn protestations from the Russian Government that all the past transgressions of the White Russian emigres had been forgiven.They were being exhorted to help The Red Army to fight the Japanese during the Korean and Manchurian Campaigns. Despite all of this, we, who enthusiastically threw ourselves into the task of helping the Motherland, were, at War's end, almost without exception, thrown into the Gulag camps of Siberia, Magadan, Kolyma and Chukotka.

I met Ellers in May 1947 in a transit camp on Pervaya Rechka ("The First River ") in Vladivostok. Zhenka was as cheerful as always. He was already working as a foreman on a construction site inside the camp and was full of humour, jokes and critical comments.Even though we were both very depressed underneath this external bravado, neither of us had any idea that it was our last meeting...

After my release from Gulag, I arrived in Magadan from Chukotka where I started making enquiries about my relatives and friends.My enquiries unearthed a rumour that Ellers had been executed by a firing squad....

I was absolutely flabbergasted. Why ? What possible crime could he have committed? It was, of course, always possible that he had been unable to put up with the humiliations meted out to the inmates of the Gulag and murdered somebody in a fit of rage. Is that what it was ?

I made some inquiries from the Administration of the Gulag but was told that only members of the immediate family were entitled to such information. I passed on the rumour to Eugene's wife, Valentina, who was by then in The USA. That is where the matter rested for a long time...

Another forty years passed, and only very recently I received a document which explained what happened...

After Eugene Avgustovich had served six years of his first sentence, which meant that he was due for release in two (or, with remissions, even fewer) years' time, some low form of humanity from the Prosecutor's Office decided to "show his vigilance". This no doubt was meant to further the scoundrel's career and to earn him the gratitude of his superiors.

Be as it may, that creep dug out and revived Ellers' case which had already earned Eugene his sentence in 1946. It has to be said that such "revisions" were fashionable at the beginning of the 1950's...

As a result of this act, instead of a pending release, Ellers was taken to Moscow and tried for the second time on the 16th of May 1952. The Military Branch of The Supreme Court consisting of three generals issued a judgement No EN 02711 which said, in part : "...sentenced in accordance with the Law of the 7th of August 1932 to 25 years of penal servitude. In addition to that, in accordance with Article 58.1 "a"of The Penal Code of The Russian Federation and taking into consideration all the circumstances of the committed crimes, the accused is to be executed by a firing squad,with his personal belongings being seized and he being deprived of his civil rights for a period of five years **(deprivation of a murdered man of his civil rights!-- V. G. Y.).** The sums of 150 000 roubles and 1 884 000 Korean won are to be transferred to the Engineering Branch of the TOF (Far Eastern Fleet) as a compensation for the occasioned harm."

Eugene denied the accusations and later appealed for clemency... He stayed on the death row for more than a month...It is impossible to imagine his mental anguish and thoughts during those terrible days and nights!...

Alas!...On the 28 th of June 1952 The Supreme Court of The Soviet Union refused to alter the verdict and the condemned man was murdered with a bullet fired through the back of his skull...

However, forty three years later, on the 28th of September 1995, The Supreme Court of The Russian Federation quashed the conviction and declared the innocence of this unfortunate human being...

When I read those documents, I felt as if I was sitting alongside my friend in that horrifying solitary confinement cell for condemned people. In my mind's eye I joined him on the last walk down the concrete steps to the eerie cellar from which there was no return...

Sleep eluded me for several nights after that experience...

Chapter 17. THE LAST FEW YEARS OF NOVINA.

1. TIGER KILLERS.

From the beginning of the War in the Pacific between the USA and Japan and even earlier--from the beginning of the War between Germany and Russia, the flow of holidaymakers to Novina began to slow down and ultimately stopped completely. There were a few people who occasionally managed to break through the travel restrictions but the mass arrival was definitely over.

Luckily for us, this no longer made much difference because deer farming for the production of pantui (soft deer horns) and hunting gave us a lot more income than all summer tourists put together. By that time we were deriving a large income from the rich game resources of South-Eastern Manchuria which borders Korea.

A drama occurred during one of our hunting expeditions while I was enjoying my tour of "The Far Eastern Babylon".

Shortly after the New Year (1942), father and my youngest brother Yuri decided to look for game in the Manchurian mountains. When they arrived in the village of Chungou where all the males of our family had been hunting during the previous autumn, they were confronted by a panic-stricken population. The farmers told them that tigers were terrorising the hamlet having killed a wood-cutter and a few horses and bullocks. The terrorised farmers were unable to provide any firewood for their needs because four tigers established themselves in the taiga (virgin forest) surrounding their houses.

Father and Yuri were woken up long before dawn on a cold January night by their host, a Korean peasant, who had a prophetic dream in which he saw dead people wearing striped gowns.

"If you are prepared to brave the frost and the gale blowing outisde, you will most certainly kill some tigers today!"-- he told them.

The hunters left at dawn. The small group, comprised Yankovsky Senior, his son, a Korean porter and a pack of dogs. Soon they discovered tiger tracks and observed a short while later that one beast had separated from the pride. They were combing some high mountain ranges when Senior saw a young tigress on the slope of a hill and slaughtered her with the first shot. At the same time an old tigress raced across a gully and, as the hunters were to discover later, set up an ambush to avenge the death of her cub.

The animal killers were running along a mountain ridge trying to cut across the mother's path, when they heard an almighty roar...Yuri Junior thought that he saw a large range motor car tyre tube flying through the air, until he realised that it was the old tigress exacting her revenge on the killer of her offspring. She was flying through the air, reminiscent of a dragon on an old Chinese engraving. Her front paws were outstretched and the tail looked like a perfect arch!

Junior was unable to raise his gun, as he was tangled up in a clump of thorny aralias, commonly referred to as "the devil's trees", but saw the old boy shoot the tigress in the mouth just before they collided. Yuri saw his father's rifle fly in the air after the impact like the propeller of an aeroplane, whereupon the irate mother grabbed hold of Yuri Michailovich as if he were a mere mouse and threw him from the top of a high snow-covered rock. Both the hunter and the hunted then started rolling down the steep incline.

When Junior finally managed to extricate himself from the clutches of "the devil's trees", he saw a distressing sight : the striped orange back of the avenger rolling down the hill, with what appeared to have been lifeless legs of Senior dangling hopelessly under the beast. Yuri was unable to shoot because the bullet would have killed both combatants. Luckily for the old man, the tigress hit an old burnt out stump and slid off the back of her victim, which allowed my brother to hit her with four bullets. As he was firing he heard : "Luylya (one of the diminutive forms of the name 'Yuri'), shoot!". It was obvious that the stunned father had not heard his son's shots...

The old hunter was in a sorry state. He lost his hat and the congealed blood from his wounds formed a clot on his cheek which his horrified son mistook for a torn-out eye! The porter raced to Senior's assistance, helped him to his feet and found the hat and the rifle, both lying in the snow.

The dead tigers were dragged into a gully through which the loggers transported felled timber on their sleighs. Timber was thrown off two sleighs and replaced with orange carcasses which were securely fastened to them. The unfortunate bullocks which were expected to drag the macabre load, broke away and disappeared out of sight leaving their handlers behind...

The carriages nevertheless made it to the hamlet of Chungou, confronting the awe-struck villagers with the sight of frightening visitors in striped gowns! The village was now free from danger, and the peasants were overjoyed!

Father had been fairly severely dealt with by the cub's mother and his injuries took about a week to heal. The tigress' claws left about twenty deep scratches on his head and body. He was lucky in that his bullet damaged the animal's jaw. He would have been unlikely to come out of the encounter alive if the mother had been in full possession of her faculties.

However, that temporary setback did not dampen the ardour of the old hunter, and he resumed the killing as soon as he was able to raise a gun to his shoulder. The hunters tracked down a third tiger, a male this time, and it fell to Yankovsky Junior to kill that noble beast.

I was in Shanghai at the time of that hunt and was elated to receive a telegram written in Japanese : "Tora sambiki totta" ("We killed three tigers").

Three years later Yankovsky Senior published a book in Harbin entitled : "Half a Century on the Trail of the Tigers" . In it he described his first killing at age fifteen, that of a tigress which dragged off a horse their beloved "uncle"--their mentor Platon Fedoroff. In this deed Senior was assisted by his brother Alexander.

Three years after the publication of that book a meeting took place between Yuri Michailovich and his youngest son. Fate and SMERSH (one of Russian Secret Service Organisations) combined in bringing about that meeting. It took place in the faraway town of Novosibirsk, at a transit station between concentration camps ran by the Gulag. They spent the whole night sitting on a prison bunk reminiscing of the past.

It seemed that only yesterday they were tiger hunters, men who were as free as the nature surrounding them. And here--in the Gulag--they had been turned into captives stripped of all human rights...Could they have ever imagined anything like it?

What exactly did father and son say to each other, what did they recall in the stinking transit barracks, surrounded by other, equally innocent captives ? Is it possible that during that last encounter they were forced to endure the insulting jibes of the revolting scum with whom they were forced to share their imprisonment --the so-called "Juniors" (short-term prisoners, usually hardened criminals) ?

When I think of that night, a tightness develops in my throat, and it gets difficult to breathe...

My grief is unbearable because both father and son are no longer alive....

2. FATHER TAKES A BRIDE.

One fine sunny morning in March 1941 Father was returning from a hunting trip in Manchuria with his three sons. The winter season had just ended, and it was time to go home to Korea. Our party was preceded by a pack of motley hunting dogs lazily mincing towards their final destination. Behind us was a caravan of several two-wheeled carts, drawn by huge red bullocks, which contained our hunting trophies : two frozen carcassees of orange-coloured leopards, one carcass each of a brown and black bear, a few dozen wild pigs and more than a hundred does. When we finally reached the border, we had trouble fitting our booty on two large trucks.

We were within a couple of hours' walk from the border River Tumangan when Father started a conversation which he must have been preparing for a long time.

It transpired that despite being sixty two years of age, the old man decided to remarry. The gist of his message, delivered with obvious insincerity, was that his adult sons apparently needed a new mother.The simple fact, however, was that our mother died five years ago and none of us had the slightest need for a new one.Naturally, we voiced our violent objections to that ill-conceived idea.

"Get yourself a housekeeper, Dad, get a secretary, a housemaid --get anybody you want-- but, for Heaven's sake, don't call her a wife! We do not need a stepmother --she will only destroy the family ! Just think about that!!"

Stubborn as always, Yuri Michailovich refused to listen to reason. He went to Shanghai in the summer of 1941 and returned with a middle - aged dowager, the portly hooknosed Olga Petrovna...

"The young lovers" were married with considerable pomp and circumstance in our family church in Novina, built out of huge granite boulders and standing on a high hill. A steep stone staircase led to the shrine. Most newlyweds had their photos taken on its steps, with Yuri and Olga being no exception.

The nuptial was conducted by the parish priest Father John Trostiansky who hailed from Harbin but, accompanied by his wife, moved to Novina a few years earlier. The service was attended by a large crowd of guests. In accordance with the Orthodox custom, crowns were held above the heads of the marrying couple, while the choir sang religious hymns.

A lavish reception was held in the Theatre Building after the wedding ceremony. Toasts and speeches abounded... Wine was flowing like a river...

`Soon after the wedding, Olga Petrovna started behaving like the mistress of the household, forcing herself onto a business which was built up by others long before her arrival. Such insensitive conduct could not but insult the feelings of Yankovsky Senior's adult offspring, but he refused to take any notice of the developing problem, always supporting his new bride.

The break-up of the family was soon to follow...

His youngest son Yuri was conscripted into the Manchukuo Army, and I started making plans for the establishment of an independent household...

Chapter 18. A NEW BEGINNING.

1. THE TIGER HAMLET.

Having occupied Manchuria, the Japanese started actively encouraging farming. Farmers were given grants of land and enjoyed "tax holidays" lasting for several years. Ownership of guns was permitted, with the dual purpose of combating the Hung Hu Tse bandits and of hunting. Many Russian emigres, including myself, took advantage of those special conditions.

I looked up a large tract of land near the Maygetsko Station in Manchuria, which is within a few hours' train ride from the Korean border. It consisted of arable land and a forest. I was able to lease it and obtain an option for an outright purchase at a later date. I named my acquisition "The Tiger Hamlet".

In order to finalise the purchase, I had to make several trips to the provincial centre of Yangtsi, which was called "Kanto" in Japanese.

The formalities included liaison with the so-called "Japanese Military Mission", a sinister establishment which was well known to all the inhabitants of Manchuria, and which was in charge of the affairs of the White Russian emigres in Manchuria. Its Russian acronym was "YVM" ("**Y**aponskaya **V**oyennaya **M**issiya") but everybody simply called it "The Mission" ("Missiya").

The head of The Mission in Kanto was colonel Taki--an extremely tough character-- who was feared by his Japanese subordinates, but was fond of helping Russians who showed initiative. As could be expected of this type of person, he had his favourites, the main one being the leader of the Russian Section of the Mission, one Leonid Guttman, with whom I had only a nodding acquaintance.

On colonel Taki's recommendation the Police Department supplied me, free of charge, with three German military rifles and a box of two thousand cartridges. This was a great help because supply of ammunition for our British Enfield rifles was running out, and hostilities in the vicinity of Shanghai made it no longer possible to obtain replacements from that area.

Whilst travelling between Maygetsko and Kanto in winter I often saw many animal tracks crossing the railway line. They looked like tracks of wild deer to me. Therefore, as soon as I completed all the necessary legal formalities connected with the acquisition of the Tiger Hamlet, I took a trip to that area.

Accompanied by my Korean assistant Kham Chi Goni I arrived at a mixed Chinese - Korean village which was near the area where I had seen the animal tracks. We decided to stay with a local farmer whom we asked whether there were many wild deer in the nearby mountains. The man growled disapprovingly :

"Yes, there are 'norgadji' (wild deer) in the mountains but they are impossible to get. For example, only a short while ago three of the best shots from the local Manchurian regiment spent a whole week chasing them and only managed to kill three deer!"

My trusted companion Kham Chi Goni smiled knowingly :

"This is hardly surprising! Soldiers are not hunters ! Wait till tomorrow and you will see!"...

To be honest, like my friend, I did not doubt that we would be successful but the result exceeded all expectations...

We spent seventeen days hunting the game and a couple of days organising the transport of dead animals by rail. During that time I killed one hundred and four does, one fat wild boar who had been damaging the potato crop, and, last but not least, a red fox.

I made enough money to buy all the necessary building materials for the five-roomed house and sheds I was going to build on my land. I even had enough left over to buy a bullock with a cart and a large bag of rice, which was normally hard to get due to the wartime shortages.. An experienced builder by the name of Pyotr (Peter) Chistyakov joined me at the hamlet in the spring of 1942. He moved to Manchuria from Korea and was destined to become the second husband of my sister, the poetess Victoria Yankovsky.

A gang of Chinese builders' labourers hired by us dug the trenches for the foundations and prepared a site for the septic tank. Other artisans started the building of the house. Work was proceeding apace.

I was making plans to bring my young wife Irma from Korea in the autumn of that year to join me in our new house...

2. A SECOND FATAL WEDDING.

During one of my visits to Kanto I received an invitation to a wedding, the second such fatal occasion in the last few years.

This time it was the turn of colonel Taki's favourite, Leonid Guttman, whom I have already mentioned . He was marrying a waitress from the local cafe, "Dai Kanto" ("Great Kanto"), a Korean lass by the name of Galya, who became "Russified" (Note: This is a term which had been frequently used in old Russia in connection with members of ethnic minorities who became Orthodox Christians and generally adopted a "Russian"way of life, abandoning their own cultural heritage).

As I have already said, I hardly knew the prospective groom, but did not want to offend him by refusing to attend. Besides, I had been on good terms with some of his colleagues from The Japanese Military Mission.

Guttman was the de facto owner of "Dai Kanto". That establishment was a secret rendezvous address used by The Mission and gave Colonel Taki's favourite a chance to make some money on the side. Its second function was as a location for secret eavesdropping on Russian radio broadcasts. The second floor of the cafe was equipped as living and working quarters for several employees of The Mission engaged in these activities.

As expected, the wedding reception was held in Guttman's cafe which was closed for other customers on that night. The newlyweds were sitting at the centre table. A striking Oriental beauty, Galya looked stunning in the wedding gown. She behaved as befits an Oriental charmer, receiving the congratulations of the guests with great dignity, with eyes downcast and a modest smile on her face. Guttman sported a dark blue suit and conducted himself very officiously indeed, lest anybody would forget that he was an important senior person! As for colonel Taki, he would not lower himself to attend such an occasion!

Following a well-established Russian custom, the guests ate, drank and sang a lot. The party became very boisterous indeed after the newlyweds left for their quarters.

At some stage of the proceedings I came to the conclusion that I had too much of a good thing and decided to have a break. I repaired to the back room and stayed there perhaps for half an hour, until I felt normal again. I hate being in a condition where somebody can point a finger at me or, worse still, make fun of my situation!

When I came back, the womenfolk were all gone and the remaining males were in a happy mood. The fellows were shouting to me :

"Pity you missed the fight! You see, some Japs were trying to gate crash the wedding demanding to be let in! No matter how many times we told them that this was a wedding reception, they kept barging in! And they were rude to boot! Never mind, we taught them a lesson by bashing up a couple of their number! We let the slanty-eyed ones know that it was a Russian party!"

The revelry continued unabated until all of a sudden there was a rap on the front door, and a detachment of police appeared at the entrance, consisting of an officer and four lower ranks. They came in and started questioning the guests.

The perpetrators of the bashing knew that I spoke good Japanese and pushed me forward as an interpreter. The officer and I stood opposite each other in the middle of the hall, with his subordinates forming a semicircle behind his back. "Kay-boo-kho"--a Japanese rank roughly equivalent to that of a captain --was polite but firm. He stated that one of the plaintiffs lost an eye as a result of the assault and, being a member of the military, the guilty person would have to be charged ; there was no way the police could overlook the offence...

I explained to the officer that I had not been present during the fight but that, according to the others present, the fight was started by the gatecrashers, and therefore they were responsible for the consequences.

The police left but we continued to party. Part of the "fun" consisted of an Oriental wrestling game where contestants place their forearms on a table, with the elbows resting on its surface. They then link their palms and start pressing each other's arms towards the surface of the table, keeping the elbows in place. The game is won when one's opponent's forearm is forced against the surface of the table. The contest lasted for quite some time but the final bout was between me and the winner of the "heats".

I must say without false modesty that in that game I was without peer, and took only a few seconds to annihilate my opponent by forcing his forearm flat against the table. The loser got very uptight and decided to engage in a Greko-Roman wrestling match. All red in the face, he grabbed me around the waist, and we both collapsed on the floor. I quickly got on top of my opponent but bumped my head against the concrete floor in the process, splitting the skin, which produced quite a lot of blood. Some of the blood stained my military-- style jacket. But as we were all pretty drunk at the time, we soon made up and finished the party with the bucks paying a collective visit to the local Chinese "tea houses"...

After that memorable wedding I and my employee Pavel (Paul) Kalistratovich Zhukov decided to travel back to the Tiger Hamlet.

Zhukov was a former soldier in the Army of the White General Vladimir Oskarovich Kappel. After the end of the Russian Civil War he spent some time working as a driver for the Japanese Military Mission.

Anyway, Zhukov and I arrived at the Maygetsko Station by the evening of the day following the wedding and stopped for the night in a Korean inn. Our plan was to continue the journey to The Tiger Hamlet the following day.

After breakfast on the day of our intended departure, I was asked to go to the local police station. I had no inkling as to the reason for the invitation but went there with a completely clear conscience and not expecting any trouble, because I was very friendly with the local superintendent.

When I entered his office I was surprised to see a completely strange face behind his desk. It belonged to quite a handsome Korean with a narrow face which surprised me with its particularly cranky and menacing expression. He had three stars on his shoulder straps which designated his rank as "koiboo"---similar to a major.

As I found out later, Pak- Arai (his name) was a former officer of the gendarmes (secret police) in the town of Hung Chung, on the Russian border, where he was known for his unbelievable cruelty. When I greeted him, he replied with a shouted command: "Attention!!! Listen, you criminal, I am going to teach you a lesson.!"

"Search him!"---he ordered his subordinates. "Put him in handcuffs and leg irons! Tie him up in accordance with regulations and throw him into a cell!"

His offsiders grabbed me from three sides, even though I made no attempt to resist. I realised that there was no point in any defiance as, quite clearly, the whole thing was a giant misunderstanding. However, there is a big difference between understanding the situation and being treated like a dangerous criminal !

I was taken through a narrow passageway and thrown into an iron cell-cum-cage which was separated from the passageway by thick iron rods. My captors placed me face down on the floor and tightened the handcuffs behind my back in such a way that any movement caused them to penetrate my wrists. The more one moved, the deeper they penetrated the wrists.

They did not have any leg irons but knew exactly what the sadist Pak -Arai meant by "tying me up in accordance with regulations". The rope which was tying my legs to the back was made to pass under my throat, and any attempt to move them led to self-asphyxiation!

It was soon obvious to me that I could not survive in such a position, because my body was bent in the shape of a diving fish and the rope was inexorably choking me. It seemed that "The Grim Reaper" was standing at the threshold of the cell...But the survival instinct brought a solution to the deadly impasse, and I started to crawl towards the wall, slowly at first, almost like a turtle. Having reached it, I turned with great difficulty and pushed my legs against the wall, reducing the pressure from the rope.Breathing became much easier...

All of a sudden I heard a commotion in the corridor and realised to my horror that the sentries were dragging a completely innocent Zhukov in my direction ! I knew from his moans and wheezes that he was tied up in the same way as I. He was thrown into a cell next to mine, and even though we were separated by a thin wall, we managed to exchange a few words before falling silent.

Half an hour later, I heard a cry :

"Valery Yuryevich! I am dying!!"...

"Hang on, Kalystratych (abbreviated patronymic of Zhukov)! Just try to put up with it! Turn on one side and push your feet against the wall! I promise you--it is all a mistake - they'll sort it out!"

Zhukov moved about for a while and then quietened down.

A short while later there was a sound of a lock being opened, and I saw a familiar face of my acquaintance --a junior police officer, an ethnic Korean. The lad knew of my friendship with his former boss and decided to help us. He whispered.

"I am going to loosen the ropes on both of you, but don't let on...The investigators from Kanto won't be long --they have already left..."

We were immediately able to breathe much easier and our legs were no longer badly cramped. The officer's action was very humane, and he himself risked dire consequences for his kindness.

Early in the evening I was unshackled and led into the superintendent's office.Three officers were sitting in the room : Pak -Arai and two plainclothed Japanese policemen from the District Office, one of whom I knew. When the trio started cross-examining me, I realised that they were given the task of finding the person responsible for inflicting eye injuries to the Japanese official. However, they were not allowed to sheet the blame to any of the employees of The Japanese Military Mission, because that organisation occupied a higher position in the police hierarchy. That meant that not being a member of the Mission, I was their obvious source of information regarding the identity of the culprit. Another reason for their interest lay in the fact that blood on my jacket and a wound on the forehead made me the prime suspect.

The Japanese interrogators were restrained although persistent in their questioning. However, the new superintendent of the Maygetsko Police, the professional sadist Pak- Arai was relentless (Note: The hyphenated name "Pak-Arai" shows that the man being described here was an ethnic Korean, as stated earlier. Like many other ambitious Koreans during the Japanese occupation, he added a Japanese surname "Arai" to his Korean surname of "Pak"). He shouted :

"You will talk and you will name the guilty ones! Did you say 'no'? Bring a bucket full of water and a tea pot !"---he ordered his underlings.

His request was instantly obeyed, and the required implements landed on the floor with a sickening thud. Not having experienced before what was intended for me, I nevertheless knew full well what to expect.

The tortured person is placed in a supine position on a bench, and water is poured down his throat through the mouth or nose, with red pepper being added on some occasions. This procedure continues until the absorbed water makes the victim look like a toad. At that point the torturers press on his stomach until the water is expelled from the body, after which the torture is repeated. Very few victims manage to survive that ordeal.

This, then, was what I was about to face, with Arai saying mockingly :

"Don't tell me that you are not afraid!"

"Of course I am afraid to be maimed but there is nothing I can add. I already told you that I was not present during the fight. How could I have seen anything?"

It was getting close to dawn and everybody was getting tired. The investigators felt that they were getting nowhere which prompted my acquaintance from Kanto to say to me:

"Look, we are going to take you back to your cell where you can have a rest. We need a rest too. I advise you to give this matter a lot of thought. Think particularly how you can prove your innocence. After all, the wound on your forehead speaks volumes for your guilt! Think hard!..."

My handcuffs were taken off and he offered me a cigarette of the "Sikisima" brand. Frankly, I did not like that insipid brand but nevertheless enjoyed inhaling it on that occasion.

"All right, I'll think things over, but please, let Zhukov go ! He has nothing to do with the whole thing!"

When being led to my den, I was pleased to see that Zhukov's cell was empty.

With my arms and legs free from shackles, I paced the cell from corner to corner, like a caged animal and never stopped thinking for one moment. And all of a sudden -- EUREKA!!!... I found the proof of my innocence!

When the following morning I finally appeared before the well-rested trio, I told them:

"Ask the officer ("kay-boo") who conducted the preliminary investigation during which I acted as an interpreter. Let him tell you whether there was a wound on my forehead! We stood right opposite each other, with a lamp shining in my face! He must remember what I looked like!"

My argument proved weighty enough, and it seems that the kay-boo was asked to give his statement over the phone, because I was released a couple of hours later.Not only that, but I even received an apology !It has to be said that the Japanese are sticklers for protocol...

Arai, of course, made no apologies, ordering me instead to leave my coat at the police station for forensic tests.

The coat was soon returned but the memories of the nightmarish hours in the cell stayed with me for a long time, and my hands and wrists took a long while to recover from the bruises and the numbness produced by my ordeal.

3. THE TIGER HAMLET COMES OF AGE

Despite my unpleasant experience, The Tiger Hamlet continued to grow and prosper. New settlers, mostly relatives and friends, kept joining me. In addition to Pyotr Chistyakov and his wife Kira, the following people took up residence in the hamlet :

Valentin Valkov and his wife Nata, the step-daughter of my brother Arseny, who built their own cottage;

A former employee of The Japanese Military Mission Pyotr (Peter) Fedotovich Shelomentsev ;

A former employee of The Mission Pavel (Paul) Kalistratovich Zhukov and his wife.

We built two "fanzas" (Chinese cottages) next to my house. One was occupied by my old and trusted Korean assistant Kham Chigoni, and the other--by an old friend, a professional hunter, a former officer in Ataman Semyonov's Army, Fyodor Pavlovich Solomakhin. Solomakhin was accompanied by his wife and daughter.

In spring of 1944 we were joined by Georgii (George) Nikolayevich Gusakovsky, his then wife, my sister, the poetess Victoria, nee Yankovsky, and their eighteen--months old son Or. George used to work for the firm of Brynner and Co. in Changchun (the capital of Manchukuo) but left to join me on the farm.

In the summer of 1944 my brother Yuri also came to The Tiger Hamlet, having completed his service in the Manchukuo Army.

In May 1944 we made a trip to the "Eldorado Valley ", whose correct name was Sakhadjan. We named it "Eldorado" because of an unbelievably successful hunting expedition in that location which took place two years prior to our present trip. On that occasion, during a sojourn in the valley which lasted for less than a month, our group of three hunters killed three wild boars, eight elk, seven bears and a huge tiger whose skin adorned the Harbin dining room of our uncle Boris Brynner (the father of Yul).

My young wife Irma joined the 1944 expedition. Being a great lover of exotic trips, she talked me into allowing her to come with us. She was fortunate to witness a rare occurrence on the first day of the safari.

She and I left our tent at dawn and were standing on top of a mountain. I pointed out to her two beautiful majestic male deer walking slowly in the valley.On their noble heads were soft antlers --the famous "pantui"of Tibetan medicine ! Not many hunters would have witnessed such a magnificent sight! I killed one of these innocent animals for its "pantui", with my young wife being a silent witness to the deed...

I summoned my hunting partner Shelomentsev to help me fetch some Chinese loggers who were going to transport the carcass out of the "taiga" (forest). Irma stayed bravely behind at a clearing in the forest which was covered with spring flowers . Her task was to guard the huge body of the victim.

She confessed later that she was very scared thinking that a tiger was about to come to savage the dead deer...

With the proceeds of that successful hunt we were able to buy two more Dutch cows.

We also planted a lot of vegetables and buckwheat. The harvest was plentiful.

Irma started a chicken farm and I was getting ready to transport some deer from Novina to The Tiger Hamlet.

To sum up, it seemed that our plans for a new, happy and prosperous life were about to bear fruit...

Chapter 19. THE HOLOCAUST.

1. THE LIBERATORS.

Future appeared rosy, but FATE was relentlessly preparing a future over which we, mere humans, had no control... It was called HISTORY...

On the ninth of August 1945 The Tiger Hamlet woke to the noise of aeroplanes. That was a sound accompanying the arrival of a terrifying tidal wave ---the war between Russia and Japan-- which was about to drown the best of the Russian emigres.

Who could have foreseen that destruction, that tragedy of countless thousands of innocent people who were true Russian patriots?

That tragedy was exacerbated by the fact that during a few years before the Russo-Japanese War, the White Russian emigres lived to the accompaniment of broadcasts from the Russian underground radio station "Otchisna" ("The Motherland").In the name of the Russian Government "Otchisna"exhorted the emigres to "trust New Russia, the most humane country in the world".

"Brothers and sisters"--it intoned ---"Wait for us ! We shall be soon with you! Help us in our sacred mission! Do not worry and do not doubt our word-- you have all been forgiven!!"

And everybody, but first and foremost the young people, trusted those beautiful words and could not wait to be reunited with their compatriots...

And little wonder that my brother Yuri, who had just completed his service in the Manchukuo Army and I rushed to meet "our own", as we all called them in those days. We defied the mortal danger of being annihilated by the retreating Japanese or by the advancing Red Army. In our headlong rush we survived the first encounter with the NKVD (the precursor of the KGB) when a captain wearing the hedgear of that organisation wanted to take us in for interrogation. I managed to convince him that we were heading for the Army Headquarters, and the warrior left us alone.

2. SERVING THE MOTHERLAND

I was appointed to the position of an interpreter with The Special Branch of The 25th Army of The Far Eastern Front and initially assigned to Kanto where I worked for "SMERSH" (an acronym of the Russian words "Death To The Spies") which took over the buildings of the former Japanese Military Mission, known as "Tokumu Kikan"during the Japanese occupation.

While crossing the yard one day after starting my new job, I noticed a Korean walking into the yard past the sentry. He wore a long cream-coloured national gown with a traditional sash in the shape of a bow, and a wide - brimmed straw hat. On seeing me, the visitor took off his hat bowing deeply, with a servile expression on his face :

"How do you do, 'sensei' ('teacher')", he said, "You have no idea how glad I am to see you!"

I took another look and could hardly believe my eyes : the man standing in front of me was none other than my old "friend" Pak-Arai! The radiant smile on the scoundrel's suddenly pale face was completely out of character."Please help me because I..."

My memory instantly delivered a picture of the handcuffs, the interrogation, the cell, the "regulation" ropes destroying me on its floor, the implements of torture about to be used...

I showed him to a bench near the sentry box and said :

"Please take a seat ! I'll report your request to the proper person."

I walked into the office of the Chief Investigator, Senior Lieutenant Vladimir Butsky. He and I had been conducting the interrogations of arrested gendarmes and policemen, who were now kept in the same cells where they tormented their former prisoners.

"Volodya, an important criminal is waiting on a bench outside. He is a well-known gendarme who is trying to conceal his identity. Let's ask him in!"

Lieutenant Butsky jumped to his feet :

"Hurry, let's go! Point him out to me!"

No more than three minutes had passed after my encounter with Arai but the bench was empty. The old fox managed to escape and to change his appearance because despite all our efforts to find him, he vanished without a trace.

Butsky was annoyed :

"What a slob! You shouldn't have left him with the sentry !"

He was right... I did no think fast enough because I had no experience in these matters...

Despite that unfortunate slip-up, my brother Yuri's and my careers continued without further diffiiculties. As staff interpreters of The Special Branch of The Red Army, we travelled from the town of Yang Tsing in Manchuria to Pyongyang, the newly proclaimed capital of North Korea where we worked till January 1946. Together with two counter-intelligence officers, Vladimir Butsky and Nikolai Podgorny, we occupied a separate flat rented for us by "the office", ate in the officers' mess and were being paid one thousand roubles a month each. Many of our free evenings were spent in the company of Korean geisha girls.

It was said that our section worked in accordance with the system established by Stalin, namely from five o'clock in the afternoon till almost the following morning. During those hours we used to interrogate gendarmes, public servants and policemen arrested by the new authorities,often acting as court interpreters by day.

Another daytime occupation consisted of working in the Headquarters of the Army Rearguard on contracts negotiated between Korean merchants and The Army. That was a very lucrative pastime because, in accordance with a long- established tradition, Korean merchants rewarded the interpreters with large sums of money...

3. NORTH KOREA'S NEW LEADER.

A historical event took place in October of 1946, heralded by the appearance of tiny "U2" planes over Pyongyang which were showering its streets with leaflets. So enthusiastic was the populace to collect them that a few young lads were run over by motor cars in the process.

The leaflets informed the masses that the following day, the 14th of October 1946, a meeting was going to take place between the people and "The National Hero"--Kim Il Sung --on the main thoroughfare of the capital --the Moranbong Square. As interpreters, Yuri and I were expected to unobtrusively eavesdrop on conversations between members of the public during that momentous event.

Our deatchnment was posted to the Moranbong Mountain dominating the centre of Pyongyang. The summit of that mountain is surrounded by a wall into which are embedded cannon balls dating back to the Chinese siege of the Northern Capital of Korea which took place in the seventeenth century.

In recent times a large stadium had been built inside the fortress. A rostrum containing a platform and a single wooden bench were erected in the south-eastern corner of the stadium for the meeting. A lectern surrounded by a low barrier stood on the platform .

Members of the elite were gathered on the rostrum. The Commander of the Twenty Fifth Army Colonel - General Chistyakov sat at one end of the bench, with he Member of The Military Council Lieutenant-General Lebedev occupying the other. Between them, in the centre of the bench, was an empty space . Invited dignitaries, other officers and we two interpreters were crowding behind them.

The stadium was filled to capacity. I observed that a group of young people were assembled in front of the podium,all of them, regardless of gender, holding huge bouquets of magnificent autumnal asters and chrysanthemums.

There were a lot of speeches in Korean and Russian on the subject of liberation of Korea from the Japanese occupiers, with instant translation into either language, to ensure that both sides understood them. Particularly memorable was an emotional speech by Pak Den Ai, a well known revolutionary, a native of Russia and a perfect Russian speaker, who spent many years in a Japanese prison. That short portly Korean woman was appointed Minister of Culture in the new Korean Government. However, as I read soon after, she managed to displease her new masters and finished up being thrown back in jail.

The excitement of the crowd grew in anticipation of the appearance of the hero of the occasion who was nowhere to be seen. At long last, a Korean officer mounted the podium.His name was Li and he was wearing the uniform of a Major of the Red Army. Li announced in two languages:

"You will now hear a speech by the hero of the Korean people Comrade Kim Il Sung!"

The scenario of the political show was faultless.

The instant Li finished speaking, a hitherto hidden trapdoor opened in front of our generals, and --like a Jack in the Box---out jumped a fit young man dressed in a brown business suit with an Order of he Red Banner on the lapel. I saw his dark angular face, black eyebrows and neatly brushed back black hair,and immediately remembered these features, even though he was beginning to show his age.

Kim took up a position behind the lectern and addressed the assembled crowd in well modulated Korean.

No sooner did he utter the first words than pandemonium broke out! The youngsters rushed towards the podium carrying bouquets which fell apart showering the orator and his entourage with white, pink and mauve petals of asters and chrysanthemums.There were screams of:

"Vansu Manse! (Ten thousand years live The Leader!)".

Incoherent moans, tears of joy and national pride accompanied the verbal performance. Amateur photographers scrambled over each other, standing on other people's shoulders and heads and blazing away with their cameras!

That was indeed a hysterically historical moment!

Having finished his obviously well rehearsed speech, Kim, the recent guerrilla fighter who distinguished himself in battles with the Japanese, retired to the bench where he took up a position between the generals. Now I knew why one space between those men had been left empty.

The speeches continued but the generals and Kim left the podium and departed in an armoured car.

On that day North Korea acquired its new Leader...

As for me, the moment I saw Kim I remembered an incident which took place in Manchuria five years earlier. An important Japanese police officer resplendid in a khaki uniform with gold-braided shoulder straps, was handing me a permit to hunt in the vicinity of the legendary extinct volcano Paektu-San.That region was rich in game but had a bad reputation as a sanctuary for the Korean guerrillas led by their famous "ataman" (chief).

I was overjoyed at having received the coveted document with its large red seal and was about to take my leave when the samurai told me to stay. The officer asked :

"How much do you get for a dead tiger ?"

"About three thousand yen for a large male", replied I after making a rough mental estimate.

The policeman nodded and produced a small photograph from his desk. Putting it in front of me he said :

"We are prepared to pay ten thousand yen for this tiger! This is Kin Ichi Sei!"

I was looking at a young but strong-willed visage of a man with dark eyebrows and short brushed back hair, wearing a student's uniform.

Right ! That's what he is like--Kim Il Sung-- (or "Kin Sichi Sei"in the Japanese pronunciation of the characters making up his name)! Of course I knew of him ! However, we had no intention of fighting the Korean guerrillas. In fact, we were sympathetic to their cause.

My reply was diplomatic :

"Esteemed Head of Branch ! We only hunt four-legged predators!"...

I could see that he was annoyed at my response.

Putting the photograph away, he growled :

"Suit yourself..But remember : not a word about this conversation to anybody !"

And on that momentous day in October 1945 I remembered that old photograph when looking at the guest of our generals. The only thing was that he was much younger looking then. There was a time when I felt great admiration for that unusual person. But I could not imagine then the future actions of that self- proclaimed patriot, who made a career based on that perception of him by others. Having made his career as a patriot, he started a fratricidal war in the mid -1950's in order to pander to his party and personal ambitions.That war cost hundreds of thousands of lives of his people as well as of his Chinese brothers. It also took the lives of untold numbers of Russians who became embroiled in that bloody adventure.

That battle which he lost, devastated his country and nearly cost him his "crown". He was back where he started from but, like his idols Stalin and Mao, failed to learn from history. A clear example of that insanity are new ambitious plans which his heirs are currently attempting to reinforce with a threat of nuclear weapons, completely ignoring world public opinion.

I have radically changed my attitude towards that individual....

Chapter 20. GULAG.

1. THE BETRAYAL.

...War scattered our family all over the world. During the six months when Yuri and I worked for the new masters we had not received a single letter. It was extremely worrying that there was no news from Novina because we heard rumours that most of the inhabitants of The Tiger Hamlet moved there. They included my wife Irma who was expecting our first child.

Despite the fact that I many times applied for a short leave of absence to visit Novina, it was invariably refused. Lieutenant-Colonel Demidov who was in charge of The Investigation Branch kept saying that there was too much work at hand. He promised to let me go as soon as there was the slightest opportunity to relieve me.

On one of my days off I was visited by a friend of mine, a counter-intelligence officer who was drunk to the point of being practically incoherent. I was alone in the flat and, having sworn me to secrecy, he told me that he recently overheard a conversation about my impending arrest. The most amazing thing about that episode was his open-hearted advice to me and my brother Yuri to escape as soon as possible across the thirty eighth parallel into the American Zone.

I was surprised and even outraged. Why would anybody want to arrest me? Was it because the Japanese enlisted me to monitor and to record Russian radio broadcasts? Well, first of all, those were open broadcasts which were part of world-wide Russian propaganda. Secondly, I made a full disclosure of that job in my curriculum vitae when applying for a position with the Russians.

No lesser a person than the esteemed Member of The War Council of the Twenty Fifth Army General Lebedev who studied my C.V., made the following official pronouncement:

"These are minor matters. All emigres who did not take an active part in anti-Soviet activities have been pardoned. That is beyond dispute..."

I do not know to this day why my friend was risking so much by warning us. He must have beem a kind and decent person. Unfortunately, I took the words of a counter--intelligence officer, about whom I knew very little, as a frame-up. I felt that if brother and I really decided to escape, we would then be arrested during the attempt...

I have to say that at least on a superficial level I noticed no change in the attitude of my superiors to me. Moreover, I was given permission to travel to Novina and Lieutenant Colonel Demidov invited me to a store filled with confiscated guns as a reward for my conscientious work.

"I know that you are a hunter and are fond of all kinds of weapons. Here you are--select whatever you want and take it home. I am not going to limit your leave. We'll send you a special invitation when you are needed."

I was very surprised to see my own Mowser rifle among the pile of weapons. It was the gun I brought with me from Shanghai. I also helped myself to a five-shooter semi-automatic fowling piece Browning and a double-barrelled shotgun.

Demidov shook me warmly by the hand :

"You will travel to the town of Kanto with Captain Nikolayev. They are short of interpreters, and you will help them for a day or two--and then -- off home to Novina!"

.....It was the twenty fourth of January 1946, and for the first time that winter there was deep fluffy snow on the streets of Pyongyang. Brother Yuri and Senior Lieutenant Butsky came to see me off at the station.

We stood on the platform waiting for the train and I was surprised to see that Yuri was barely managing to hold back tears. I could not understand his emotions because he too was due for home leave in the next few days...

.....Only seventeen years after that day did I find out the reason. By then we had been both released from imprisonment, wrote to each other and arranged to meet in Moscow. It turned out that he had good reason to be sad, as he was ready to flee to the South in the morning of the following day. But...he was arrested at dawn of that day! It meant that he was arrested even before me.

He wanted to escape in company of his Korean girlfriend. Her role in the affair remains a mystery. She could, of course, have been a secret agent who betrayed her lover but, on the other hand, she could herself had been arrested and thrown into a Gulag camp. Very many Korean men and women were prisoners of Gulag.

Nikolayev and I arrived in Kanto in the early evening of the 25th of January 1946. The train left on the remainder of its journey to the North East, and some soldiers helped me to carry my substantial luggage to the officers' quarters.In addition to the guns, I was carrying an enormous quantity of presents for my wife Irma, our future child, her friend (who was my cousin Tanya), and for all the numerous relatives awaiting me in Novina. Nikolayev showed me to a vacant bunk and ordered supper which included a large bottle of Korean vodka.Seeing that the following day was a Sunday he suggested that we go hunting pheasants and wild deer. I declined in these terms:

"Look, let's do some work tonight, tomorrow and for another couple of days so as to finish it soon. I can't wait to get home. Just to think that I haven't seen my family for six months!"

I picked up an Army newspaper from the table and started reading the latest news from the Divisional Press. The light was poor, coming from a single unshaded lamp hanging from the ceiling.That peaceful pastime was interrupted by the appearance on the threshold of a tiny man wearing a major's uniform. He beckoned to my colleague :

"Captain Nikolayev, come and see me for a minute!"

Nikolayev left and came back rather quickly but instead of sitting down started circling the table in a most peculiar manner. I looked up at him:

"What are you up to ? Sit down!"

My mate sat down resting his head on the elbow and suddenly blurted out:

"Wee-ll, you were in such a hurry to get home, and here I am having to arrest you!"

I got terribly annoyed :

"You are joking, of course!"

He shook his head :

"No. I am under orders. Empty your pockets !"

He turned to the officer in charge of our barracks:

"Levchenko, you'll be the witness. You will sign the record of evidence after I search Valery."

Having conducted the search, a record of evidence was prepared. It mentioned money in Russian roubles, in Japanese yen and the "gobi" (currency) of Manchukuo. Included were also all the presents for my near and dear ones, including a platinum watch and a ring with a large diamond which I bought in Pyongyang for Irma. Neither did Nikolayev forget the guns, my camera and a golden engagement ring which he called "a ring made from yellow metal". The original was written on yellowish paper, with one copy produced with the aid of copying paper. Nikolayev handed the copy to me :

"Keep it..I think they will soon sort things out for you but for now I must call the escort to take you to jail. Make sure to take warm clothing and underwear ; don't forget your toiletries ; all these things might come handy. I would not be surprised if the investigation were to take a couple of months. Oh yes, we had many cases of spotted typhys in jail but we disinfected the place, so you have nothing to worry about".

2. UNDER INVESTIGATION.

It was late at night when two submachine-gun toting soldiers took me to jail, an old building which had been constructed by the Japanese. It was surrounded by a huge brick wall and had an odour peculiar to all jails. They led me through a long corridor with a concrete floor and opened the door of a cell used for solitary confinement. In went my suitcases, and the lock was shut with a loud bang...

Much later I had an opportunity to compare that dungeon with a typical prison of the Gulag. I must say that my first place of incarceration was absolutely luxurious compared with the "comforts"of those hovels. For example, my present single cell would have housed anywhere between 10 to 15 prisoners in Russia. It had a wooden floor, a trestle - bed and a table of sorts. In one corner, under the window, was located a toilet which was emptied from outside. I collapsed on the bed and fell into a deep sleep...

I was woken by the squeaks of a small platform which was used by one of the inmates to transport the prison breakfast consisting of a "kasha" (gruel) made of a mixture of compressed beans and large potatoes. He knocked on my door and pushed the "kasha"through a special window, reminiscent of a feeding trough in horse stables. For the next three days I was practically unable to eat that mush, but it has to be said that, given enough time, one gets used to anything.Mercifully, that kasha was later replaced with the soldiers' rations of another type of gruel augmented with soup and bread.

A few days after my incarceration I received a visit from the tiny major who turned out to be the officer in charge of the Investigation Branch of the 40th Division by the name of Novikov. He sat down on my bed and had a friendly yarn. It transpired that I was not actually arrested but "detained"and Novikov promised to conduct a speedy "investigation"and most probably let me go home. As a detainee, I was allowed to walk along the corridor and in the prison yard although I had to sleep in the lockup.

The major asked me to give Russian lessons to the Korean governor of the jail.In addition to that I was given the right to teach Russian to a group of "detained" Korean students who shared the same jail with me. Their relatives brought lavish food parcels which they were keen to share with their "songzay" (teacher).

In contrast with the Russian prisons, which I had yet to get to know, my first prison, built by the Japanese, had glass in the top part of the doors which was admittedly protected by a grill. The glass could be easily moved and this enabled prisoners to hold conversations between cells. I would set an assignment and question my students on their progress before starting the next one.

The evenings were spent with major Novikov who was in charge of my political indoctrination. He used to supply me with the works of Marx and Lenin which was just as well, because I would not have touched them with a barge pole under different circumstances.

Unfortunately I succumbed to the spotted typhys, having evidently been bitten by a louse which managed to survive the disinfectants (<u>Note:</u> Spotted typhys is transmitted by lice much as malaria is transmitted by mosquitoes). My temperature rose alarmingly and I started hallucinating.

I saw a fat dark-skinned deity which was moaning under a palm tree somewhere (search me why!!!) in Taiwan. It was upset because a red wolf had devoured its liver...

On another occasion my wife Irma and Father John (the priest from Novina) came into my cell and asked me to light a candle which would not burn...

The last vision was that of Stalin whose torso appeared in the window of my cell. We had a good chat and he invited me to attend a conference at 2300 hours and gave me a rank of a Major-General before taking his leave. When the time for the meeting drew close, I demanded to be released. Having been refused, I went berserk and smashed the glass on top of the door with a hand basin. An alarmed warder called the officer of the guard. The intelligent sergeant realised that I lost my mind and calmed me down with the explanation that the meeting had been postponed and that I had been instructed to catch up on some sleep instead...

My last recollection of that period is of being carried to the hospital on a blanket. I remember nothing else about my illness because I lost consciousness.

When I came to I saw another prisoner sitting at my feet and injecting me into the groin with a huge needle. He was a Korean medical doctor with a smashed face who had evidently undergone a "detailed interrogation". The injection was my only means of nourishment as I was not capable of taking either food or drink by any other means. Seeing that I came to, he smiled with his crushed lips and croaked :

"Well, you are alive after all! Frankly, I did no think that you would wake up..Your temperature was mostly forty one degrees, even forty two on many occasions! These injections were the only thing which was sustaining you..."

My recovery was very painful because my stomach lost its capacity to function normally and I had to learn to walk with the aid of a walking stick. However, my appetite was enormous. I used to devour three sets of rations : the normal prison one followed by another one from the soldiers, and one more from my students. Soon I became grossly overweight, in a way never before experienced in my life. I started to exercise on the door jamb, lifting myself up by the arms, and finished up tearing the door out of the wall because of my weight. Both the door and I collapsed on the floor...

Towards summer of 1946 I was able to walk outside into the prison yard. I used to lie down on the grass under the wall whose upper edge was covered with broken glass, read for many hours on end and plan an escape. I had no idea what was happening at home. I did not know that Yuri had been arrested or that my father was about to be arrested and sent to Gulag. Neither did I have any inkling of the plans our new masters had for my brother Arseny and cousin Tanya. The only thing I knew quite clearly was that should I escape, they would suffer, and that stopped me in my tracks.

I befriended the officer of the watch, a very intelligent sergeant. We used to play checkers and drink the good old vodka which I was able to buy with the money I had on me during the arrest and which the prison authorities were allowed to release for such a purpose. The lad kept giving me encouraging news. He told me, for example, that he overheard officers from Headquarters discussing me and saying that I was about to be "kicked out and sent home". Another comforting sign was that Novikov, the investigator, told me to write to my wife Irma informing her that I had been sent on a long assignment but would be home soon.

It seems that the whole question of how to treat our family was being discussed at a high level, because otherwise there would have been no sense in keeping me under investigation for such a long time, without effecting a formal arrest.

Ominous signs appeared when I read about a hostile speech by Winston Churchill in Fulton, reported in an army paper shown to me by Novikov. The next sinister sign was the death sentence meted out to Ataman (Cossack General) Semyonov (a White Commander famous in The Far East) and other White Generals. The really menacing part was that they were alleged to have stated that all young Russian emigres were prepared to fight against the Communist Regime. That news was very depressing.I became very worried indeed.

3. CONDEMNED.

In August 1946 I was summoned to see Nikolayev who showed me a formal warrant for my arrest. My treatment underwent an immediate change. My head was shaven and I was deprived of any freedom of movement.

The court case took place in October of the same year. All my "sins" were sheeted home to me :

My White Russian passport

Listening to Soviet radio broadcasts

Payment of contributions demanded by the Japanese for the prosecution of the war against China (how could one dare refuse such a request?)

They remembered my trip to Shanghai in 1941. Why did I go? Whose assignment was I carrying out?

That was another one of those crazy accusations! What assignment? My aunt asked me to come to help her settle the affairs of her husband, my uncle Paul, who had been murdered by terrorists!

Members of the Military Tribunal were each trying their own line of questioning.

The court room was familiar to me because of my recent work in The Special Branch. The "troika" (three members of the Tribunal) sat in the centre at a table covered with a red cloth. The secretary occupied a smaller table whose cloth was green . There was a third table for the interpreters which my brother and I used to occupy but today's proceedings did not need interpreters to subject me to cross - examination.

I stood to attention in front of the table representing myself. Here is what I said :

"Yes, I listened to the radio.

Yes, I paid war taxes.

But I ask the Tribunal to understand that the Japanese were completely in charge in Korea and Manchuria.It was, of course, possible to try to outsmart them, to avoid their requests or assignments but direct disobedience spelt death. However, I did not betray The Motherland.

I hope that The Tribunal will take this into consideration..."

I was naive enough to think that I would be acquitted. Therefore when I heard :

"Six years in the Correctional Labour Camps", I barely managed to stay on my feet.

I felt like an animal surrounded by a pack of well-trained hounds. One breathless beast was barking at me from the front, with the second one attacking from the rear, and the third one...

I was allowed the last word.

"I ask for all my personal belongings, as listed after my arrest, to be given to my wife who otherwise would be left destitute."

They remembered...Heavens!!! The belongings!!! They forgot them, darn it!!!

"Secretary, add : 'Six years with the confiscation of all personal belongings!'..."

When I got back to my cell I, for the first time in my life, fell on my knees and barely managed to crawl to the mug full of water. I appealed asking for my case to be reconsidered...

I was taken to Pyongyang for the so-called "appeal hearing" in December with five Korean prisoners, all of us shackled together (yes, we were even taken to the toilet together, all five of us).

The new tribunal consisted of my former colleagues. During a break in the proceedings, one colonel whom I knew well whispered to me :

"Steel yourself. There will be no reduction in sentence. The District Authorities have done us like a dinner.They reckon that the first Tribunal was too lenient with you. Try to be strong."

And here it was ---the new sentence :

"Ten years of Corrective Labour Camps".

I felt as if my legs were suddenly filled with lead..

There followed a trip to Seisin for questioning in the presence of my father.

I found out that three people had been arrested : Father, cousin Tatiana (Tanya) and Ellers...

Back to Pyongyang from Seisin and, finally --transportation to Vladivostok in Russia.

4. HOME SWEET HOME.

The train carrying prisoners from Pyongyang arrived at the "Vtoraya Rechka" ("Second River ") railway goods yard in Vladivostok just after dawn on a dark February morning in

1947. The prisoners were taken from the train, formed into groups of five and led along steep city streets covered in pre - revolutionary cobblestones. They were escorted by vicious guards armed with automatic weapons and accompanied by growling alsatians.

My God ! How squalid, dirty and gloomy had become my native city in twenty five years! Hunched squat unfeminine-looking women dressed in patched quilted jackets and wearing army boots were dragging themselves along the sides of the roads.An unshaven lorry driver dressed in oil soaked overalls, using choice four-letter words, was turning the starting handle of his vehicle which refused to get going...

Not a single soul was taking the slightest bit of notice of a whole herd of prisoners. It was clear that this was a common sight for the inhabitants of Vladivostok. The only attention came from the soldiers who were escorting us, with their incessant shouts of :

"Keep up! Do not fall back!"

At long last our column creeps through the archway of the smelly prison on the Partisan ("Guerrilla") Avenue. A soup (it consists of tiny, the size of lead shot, unwashed potatoes), and a small moist piece of black bread are served.Following that meal we march to a Gulag camp called "The Sixth Kilometre".

At the beginning of March 1947 we were loaded into lorries and taken to the Diomid Bay near Vladivostok. The lorries travelled along the Pushkinskaya Street, past the house of our grandmother, "Boosya -Alya" Sheveleva, a house which I knew since my childhood and which evoked sad memories of happy times.

In Diomid Bay we were given the task of unloading carriages containing lime and cement. The work was true hard labour because the materials were not bagged and the poisonous dust filled our noses, mouths and eyes. We had to work ten hours a day on starvation rations. There were no washing facilities, and the only way to reduce the unbearable itch was to bash one's pants and coat against a telegraph pole.

Before very long, many prisoners began suffering from "night-blindness", an affliction caused by inadequate nourishment and lack of vitamins. To try to effect a cure, authorities started giving some prisoners a spoon of fish oil after the evening meal. Since the oil was not given to all prisoners, the "lucky ones" would not swallow it but carry the medication to the barracks in their mouth instead. There they would spit it out into a common pot!

A conspiracy was brewing in our work detachment under the motto :

"Escape or death!"

We formed a group of prospective escapees which contained some of my Manchurian compatriots. One of them was a fearless hunter by the name of Fyedya (Theodore) Shepkin. The second organiser of a break-out was a man who had travelled with me from Korea to Vladivostok--a Russian lieutenant by the name of Vladimir Rozanov, who was sent to Gulag for having a Korean girlfriend. He was a real daredevil who was ready to make a run for it at any moment. During our transfer from Pyongyang Rozanov used to whisper into my ear :

"Let's ask the guards to let us step outside to get some warmth. Once we are out, we can kill them with an axe used to break up coal. Then it will be a simple matter to escape into the forest.."

My reply was :

"Nothing can possibly come of it. We are surrounded by snow. They'll track us down like rabbits and shoot us dead.."

On arrival in the Diomid Bay we were betrayed by a stool pigeon. The upshot of it was that our work detachment was broken up. The lads from Manchuria were sent to prison and Rozanov and I were forced to walk back to the "Sixth Kilometre Camp"under the supervision of a guard. It was in that camp that I saw my father for the last time in our lives....

As a potential escapee, I was placed into a "ZUR" (Russian acronym for the words "Zone of Intensive Supervision"). My father happened to be in the same Gulag camp as I, and found out about my transfer from the "'Zek' wireless" and walked over to the mesh separating the "ZUR"from the rest of the camp. (Note : The word "zek"is a short form of the Russian word "Zakluchonny"----"Prisoner". The victims of the Gulag were known as "zeks")

I noticed that he still looked quite cheerful, with his full moustache, a Rover Scout hat and high laced-up boots. We greeted each other and shook hands through the holes in the mesh, the same type of mesh we used in Sedemi to incarcerate deer...

We did not moan or cry but conversed in a business-like manner. Father said :

"Well, how do you like this stuff? Remember how you argued with me insisting that everything was fine now in Russia and that The Motherland had pardoned everybody...?"

He was absolutely right...In common with most young men of my generation, I had been got at by Soviet radio propaganda and was full of patriotic sentiments.Yes, begorra, I did argue with him in a most intemperate way!

Other zeks kept hanging around trying to eavesdrop on our conversation, which forced us to continue in English.

"Papa"---I said---"Look at those mountains in the west. Do you think that Manchuria is behind them?"

"I understand what you are getting at"---he replied. "You are right, the border is close to those mountains but the risk is far too great.It would have been different if you and I could make for them together...No, I think you will be better off putting up with things.. After all, you are still very young.. It is I who will find the imprisonment much harder..."

"Do you smoke?"---- he asked after a short pause.

Father never smoked himself and hated the smell of tobacco. I knew that I was going to upset him with my reply but confessed that I did, indeed, smoke.

"A shame, but what can be done? Wait here, I'll get you something" .

He went into his barracks and brought me a packet of leaf tobacco wrapped in an old worn sock which had obviously been washed innumerable times.

The guards saw what he was doing and one of them screamed :

"Don't come near each other!"

Nevertheless, father managed to tell me that he and Ellers, who was by that time a foreman on a building project inside the camp, were going to try to talk the authorities into allowing me to spend the night in their barracks. They were going to brew me some coffee they received in a parcel from relatives in Korea....

It seems that their request had been denied...

I was not aware of that and spent the whole night tossing and turning on the narrow shelves which passed for beds in the ZUR barracks, waiting to be called over.

In the morning of the following day I was again forced to join a group of zeks on the way to another destination.

Father tried to walk up to my lorry but was stopped by an ominous shouted command:

"Don't approach them!"

He walked back and waved...

I waved back...

I have never seen him again...

5. ESCAPE.

On the 20th of May 1947 I arrived in the Gulag camp by the name of Tavrichanka. Our party was transported in two one -and - a -half tonne lorries. The camp, which had been previously occupied by Japanese prisoners of war, was part of a mine complex.

From the very first day Rozanov and I started preparing for an escape.Our plan was to short circuit the electricty supply and to scale the three metre high wall. That structure was protected by five rows of barbed wire mounted on supports which were directed towards the inner yard. We decided that that was the only way to freedom.

A dilapidated house converted by the Japanese into a kitchen was sitting in the middle of the prison yard. In it we found a few shelves and racks which I converted into three ladders. Two of them were immediately stolen by the inmates, but the third one survived because it was hidden behind a long toilet, with seats designed to accommodate twenty zeks at a "sitting". We also purloined a roll of twine from the barracks for the disabled, where aged prisoners were making fishing nets.

The twine had to be twisted into a rope which could then be used to throw a piece of wire over the electrified fence to cause a short circuit. Three Russian Army deserters from Port Arthur (an old Russian fortress near the present day Chinese city of Dalian, formerly, Dalnyi, which was recaptured by Russia from the Japanese at the end of World War II) caught us "red-handed" and demanded to be included in the escape plan as payment for their silence. We were forced to accede to their demands.

The first two attempts to short out the electricity failed dismally because the wire was too thin and melted without disconnecting the supply. We only managed to cause the lights to "blink"after which they would get back to normal.Every time we had to run for our lives to avoid being spotted by the ferocious "bludgeoners"---trusted prisoners who were carrying heavy cudgels-- and who could have bludgeoned us to death.Luckily, we finally managed to find a piece of cable which was destined to do the trick...

It was just before dawn on the 31st of May. Thick fog which came up from the ocean was covering the watch towers. We assembled in the wooden toilet pretending to answer the call of nature. Having waited for a short while, Rozanov decided that the moment was right and threw the cable over the fence. There was a steel nut attached to the end of the cable, and it immediately entwined itself around the fence wire. A crackling sound followed, and the lights went out!

I grabbed the ladder and stepped over the "no-man's land" which consisted of a metre-high fence of barbed wire surrounding the camp and separating the inmates from the main wall. That action immediately put me at risk of being shot without warning...I made another step...

The next question was : is the ladder long enough? Luckily it was. With the ladder resting against one of the supports holding up the barbed wire, I scrambled up it like a cat, throwing a pair of cotton wool padded trousers over the barbed wire, jumped onto them, lay flat on my stomach for a moment and fell over the outside fence to freedom. The others followed suit, with the rusty wire making a frightening scraping sound.

There was a yell from one of the towers :

"Who is it ? Where are you going ?"

Then followed three rapid shots : "Pow ! Pow !Pow!"

The bullets whizzed over our heads...

We raced away, puffing and breathless, quickly passing the settlement and heading for the hills...

I had no doubt that the noise and shooting would be followed by a pursuit involving guard dogs. Therefore, once we left the township, I made a sharp turn towards a bog where the alsatians would not be able to pick up our scent. As additional insurance, I even sprinkled some of the priceless cut tobacco leaf over our tracks,

I kept sprinting ahead with Volodya Rozanov keeping up with me and the rest of the group beginning to lag behind, extending our line. It was getting light and I headed for some hills overgrown with trees. However, our deserter fellow travellers were unable to keep up with us.

"Slow down! Don't run so fast, hunter, you ! Can't you see that we can't run like you!?"

We stopped and allowed them to catch up with us at the edge of the forest. No sooner did we resume our flight than we ran into a ploughed field at whose edge was a small house with three ganders running to its gate flapping their wings. At the other edge of the field stood a bucket of cut potatoes waiting to be planted. Volodka (Rozanov) who was small of stature and quick on his feet, needed only three leaps to catch up with the ganders and to grab one of them by the neck. I got hold of the potatoes, and our whole group raced into the forest looking for all the world like a pack of jackals.

Our flight continued until we ran out of breath, after which we stopped in a gully in the thicket and lit a camp fire. We boiled the gander and the potatoes in the bucket, and filled our bellies for the first time in many days....

Having got up after a short rest we heard a small plane buzzing in the vicinity. It seemed that our jailers were already searching for us. I started leading our group towards the north-west, realising that if we were to make it to the border with Manchuria, we had to cross the Suifunhe River. At that moment one of the quick-witted criminals spotted in a small hollow a chicken coop belonging to a collective farm and decided to post me as lookout, with Rozanov joining the others on "the job". They came back very soon carrying thirteen chooks in several bags!

Following that raid we collapsed on the ground and fell asleep under some oak trees. The morning saw us at the banks of the river where we boiled a couple of chooks. One lucky black chicken managed to break loose and disappear into the bushes.

We soon spotted a carriageway leading to the river. The stream split into three arms at that spot. The spring floods had passed, and having decided that the river arms could be easily crossed on foot, I started the crossing using a stick for support. The water did not feel cold despite the fact that I was only wearing torn trousers and worn shoes. I was a third of the way across, fully expecting the others to follow me, when I heard cries behind my back. Turning around, I saw the rest of the group standing on the banks of the river shouting accusingly :

"Let's go back ! We are afraid because we can't swim! You promised not to leave us alone, and you also have two chooks in your bag! Come on, let's keep walking along this bank until we find a boat and cross without any risk!..."

The worst feature of this hysterical choir of cowards was the voice of the man whom I regarded as my trusted friend --Vladimir Rozanov! He obviously betrayed me and joined the criminal gang, with me being regarded by all of them now as "a despicable intellectual"--one man against four...

I had to give in, and all of us started walking slowly along the left bank of the Suifunhe, losing precious time needed to increase the gap between us and our tormentors and stupidly devouring chickens which were a veritable gift from heaven!

The gang stopped taking any notice of me and continued to rob settlements which themselves were short of food (that was the spring of 1947 !) leaving a trace of petty crimes behind our group. To make matters worse, all they managed to purloin were an axe, a scythe and a few crusts of practically inedible bread made from bran ! Three days were stupidly wasted...

At long last, in the darkness of the night, we found two boats chained to the shore near a village called Razdolnoye. It took us a long time to smash the locks using some river stones. One boat sank in the process and we had to crowd into the second one to cross the river using our hands and a few planks as oars. Having "crossed" the stream, we realised that we landed on an island ! Another boat had to be stolen almost in full view of some fisherman, until we finally made it to the opposite shore.

Instead of moving on, "The Brotherhood" walked towards a village in the hope of catching a sucking-pig. That attempt failed dismally, with the petty criminals having to run for their lives from some irate peasant women... It was quite astonishing that nobody followed us...

Finally, we managed to cross the highway and the railway leading from Razdolnoye to the Korean border. Following that feat we climbed a nearby hill and fell asleep because we were collapsing from exhaustion.

I woke up at dawn and took a good look around after making my way to the summit of our hill. The spring morning was cool and fresh. The grass was turning green after a long winter. A pheasant cock was shrieking somewhere close by, reminding me of the happy days when I was free. It was like a fairy tale after eighteen months in captivity! Right ahead of me I could see the peaks of The Blue Ridge--that was the border !! We could make it there by nightfall. There was, of course, the risk of being spotted by border guards and receiving a bullet for my efforts, but it was infinitely better to die a free man than a prisoner of the stinking Gulag! I decided to wake up the rest of the group and to start walking at once.

When I returned to the camp, the others were sleeping like a herd of wild pigs, and I had a lot of difficulty waking them up. "The border is in sight ! Let's go!"

"Naah ! Unlike you, we cannot eat snakes and frogs ! There is no way we are going to go anywhere until we catch a calf or a sheep and have a good feed. Don't forget, you gave us your word to stick together !"

That "word", curse it, was choking me. It would not let me send them to hell and walk away on my own, even though I realised full well that "The Brotherhood" held nothing sacred and that, given half a chance, they would sell me for a few cents ! However, I was unable to break my word ---such was my upbringing, going right back to my childhood days...

To make matters worse, Rozanov and one of the trio, a shorty by the name of Ivanov, announced that they were sick and unable to go on. They were weak, they said, and had to have something to eat. Therefore, having waited till it got dark, the three of us went in search of a calf or a heifer to steal. The clumsy deserter Vovka decided to blunder into the yard of a collective farm where he was set upon by the watchmen, and we were unable to rescue him. Much later we found out that, having been beaten up by the farmers, he told them where the rest of the fugitives were hiding.

The older deserter and I returned by dawn to the rocky peak where our "patients" were lying. In the neighbouring gully we saw a flock of sheep in charge of a shepherd. We walked down the mountain, sneaked up to the flock through the forest and tied up its guardian.

While we were at it, we heard the sound of automatic weapons. With the blunt end of an axe I managed to fell a lamb which was running past. We ran away and hid in the forest where we cut up our quarry, roasted it and had a good meal after which we fell asleep under a fallen cedar tree...

The fairy tale ended on the 5th of June 1947 when two officers and five soldiers armed with automatic weapons caught up with us. They were helped by a pack of savage alsatians. The soldiers were cursing under their breath :

"Because of you we spent three nights feeding mosquitoes !"

One of them hit me over the head with the butt of his automatic weapon. The officer shouted at him :

"Don't you dare !"

But it was too late : one of my eardrums was ruined forever....

We were handcuffed and taken to the headquarters of the detachment which was hunting for us. They set up shop in the office of "The Seventeenth Party Congress Collective Farm". As soon as we were brought in, the Lieutenant Colonel in charge of the operations made a jubilant phone call to his chief :

"Comrade General ! The fugitives have been captured !....

What ? Yes, the ataman (leader) of the gang, the White Guard, has also been apprehended ! Yes, yes, he is here, with me!"

He turned to me :

"Well, you reptile ! Aren't you lucky ! The death sentence was abolished yesterday. Otherwise you would have been surely shot !!"

6. RETRIBUTION.

I spent the following three months in the remand prison of the town of Ussuriysk where I shared a cell with a Japanese general Hasabe, a major of the Chang Kai Sheck (Leader of Chinese Nationalists) Army by the name of Dzu, and Kovalev, a Russian lieutenant who had been under investigation for eighteen months. Kovalev was a veteran of The Second World War but the authorities remembered that he had been imprisoned by the Finns during the

Russo-Finnish War of 1940, and started criminal proceedings against him. He was always ravenously hungry and was severely depressed and paranoid.

The prison day started at six o'clock in the morning when we had to get up and receive a small piece of moist black bread each. Half an hour after the first rations, we were given nine grams of sugar and a mug of hot water. The three of us waited for the second issue of rations so as to drink the sweetened water while eating the bread, but poor Kovalev was incapable of waiting. He cried but ate the dry bread before receiving the water and sugar. For some reason, best known to himself, he suspected that the Chinaman was being secretly given extra food and attacked the poor fellow with a wash-basin. We had to forcibly restrain him to calm him down.

Hasabe had a good command of the Russian language. His stories were very entertaining ; for example, he told us that during The First World War he was appointed a Military Attache to the Headquarters of Tsar Nicolas The Second. He also remembered his days as a spy in Paris and the exotic French houses of ill repute.

Another one of his stories was typical of post-revolutionary Russia...

It seems that in company of three other Japanese diplomats he was travelling by train from the City of Dairen (Formerly Russian Dalnyi, near Korea, which had been ceded to Japan after the Russo-Japanese War of 1904-1906) to Moscow. According to the Japanese tradition, passengers travelling first class leave their shoes outside their sleeping carriage so as to have them cleaned overnight by the railway staff. Knowing Soviet customs, Hasabe stopped leaving his shoes outside as soon as the train entered Soviet territory which was after it left the Manchuria Station. Hasabe's colleagues expected to receive their cleaned shoes the following morning and were quite surprised that they were waiting in vain....

The master of the train was severely put out by that event, and managed with great difficulty to get hold of three pairs of torn slippers during the stopover in Irkutsk, a town located on Lake Baikal. The embarrassed diplomats had to wear them when greeting their confreres in Moscow...

Hasabe remembered his suits which, being a diplomat, he had tailor-made in various capital cities. I joined in, remembering the suits left in my home. I counted two dinner suits, three warm business suits, four summer outfits and some sports get-ups, a total of twelve attires.

We had our conversation before "lights out", after which prisoners had to stay silent, but all of a sudden the lock on our door emitted a scraping noise, and the malnourished shape of one of our warders appeared on the threshold. He gave me a look full of contempt and pronounced :

"Make sure that when you lie you don't stretch credibility beyond breaking point! Twelve suits, indeed !!"

He silently shut the door and left us alone....

For this and other inhabitants of the Soviet Union my story was an impossible tall tale !

Hunger was the natural state of the prisoners of Gulag, and for that reason we often discussed food. Poor depressed Kovalev begged us to shut up, and Hasabe and I conducted these discussions in Japanese. During our walks in the prison yard I would surreptitiously pick a few shoots of goose -foot (weed) growing near the fence and use it as a garnish for the soup we received for lunch.

The food was placed into our feeding trough by a young cook --an attractive strong and healthy filly by the name of Mashka. When looking at her pink bare arms one day, I astonished my fellow inmates by saying :

"When she pokes her arm into our feeding trough tomorrow I'll tear it off and eat it!" The Asians looked at me in disbelief but sad and pitiful Korolev started to cry...

I was lucky when it came to the preliminary investigation into my escape. The investigator was a very decent fellow by the name of Captain Shevchenko. It may sound strange, but he commiserated with me. He even gave me some food and cigarettes. It is quite possible that he was able to explain the reason for my escape in a way which ultimately led to a review of my case.

My third court case in the Gulag system took place in August 1947. Each member of our group "earned" twenty five years imprisonment in the Gulag's "Corrective Labour Camps".

We were taken to jail immediately after the court case.Four Chinese prisoners were added to our group, making it a total of nine.For a short while we were on our own in the prison entrance where somebody left half a bag of newly harvested potatoes. It took us only ten minutes to devour all of these uncleaned potatoes which were still covered in soil.The nine of us were champing like a herd of piglets...

My further translocations continued without the rest of my group. I was taken from Ussuriysk to Khabarovsk from where I was transferred to the Vanino Bay on the Pacific Ocean, opposite the Island of Sakhalin.

It was December 1947 and the cold was absolutely savage. One thousand prisoners were loaded into each of the four holds of the motor vessel "Krasnogvardeyets" ("The Red Guard"). That ship was one of the Liberty type vessels which the USA gave to Russia under the "lend-lease" agreement which existed during The Second World War between the two countries. It was intended for the transport of cargo. However, the Gulag bosses "adapted"it for the transport of the "human cargo"of its slaves.

The holds were equipped with three levels of benches made of raw timber, but no provision was made for any kind of heating...In order to escape death by freezing, the zeks (prisoners) had to dance around the hold, which they did either on their own or in pairs and even groups, forming dancing rings. I would venture to say that if that ship was transporting cattle, the agency responsible for it would not have been allowed to send its cargo to a certain death...

The bizarre "ball" was lit by electric lamps and the walls of the hold were covered in ice. At the height of the "merryment" the ship started rolling, and one set of shelves collapsed on the floor. A blood-curdling scream followed that accident. People who found themselves underneath the collapsed shelves were squashed like pancakes. That did not disturb the Gulag authorities who "wrote off" the victims by throwing them overboard.

The nightmare lasted for five days. By the time we reached the port of Nakhodka (near Vladivostok) only a few hundred "human cattle" were able to walk off the ship unaided. I was on top of the world during the trip because the large toe on may left foot was badly frost - bitten and I spent the journey in the prison hospital which seemed like a true paradise. Never did I experience such a comfort during my Gulag days!

In July 1948 an identical motor vessel, this time named "Stepan Razin", took me to Chukotka (on the Arctic Circle, near the Bering Strait, opposite Alaska). The food consisted of dried bread, plus some weak soup and a mug of water once a day. The trip lasted for almost six weeks and involved crossing five seas, with the final destination being the Port of Pevek (on The Chukchi Sea, in The Arctic Ocean, just north of The Arctic Circle). It was already snowing when we arrived there on the twenty ninth of August.

Upon arrival in Pevek, prisoners were taken to various mines. I was moved to a mine called "Krasnoarmeysky" ("Red Army Mine") which was involved in the mining of tin, whose ore is called "cassiterite".

My job was to obtain cassiterite with a pick and to load it into wheel barrows which I then emptied into iron sleighs and took out of the mine. Another job involved digging forty five centimetre deep holes in the ground for blasting of the ore. I had to use a crow bar and worked in open air in extreme cold.

Yet another task consisted of carrying on my back of ore samples for assessment by the Ore Exploration Bureau. I carried them out of the mines, after which I had to wash, dry and blast them with compressed air. The treated samples were then tested to determine the percentage of metal contained in them.

Many times I thought that I would not to live to see another day and would die of starvation, as I did not get enough black bread to sustain life.

However, quite unexpectedly, my sentence was reviewed in winter of 1949. I was allowed to serve a total of additional ten years which meant that I could work without the supervision of an armed guard. That gave me a chance to earn a few extra pieces of bread. The effect was almost immediate, because three weeks after the increase in my rations I realised that I was beginning to gain weight. My previously bare bones were acquiring a cover of flesh, which was noticeable when I was having my shower.

A further improvement was the reduction in the length of sentence for exceeding the production quota. Whenever I achieved 121% of the daily quota, a day of incarceration was regarded as being equal to three.

The result of all this was that in August 1952 (four years after arrival in Pevek) I was released from The Gulag and issued with the first official papers since my arrival on Russian soil. It was a "Release Certificate" which stated (I quote verbatim) :

"This document is not an internal passport, and it cannot be used to obtain a 'Propiska'. (<u>Note</u> : The term for internal registration in Russian is "Propiska". Without a "Propiska", a citizen cannot "officially" take up residence anywhere).

Chapter 21. BEYOND GULAG.

1. THE FIRST TENTATIVE STEPS.

The release document from the Gulag did not allow me to leave Chukotka but I was allowed to find private lodgings and work for wages. I took up residence at the "Yuzhny" ("Southern") mine staying there for nearly three years. I started work as a mining foreman and later obtained the position of a manager of an instrument laboratory. My work was rewarded by a number of written commendations and bonuses.

At long last, I was allowed to leave Chukotka in 1955 and fly to the town of Magadan (located near the 60th parallel, on the Sea of Okhotsk, on the Pacific Coast). There I made enquiries through the Gulag Head Office and found the addresses of my father, my brother Yuri and cousin Tanya. I sent them as much money as I could afford, in order to improve their financial position.

Enquiries through the Association of Russian Citizens in Harbin established that my wife Irma and my young son Sergey left for Canada.

Whilst holidaying in Magadan, I went hunting wild geese with my Manchurian countryman, an "old believer" (a member of the branch of the Russian Orthodox Church which broke away from the main body in the 17th century) by the name of Kovyazin. We were hunting near the settlement of Talon, in the vicinity of some women's Gulag camps. In one of these camps I met a "white slave" who was expecting to be released in the near future.

Her name was Irina Kazimirovna. Thirteen years before our meeting she was a schoolgirl in the Russian town of Saratov (on the Volga River, in Southern Russia). Her "crime" consited of reading a poem at a birthday party given to one of her high school friends. The poem belonged to a well known poet Sergey Yesenin and was entitled "Return to the Motherland".

We married on the 27th of March 1956 in a small government Registry Office in Magadan, with the marriage licence costing us fifteen roubles. The female office manager who performed the ceremony did not utter one word of congratulations or encouragement at its conclusion.

My cousin Tanya was released from imprisonment at the time of my marriage and lived in the town of Taishet (Siberia) where she was awaiting the release of her uncle, my father Yuri (George) Michailovich Yankovsky. Tanya wanted to bring my father with her to join us in Magadan. Unfortunately, dad did not live to see freedom. He caught a cold and died in a Gulag hospital a few weeks before being released.

My brother Yuri was released from Gulag in Central Asia and stayed there after the camp. We met in Moscow in 1962, seventeen years after the memorable farewell in

Pyongyang. The meeting took place after we wrote to each other to establish a suitable time for it .

Irene's (Irina's) and my son Arseny was born in Magadan in 1959. At that time she was working as a proofreader of a local newspaper, and I had a position as a forester in the Magadan Forestry Department.

Our jobs enabled us to save enough money to buy an apartment in Vladivostok where we went to live after I was pensioned off in 1966. At that time our son was being treated for chronic pneumonia in Moscow but subsequently joined us in our flat. However, it soon became apparent that he could not live in the humid climate of Vladivostok.That forced us to move to the town of Vladimir (About 200 km east of Moscow) where we have lived since 1968.

I started writing stories and articles for various magazines and published seven books. Here are some of their titles (all of them are only available in Russian):

"Nenoony The Four -Eyed" (the story of my grandfather Michael Yankovsky)

"A Long Return" (the story of my imprisonment in the Gulag)

Some books about hunting and Korea (again, only in Russian) :

"Tigers, Deer and Gingseng"

"The Peninsula "

"The Heirs of Nenoony"

2. A TRIP INTO THE PAST.

It took fifteen years of applications, followed by refusals, to finally get permission to visit my family on the American Continent. That permission was given by Gorbachev's Administration in 1986. I could not believe that I was actually on my way until I heard the stewardess on the Aeroflot Plane "IL-86" announce that we were flying over Oslo...

At the Vancouver Airport I was met by my first wife Irma and a man with a greying beard, my son Sergey (Serge) who, for the first time in 40 years, called me "Papa".Having obtained a fortnight's leave, Serge took me all over Vancouver and its surroundings, showing me museums, ice hockey, horse races, the Island of Victoria and an Indian village. It was quite an eye opener to see its two-storeyed cottages, cars, and motorised fishing trawlers. Native Indians enjoy fishing rights which are denied to the whites..

Irma and I spent a lot of time in vivid descriptions of events of the intervening four decades..

Following the Canadian leg of the trip, I flew to San Francisco to meet my dear and near ones, and friends from the days of my youth. I stayed with my cousin Oleg Shevelev, my sisters Musa and Victoria and with the family of Vova Shevelev, the son of my late cousin Gleb.

My longest stay was with widowed Nusya.

My sister Victoria's son Or, whom I nursed as an infant in the Tiger Hamlet, took me to the famous Fort Ross. He and his friend flew me along the shores of The Pacific in a charter plane to show me the unforgettable sight of whales migrating from Alaska to California.

I returned to Moscow in February 1987. I must confess that Moscow appeared very untidty compared with western cities.

On return to Vladimir I was told with great humour by Irina Kazimirovna that her tender -hearted neighbours commiserated with her in these terms :

"We are sorry for you because Valery Yuryevich is obviously not coming back. After all, he has gone back to his first family ".

3. HONOURING THE FAMILY NAME

I was determined to exonerate the memory of my father by removing the slanderous stigma of "the enemy of the people". For thirty years I petitioned the Supreme Court of the USSR to reconsider my father's case, only to be told time and again that "the case was not capable of being reconsidered". However, in 1990 The Court reconsidered that matter. We were officially notified that father's name had been completely cleared.

We have yet to receive his belongings seized during the arrest but are working on it. However, cousin Tanya and I have found the remote cemetery at which Y.(G.) M. Yankovsky, our "Papa -Tiger", finished the last ten terrifying years of his life. That cemetery is located between Taishet and Bratsk (Siberia), near a station called Chuksha.

We ordered a metal plaque engraved with the following words :

NOBLEMAN YURI MICHAILOVICH YANKOVSKY.
AUTHOR OF THE BOOK
"HALF A CENTURY IN PURSUIT OF TIGERS".
1879--1956.

Cousin Tanya was the last member of our family to have seen her uncle alive, one month before his death. She attended the thanksgiving ceremony held on the fortieth anniversary of the release of political prisoners from the Gulag camp called "Ozerlag" ("The Camp on the Lake") and, with the aid of fellow-ex-inmates, attached the plaque to a birch tree.

In September 1991 a two-metre-high bronze monument was erected in honour of my grandfather Michael Ivanovich Yankovsky on the Yankovsky Peninsula, near Vladivostok. The monument was built with the kind help of members of the Arsenyev (a well-known Russian explorer of the Far East, author of the book "Dersu Usala", later made into a world-famous film) Museum in Vladivostok. Invaluable assistance in that undertaking was rendered by an energetic member of the Museum Board Boris Alexeyevich Dyachenko and sculptor Oleg Stepanovich Kulesh.

This is the text of the inscription on the Monument:

**HE WAS A NOBLEMAN IN POLAND
AND A PRISONER IN SIBERIA.
HE EARNED RESPECT AND WAS HONOURED
IN THE USSURI REGION.**

4. THOSE WHO ESCAPED GULAG.

My sisters Musa and Victoria escaped Gulag for different reasons.

Musa lived in Shanghai which was beyond the reach of the KGB. She left that city in 1949 and reached Chile with many other refugees, migrating later to the USA.

Victoria was stranded in The Tiger Hamlet where she suffered many privations and was subjected to humiliation by riff-raff which got out of control after The War. It was not until 1953 when Musa managed to help Ora (Victoria) to find her way to the USA, in company of her new husband Peter Chistyakov and young son Or.

The only male member of the family who managed to escape the clutches of the NKVD--MGB (Precursors of the KGB) was my brother Arseny who was a very gifted individual. He and I grew up side by side, first as happy children of a well-to-do landowning family, and later--as teenagers during the tough initial years of exile.

As time went on, difficulties and successes of our daily lives and hunting expeditions were approximately evenly distributed. Together, shoulder to brotherly shoulder, we fought off attacks of the Hung Hu Tse bandits, hunted wild pigs, bears and other game. When we succeeded in killing a tiger in winter, we invariably threw off our warm mittens and exchanged handshakes. We experienced severe hunger in the taiga (Manchurian virgin forest) and spent many winter nights by a camp fire in our tent. There was friendly rivalry between us in the pursuit of the belles who spent their holidays in Novina and Lukomorye....

I moved to Manchuria in the mid-1940's but Arseny and his wife Olga stayed in Novina. Olga was several years older than my brother and left her first husband, a writer by the name of Michael Sherbakov, to marry Arseny.

At War's end Arseny was drafted from Novina to work for Russian Intelligence as an interpreter of Japanese and Korean. It was well known that his work was highly valued by his superiors. However, the situation underwent a drastic change from the beginning of 1946. Our father was arrested, followed by the arrests of cousin Tanya and our close friend--Ellers. When Arseny heard of the arrest of his brothers, he realised that he was to be next...

He went to Pyongyang accompanied by his wife, using the collection of his Russian passport as a pretext. There he got in touch with a group of smugglers who frequently crossed the 38th parallel (the border between North and South Korea) and who helped him to escape to the South after some hair-raising adventures.

As could be expected, he was accepted as an employee of the American Intelligence. After the Korean War, he went to Japan where he made a career as a businessman, becoming a Commercial Director of "Mitsubishi", one of their largest companies.

Arseny and Olga's marriage was childless which caused them to adopt a four-year old boy of mixed Japanese -American parentage. He was one of many such children who appeared in Japan during the American occupation. They christened him Grisha (Gregory) .

Following a few successful years in the employ of Mitsubishi, Arseny was able to buy a two-storeyed house in San Francisco and a dacha (holiday home) in the Californian countryside.

He used a very clever ruse to find me in Magadan....

In order to deflect attention to himself from the KGB and the CIA he started writing to me under the guise of Volodya (Vladimir) Vakhovich, our relative who perished during the Second World War. He invented a story that Vakhovich miraculously survived the sinking of the ship of his British employer by a German submarine. The story was so plausible that for a while even I believed that Vakhovich escaped death....

I started getting parcels and money transfers from "Vakhovich "which I was asked to share with Yuri and cousin Tanya. Just before I left Magadan I received a request from the local post office to collect a parcel. When I came to collect it, I was given an oblong box for which I did not have to pay any duty as it had been prepaid at the time of posting. I opened it at home and could not believe my eyes ! The parcel contained a brand new semi-automatic twelve gauge Browning shot gun !

My hunting colleagues in Magadan and I were astonished. I used that rifle during the last two winters in Kolyma, taking it to a few unforgettable hunting expeditions in search of wild geese.

Having retired, Arseny wanted to organise "pantui" (soft deer horns) deer farming in California. I sent him books of detailed instructions to help him on the way. He was expecting a visit from me and organised a guest visa, but all attempts to get permission to travel abroad met in those days with the standard answer: "Permission refused". No reasons for the refusal were ever given.

The KGB made a number of approaches to our family about Arseny. They made several overtures to me in Magadan, to Brother Yuri In Bishkek (capital of Kyrgyzstan, in Central Asia) and cousin Tanya in Novozybkovo (Western Russia), with suggestions to invite Arseny "to visit The Motherland". It was evident that they could not forgive him his escape from under the noses of their Secret Service ("SMERSH"--"Death To The Spies") organisation, to join the Americans.

They were obsessed with the idea of catching and punishing him but were unable to achieve their aim. Nevertheless, I cannot help ruminating over the theory that they did find a way of killing him. It is possible that he was surreptitiously stabbed with a poisoned umbrella or given a poison by some secret agents during a meal in a restaurant...

Be as it may, he suddenly succumbed to a mysterious illness at the time of his life when he was healthy and full of energy. It started with the paralysis of one leg, followed by the second. The arms followed...Doctors were unable to diagnose his illness but suspected poisoning.

Arseny died in San Francisco in 1978 aged 64 years and was buried at the so-called "Serbian Cemetery" where I paid my respects to his grave in 1987.

His wife Olga died a few years later.

Their beloved half-Japanese adopted son Grisha kicked Olga's crippled sister Nina (she was unable to walk) out of their home. Having accomplished that vile deed, he quickly sold off the assets of his adoptive parents and vanished, without giving a cent to any of Arseny's relatives, despite the fact that on his death bed Arseny told his cousin Gleb Shevelev:

"Olga knows everything. She will carry out my instructions".

But, alas, he left no will, and Olga and Grisha had done what suited them...

5. WE HAVE OVERCOME...

The opening of the monument to Michael Ivanovich Yankovsky took place on a sunny autumn day in September 1991....

The numerous participants of the ceremony gathered on a knoll overlooking the Sedemi Bay, many of them carrying flowers. Among the official guests were dignitaries from Vladivostok and surrounding districts, personnel of the Arsenyev Museum in Vladivostok, Local Government officials, senior staff from the State Deer Farm and the State Wharves. They all helped to finance the construction of the monument.

I came from Vladimir with my son Arseny and the director of the "Zolotye Vorota" ("Golden Gates") Publishing House Nikolai Lalakin.

The most remarkable visitor was my sister, the poetess Victoria Yankovsky who came from California with her son Or and two granddaughters, Alora and Kira.

The grand - and great-grandchildren of the legendary Captain Gek also attended the ceremony. They came to honour the memory of their forebear who shared with my grandfather the first difficulties, losses and joys of developing, in the words of Michael Yankovsky, "the land which had not been settled before."

..........WE HAD, INDEED, OVERCOME.......

Chapter 22. ACKNOWLEDGEMENTS.

The author Vladimir Krakovsky had been advising me for a long time to write this short novel. I also received many letters from Misha, the first born son of our friends Natalia Borisovna and Michael Alexandrovich Hintze, urging me to undertake this task.

Michael Michailovich emigrated to Australia with his parents at the beginning of the nineteen fifties. He retained many happy memories of Novina and Lukomorye and has kept numerous photographs of that era. A few years ago he visited us in Vladimir. We are keeping up a lively correspondence with Misha.

Last but not least, I must acknowledge that the publication of this narrative has been primarily made possible through the untiring efforts of Alexander Alexandrovich Kovzun, a research worker at the Vladimir District Library. He was the first scientist to get in touch with me and to suggest the publication of my book....

Chapter 23. CONCLUDING REMARKS IN LIEU OF AN EPILOGUE.

1. CREATION OF NOVINA

After reading the manuscript of this work prior to its publication I came to the conclusion that I omitted to relate a few relevant details of the history of the life of our family in Korea. The most important omission appears to be that I did not describe the conditions which prevailed immediately after our escape from the Communists. Neither did I explain how we succeeded in the face of overwhelming odds...

For many years I used to run my father's weekly errands by riding my bicycle fifty kilometres from Novina to Seisin. An additional task involved supplying the Seisin Post Office with short summaries of radio broadcasts we received from Vladivostok and Khabarovsk, for which I was paid forty yen a month (roughly equivalent to forty US dollars at the time). Thirty of these dollars went into the family coffers, with only ten left at my unfettered disposal. But even that modest sum was a great help to the budget of an impecunious youth.

On the way back I always brought with me a heavy load of bovine bones supplied by our grandmother which allowed the inhabitants of Novina to cook a modest soup.It was quite an effort to get the loaded bike over two high mountain passes on the return trip, and I had to literally stand on the pedals to keep it moving. I huffed and puffed and was constantly swallowing copious quantities of dust stirred up by passing motor cars. Oh how I longed to buy my own car ! But despite those difficulties (or, perhaps, because of them) I became strong enough to race to the tennis courts with my trusty racket immediately after unloading my "iron horse"!

It was not until 1932 (ten years after our arrival in Korea) that our family could afford an old 1926 Chevrolet which had the shape of an open horse cart ("phaeton"), with thick timber spokes on its wheels.

Even though it was not much to look at, the car was very reliable and capable of carrying seven people. A huge luggage rack located at the back transported huge loads. We christened that bomb "Starya" ("The Oldie") because of its age but "Number 267" (the figure engraved on its number plates) gave us good service for a few years.

We had far better cars later, but "Starya"was part of a very special period in our lives. That motor car signified the introduction of transport self-sufficiency into Novina which resulted in very noticeable improvement in our fortunes!

Returning to tennis, I must say that it was very popular in Novina. I was a good player and became the resort champion during one of the summer seasons. Another popular sport was "gorodki" (a Russian version of ten pin bowling. It is played in open air and uses homemade unsophisticated equipment). Gorodki championships were hotly contested between members of our family and the holiday makers. Between the gorodki field and the tennis courts we erected a horizontal bar and a set of parallel bars which attracted a lot of amateur athletes practically every fine evening.

A mast bearing the Russian National Flag and the "Novina"crest were located in the vicinity. The ensemble was crowned by a bell mounted on a post and used to summon the holiday-makers to breakfast, lunch, afternoon tea and dinner...

A later craze was volleyball. We had mixed teams, and the highlight of the season was the match between Novina and Lukomorye.

The Lukomorye team was headed by a great lover of sport, our uncle Borya, Boris Yulyevich Brynner, the father of Yul.

The Novina team was led by an extremely popular captain in the person of Gutya Bibinova - Rokotova --the brown-eyed olive-skinned wife of the editor of the magazine "Rubezh" ("The Border") published in Harbin. Being a wonderful human being as well as a charming woman and an all-round sports person, Gutya managed to create a highly disciplined team. She commanded complete obedience from young lads, many of whom were quite undisciplined in their daily lives. Her melodious voice, reminiscent of the sound of a silver bell, elicited smiles on the faces of normally unsmiling older men.

2. THE DEATH OF NOVINA.

Novina died in one day.It took perhaps one hour to destroy the fruits of twenty years of daily painstaking labour which went into that enterprise. But it was not only the destruction of Novina but also of the efforts and experience of generations of our family, going back to the discoverer of the Yankovsky Peninsula in 1880.

People running the Russian Secret Service Organisation SMERSH (an acronym of the Russian words "Death to the Spies") spent about a year looking into and sniffing around the Yankovsky estate.To them the place smelt like grilled meat, like something which promised a handsome booty. While the bosses of SMERSH often visited Novina and freely sampled its fruit both figuratively and literally, a black deed was being carefully crafted in a building on a hill in Seisin, a building which many years ago was the Russian Imperial Consulate in that city.

Finally, on the fourth of September 1946 (approximately one year after the end of the War), a warrant was concocted for the arrest and search of the owner of Novina, Yuri (George) Michailovich Yankovsky.The warrant for father's arrest was prepared and signed by the Senior MGB (precursor of KGB) Investigator Lieutenant Fedishin and sanctioned by Lt. Colonel Yelkin and Acting Prosecutor Vovchenko. On the day of Novina's death, the fifth of September 1946, the author of that document rolled up in person at our estate, accompanied by his assistants and witnesses. That character not only arrested Yuri Yankovsky but, under the guise of a "search", robbed Novina a long time before father's trial.In order to preserve a semblance of legality, the thieves hatched a semi-literate but fairly comprehensive list of their loot. The organisers of the robbery could not have imagined even in their wildest dreams that their masterful creation would ever see the light of day! But "tempora mutantur"---times change!...

3. SUMMARY OF THE YANKOVSKY FAMILY'S HISTORY.

The descendants of the knights who fought for the Lord's Casket in the fourteenth and fifteenth century were subjected to robbery and outrage three times during the course of the nineteenth and twentieth centuries.

My grandfather Michael Yankovsky joined a detachment of rebels from the Gorets Agricultural Institute of the Mogilev District. The detachment was instructed by the Central National Committee to seize the gold reserves of the Gorets Treasury in order to pay for the shipment of weapons which had been ordered from England and were being delivered to one of the Lithuanian ports.

The rebel students were led by Ludwig Zvezhdovsky, a Captain of the General Staff and an erstwhile aide-de-camp to the Governor. Ludwig's alias was "The Axe". The group confiscated cases filled with Tsarist gold coins loading them on horse-- driven carts taken from the local Jews. However, a punitive expedition (a detachment of regular troops fighting the rebels) caught up with them when they were about to cross the River Pronya (in Poland). The regular troops attacked the rebels with case shot fire, crushing them.

The rebels were captured and the gold returned to the Treasury. Their leader, The Axe, managed to escape, only to be arrested and executed later.

The participants of the National Uprising were classified as members of "a rebel band". Pan (Polish word for "Mr") Michael was incarcerated in the Bobruisk Jail where he underwent his first questioning on the 22nd of May 1863. He was given a particularly severe punishment because he managed to hide a pistol during his arrest.

The investigation lasted through the summer of 1863. The court case took place in September, during which an annoncement was made of the decision made by the Governor-General Muravyov, known by the nickname of "Muravyov, The Hangman."It read :

"His Excellency, The Commander of he Vilno Military District, Infantry General Muravyov, having studied the documents relating to this investigation has resolved as follows:

To confirm the decision of the Military Court convened in the city of Mogilev, in accordance with the Monarch's decree, to deal with the rebels who are former noblemen and students and who have been convicted of armed action as part of the Gorets rebel band, and robbery of the Treasury of the town of Gorki...

All accused are to be stripped of their titles as nobles, of all rights to property and to be exiled to a place of penal servitude. Their property is to be confiscated and handed over to the Treasury."

Michael Yankovsky was sentenced to seven years penal servitude. This is how the rebel came to be in Siberia, with his family, consisting of his parents and thirteen brothers and sisters, having been dispossessed and scattered over The Russian Empire.

Having served the years of hard labour near Lake Baikal (in Siberia), Michael became "a free settler" and travelled to the shores of The Pacific where, after many years of painstaking work he created a unique farm which brought fame to the peninsusla, later named after him.

His eldest son --Yuri (George) Michailovich was a worthy heir to his father's enterprise which prospered for forty two years. (******See the footnote at the end of this section**). However, The Russian Revolution hated and rejected hard working entrepreneurs and property owners, hanging and shooting them for their efforts!

This led to a second loss of our family's fortunes which culminated in our escape abroad, to Korea. We only salvaged what little we could take with us during our hurried departure.The new proletarian masters of our estate did not have to pay for our houses, horses and deer. Nevertheless, as we found out later, they had no idea about how to run our model enterprise and let it go to rack and ruin...

Korea saw the beginning of a new cycle of creative endeavour. Again we had to start from scratch, living in tents and shacks and eking out a pitiful existence. I still remember our life in a tiny Korean "fanza" (hut) during our first summer in Korea.

One day we were visited by a group of Japanese women living at the holiday resort of Ompo. They were either paying guests or geisha girls working there. One can only imagine what a terrible impression we, a group of Russian refugees, made on them, because before leaving us they surreptitiously left a five sen (cent) coin on a bench (these coins had a hole in them and used to be carried on a piece of string). They must have been afraid to insult us with an open donation. My mother was shocked when she saw the coin.

"Just think of it", she exclaimed, "we must look like beggars!".

We worked like ants overcoming all difficulties. On a practically barren terrain consisting of rocks and infertile fields we created two settlements which were as close to paradise as is imaginable. Novina was located in the mountains close to the health-giving Ompo hot springs, and the resort of Lukomorye was justly proud of its magnificent beaches.

It is of interest to note that the burglars who confiscated Novina before the court case took place did not find it necessary to make any mention of its subsidiary, the sea-side resort of Lukomorye .

CONCLUDING REMARKS IN LIEU OF AN EPILOGUE

Lukomorye with its fairy-tale fragrant forest, its beach covered in golden sand and its blue ocean disappeared without a trace, as if it had been invisible. It was simply stolen by the senior military overlords.

That ended the third and last tragic period in the life of our long-suffering family. Everything was ruined --this time forever.....

I thank God for the existence of enthusiasts who helped me to write this saga, and I want to express my sincerest thanks to them. My story contains neither a single invented name nor an untrue fact. I want to believe that my readers will find this narrative instructive and that it will serve as a monument to the generations which have forever disappeared into the Past....

***Footnote.

One year before our escape to Korea, i. e. in 1921, having made a thorough examination of our enterprise, some American businessmen approached Y. (G.) M. Yankovsky offering him two million U.S. dollars for its purchase, which in today's money amounts to at least U.S. twenty million. However, father refused their offer.

The Americans were not taking any chances, because right up to 1930 foreign concessions with extra-territorial rights existed in the U.S.S.R. (they were subject to the laws of the country of origin and not Communist laws). For example, having acquired a Swiss nationality (based on the origins of their father Y.I. Brynner), the Brynner brothers remained right up to 1930 the co-owners of lead and silver mines located on the Bay of Tetyukhe, in The Russian Maritime Provinces.

4. ARSENY YANKOVSKY'S STORY

First detachments of Soviet troops which entered "Novina", a small Russian settlement in North Korea near the port of Seisin (now Chongjin), detained most of male Russians and took them to the headquarters. Shortly afterwards they decided to use those who spoke either Korean or Japanese as interpreters.

One of Arseny's first assignments was to accompany a party sent to capture the Japanese Governor of the province who escaped into the hills together with the members of his staff. When they tracked him down, the Governor surrendered without resistance. Taking advantage of the fact that none of the officers and men spoke Japanese, Arseny who knew the Governor personally, addressed him in that language:

"Your Excellency", he said,

"I am here only because I was forced to do so."

"I am glad you came", said the Governor,

"You will be able to translate correctly for me."

After that Arseny accompanied several expeditions sent to seek out and arrest fugitive Japanese officials as well as Koreans who collaborated with them.

Eventually it was announced by the Soviet Occupation Forces that all stateless Russians would be issued with Soviet passports. In this connection lists of persons who were called upon to apply to the Soviet Embassy in Pyongyang for their passports were issued but the names of Arseny and his wife were not amongst them. This alarmed Arseny because he saw it as an indication that he was under suspicion and might possibly be arrested.

Upon careful consideration he and his wife decided to make an attempt to take refuge in the American Zone. In order to accomplish this they felt they had to get as near as possible to the American positions without arousing suspicion. So early one morning Arseny and his wife hitched a ride on a Soviet truck travelling to Pyongyang. He was wearing the Soviet military uniform issued to him as an interpreter, and the driver, taking him for an officer, addressed him as "Comrade Commander."

Upon arrival in Pyongyang they went to the Soviet Embassy and said that they had come to collect their passports. They were told that their documentes had not arrived yet and were asked to come back in a day or two. That same night they started on their walk to the American Zone.

After a while they came to a hut belonging to an old Korean who let them in and gave them some tea to drink. Then Arseny took the shotgun he was carrying with him, pointed its at the old man and told him that they were escaping to the American Zone and were looking for mountain trails which were not being guarded. Arseny ordered him to guide them, and the old man came with them and showed them the way.

When they got close to the border, he begged them to let him go, explaining to them which trail to take. Shortly afterwards they came across a group of Koreans who were cautiously travelling in the same direction. Being diriectly covered by Arseny's gun, they explained that they were smugglers on their way to collect contraband in the American Zone and carry it back to Pyongyang. They assumed that Arseny was an American spy returning trom the Soviet Zone after collecting the required information, and readily agreed to show them the way to the American lines.

The smugglers kept their promise, and in due course Arseny and his wife surrendered to the American Military Authorites and asked for political asylum.

(Note : The above is a copy of a handwritten document contained in the archives of M.A.Hintze {1900-1992} who compiled it on the basis of a discussion he had with Arseny Yankovsky in the U.S.A. in the late 1970's.)

Part Two

My initial intention was to devote the second part of my book to photographs with suitable captions. However, I soon realised that that was not enough because too many events concerning my immediate family as well as more distant members of our clan did not get an adequate airing in the first part. I therefore decided to devote the second part of my narrative to the filling in of these voids

Chapter 24. A CAR CALLED "STARYA" (THE OLD BOY) AND ITS MATES.

The desire to own a motorcar became an obsession, which was plaguing me like a chronic disease, and when pushing the pedals of my heavy bike I kept imagining that I was turning the wheel of a car. It seemed to me that the acquisition of a car would, in the words of a song by a pop star by the name of Utesov who was very popular at the time, immediately "make our life better".

However, there was no possible way we could even think of acquiring a new "Ford" or a "Chevrolet" despite the fact that they adorned the showrooms of the Seisin car dealers. Those blue, green and burgundy beauties were displayed in their windows costing less than one thousand US dollars at the time (1860 Japanese yen, to be precise), but we did not have that kind of money.... The Japanese "Nissans" and "Toyotas" were only available in the form of lorries and their quality was immeasurably inferior compared with their American rivals. Our only hope was to pick up a car at an auction. These were rare and took place only when the government unloaded its used cars. But my obsession was so strong that I used every opportunity to get behind the wheel of a car. I also spent a lot of time studying the road rules in Japanese.

When our uncle Victor was studying the road rules for his licence after we acquired a car, he learned them like poetry, without understanding most words. He would also sing the unfamiliar phrases. I was told that the government examiner was falling over with laughter during the test but uncle managed to pass! I sat for my licence before Victor and having flunked the first test, managed to pass the second one and was given a provisional licence.

We were not prepared for an auction when it was announced by the Railways Department which was selling an old greeny -- brown sedan, a huge 1926 Chevrolet whose wheels were adorned with timber spokes. It had seven seats two of which were collapsible, and a huge boot attached to the back. The opening price was 250 yen. Our financial position was very difficult indeed but Father heeded our pleas and paid that amount as, luckily, we were the only bidders. We immediately christened our purchase **"Starya"** ("The Old Boy") and welcomed it into our family.

Unfortunately we were unable to get it to go straight away. A few days were spent under the car fixing the oil pump and the brakes. But at long last I took the wheel and drove our whole family into town, which lay on a road leading through the markets. The roads were muddy and the road rules required the fitting of special brushes to the wheels under those conditions. The brushes were mounted on long shafts which required skilful navigation through the throng of buyers   I drove very carefully but unfortunately managed to catch the wide trousers of a hapless passer -by who started to scream off his head and jumping on one leg next to our car. Luckily the poor fellow sustained no injuries due to Starya's low speed.

My passengers were elated by our first trip, which signalled a major change in our lifestyle. I no longer had to swallow the dust of passing cars, which was otherwise abundant on the unsealed highways. As well, I was able to transport our houseguests and to carry various goods in the boot of "The Old Boy" instead of on the back of my bike.

Our first major car trip involved a hunting expedition. For some years we had been aware of the fact that a "Big House" of pheasants was located in the north-eastern corner of Korea, on the right hand bank of the Tumangan River. Unfortunately we could never get there on our bikes because the trip involved the crossing of a huge mountain range. We used to stop on our side of the range, in an area called "Yanchen"

The hunting rules were very strict indeed. One was not allowed to hunt water fowl till the 15th of September (as opposed to August in our country), and pheasants could only be taken from the first of November, which ensured that young birds were fully grown and which had the added advantage of being able to freeze the shot birds, as the temperatures dropped below zero at night.

Our group comprised my father (George Yankovsky), Kolya (Nick) Gusakovsky, brother Arseny and yours truly. Our chauffeur was Rhee, an old Korean friend whose nickname was "Khromonozhka" ("The Lame One").

I was not yet game to tackle such a long journey on my own.

We also took three hunting dogs --- three well-trained retrievers (pointers). It is a well-known fact that a pheasant hunt without a good dog is a waste of time, because the dog not only finds the birds but also chases and catches a wounded quarry. A wounded pheasant would otherwise outrun its assassin.

We firsts travelled east describing a large arch along the shoreline and then turned north, ultimately reaching our coveted destination, which consisted of lush fields of soy beans located on rolling hills, with the whole area teeming with pheasants.

Old pheasant males organise early morning raids on the soy plants when the beans are ripe and are about to be harvested. The old "ataman" (leader) races towards a plant and starts to hit it with its wings making a sound like a threshing machine, knocking all the beans on the ground out of their pods. The hens and their brood attack the beans, devouring them in a matter of minutes.

We started to decimate these birds, much to the delight of the local farmers who regarded them as their arch- enemies. Our group of Russian hunters pursued the pheasants up and down the hills, accompanied by the dogs. Father and I were pursuing our victims with Browning rifles, with Arseny sporting a double-barrelled shotgun and Kolya brandishing a "three – liner" which used to belong to our grandfather.

The results of our hunt were magnificent. It took us only three and a half days to slaughter 216 long-tailed, multicoloured roosters and ashen-coloured spotted hens. Father's share of this carnage were 92 birds, with Arseny and I killing 52 and 72 of them respectively. Our shortsighted Kolya only managed to shoot down two victims. It has to be said that pheasants are very crafty. They fly out of their hiding places with a tremendous din, which tends to put off an inexperienced hunter.

It is a great pity that I no longer have the photograph of our "Starya" covered in these tasty birds as if in a huge quilt.

The mistress of the "fanza" (hut) where we stayed for the hunt cooked a delicious pheasant soup with some potatoes, whose aroma spread all over the district.

Our journey ended on the fifth day, in the yard of our Seisin "fanza", by which time "Starya" completed a five hundred kilometre circle under the guidance of our lame friend Rhee, and scaled quite a few high ridges. In addition to two hundred pheasants we also killed two wild deer on the journey home. Our awkward-looking "Starya" seemed to be a stranger to the word "overload", even though its maximum speed was only forty miles per hour.

Alas, all good things come to an end.

"Novina" was developing rapidly, and after two years we realised that we needed a new, more presentable-looking car. There was no talk of an auction, which made us think of another way out.

We were acquainted with a White –Russian family who lived in Seoul. Their younger son, Lyoka, was a car salesman who promised to find us an inexpensive vehicle, and younger brother Yuri and I decided in 1934 to pay him a visit, arriving in the Korean capital by train at the beginning of May.

Lyoka's first offer was an old ruin of a Dodge which was utterly incapable of scaling the steep streets of the ancient city, but we eventually settled for a dark blue, respectable – looking Chevrolet costing more than one hundred yen, which meant that the money we brought with us could not cover its transport back to Novina by rail. It looked for a while that we were stuck.

However, having considered our predicament, I decided to undertake the hazardous fifteen hundred-kilometre journeys by road.

Unfortunately an old bomb is just that: old junk…Its brakes failed immediately after we left Seoul and we did not know of any repair shops sand had no money for repairs even if we found any. Luckily, my experience with "Starya" taught me to brake using the gear box but as every driver knows, it is very well to use this method in an emergency, but it becomes an entirely different cattle of fish when one has to navigate over endless mountain passes and through countless hair – pin bends.

The second day out of Seoul found us on the banks of a deep river with a bridge whose decking had been swept away by last year's flood leaving huge gaps, which we proceeded to plug up with branches of young oaks. Not wishing to risk the lives of my companions, I told them to cross the structure on foot and charged across the bridge on my own. The old bomb swayed from side to side but miraculously made it to the other side where I took a backward glance …the makeshift repairs had collapsed into the water and were being swept away by the river….

Unfortunately, things got worse after we passed the town of Khanko, when we encountered a group of villagers hurrying to the markets. I blew my horn, and the group moved to the right, whereupon I stepped on the accelerator so as to get out of their way, only to clip an old Korean woman carrying a basket full of apples, who made a sudden dash across my bows. I desperately tried to avoid running her over and jerked thee steering wheel to the left, straight into a ditch.

My position was parlous indeed, as my driver's licence was not valid outside our province and the permit to take the car to Novina was issued in the name of a Seoul driver, but here I was—having knocked down an old woman! My jalopy galloped along the open field and miraculously managed to make it back onto the highway, with Yuri and Lyoka screaming on top of their voices: "What the hell do you think you are doing! Stop at once!!" I ignored them and went for my life …

We were petrified expecting a police chase and panicked at the sight of any police vehicle, but, luckily, nothing happened, and early on the fourth morning of our trip, having washed our blue sedan in a brook and adorning it with flowers, we made a triumphant dash through Novina. The blue car did not receive a nickname but was simply known as "Five Hundred and Four" which was its registration number…

I spent many a sleepless night, expecting a retribution for my misdeed but none came, except when the NKVD- SMERSH (Organs of Russian terror apparatus directed against humanity) imprisoned me twelve years later in the town of Khanko "for aiding and abetting the international bourgeoisie". I would gaze at that cursed road out of the window of the first floor hallway of my prison during the short daily walks which I was allowed to undertake, and think to myself: "Maybe this is the retribution!"

Who knows—it might have been!

There were several other cars in the history of Novina but the best and most favoured of them was a blue "Ford" with a figurine of an airborne pigeon on its hood which earned it the nickname of "Dove". The unbelievable history of its acquisition for a ridiculously small sum is worth a special mention…

"The Dove" belonged originally to the administration of the Seisin prison and had only eight thousand miles on the clock, but its motor was damaged when a lazy driver failed to empty the radiator before garaging it overnight. The motor head was blown off and the administration came to the conclusion that the rest of the engine was also destroyed. However, our friends who worked as motor mechanics in a Ford garage told us that that was not necessarily the case. They advised us to grease the palm of the official in charge and to make an offer for the car. The starting price at the auction was only 140 yen, which we could well afford to risk. We made our bid and got the car!

Upon towing "The Dove" to Fords we paid nineteen dollars for a new head .The car started at once and proceeded to go like a clock. Its high suspension made light work of bad roads and its powerful acceleration would push the driver right up against the back of the seat! It had only three gears but even the third gear was powerful enough to handle steep hills.

Our Dove served us till the death of Novina and looked after the needs of passengers and cargo. It was a fitting replacement for the loyal horses which were the only form of transport available in the days of my grandfather and which he described as "carrying water one day and a warrior the next". (See Yankovsky M.I. **"Horse breeding in The South Ussuri Region"**. St. Petersburg and Khabarovsk, 1892).

Chapter 25. A POISONOUS SNAKE (MEDYANKA)

The sound of the telephone a few years ago in our flat in Vladimir rekindled old memories. The faintly accented female voice on the line was strangely familiar: Valery? This is your old friend, the sister of the writer Natalya Ilyina, Olga Laylle; I am sure you remember me, as "Goolya" don't you?

"Goolya! Good Heavens, of course! What brings you here?"

"I am in Suzdal (Note: **a Russian town appr. 30km{20 miles} north of Vladimir**) at the moment accompanying a group of tourists from Paris. My husband Maurice and your good friend from Korea, Zhenya, are with me. Zhenya lives in London now. Do you remember how she was bitten by a snake? Anyway, you and your wife are invited to a dinner to our hotel tonight…See you there".

This is how I met a long – forgotten fragment of my youth, got to know the charming Mr. Laylle and renewed my friendship with Zhenya. It was an unforgettable evening during which we remembered the distant past and the episode involving Zhenya and the snake (of a species we called "Medyanka" -{"A Copperhead", in Russian}).

I promised my friends to write a short story about that incident and to send them copies to Paris and London. **So here it goes…**

…One fine morning we returned from a hunting expedition, which we undertook at the request of the inhabitants of a nearby Korean village who begged us to protect them from wild pigs, which were mercilessly destroying their potato and soybean crops. There were three of us: my brother Arseny, cousin Gleb Shevelev and I.

We walked past the First Waterfall and crossed the Ompo River over a narrow bridge before scaling the mountain pass leading to a small plateau where we saw two "fanzas" (Korean huts) nesting under thatched roofs. Their young and old inhabitants raced to greet us and to complain about the misdeeds of the wild pigs, which lost all fear and were even rolling down the hills in broad daylight to attack the crops…

Gleb and Arseny took up a position near a well worn path which was obviously used by the wild pigs, whereas I decided to hide behind a mound of rocks in the middle of a soy bean field located about one hundred paces away from the last fanza. The farmers picked these rocks from the surrounding area and arranged them in a neat circle, which was overgrown with absinth and vines of wild lemon and served as an excellent hiding place.

I crawled into the middle of that spot and rested a short Winchester rifle which once belonged to may grandfather against a moss-covered rock. Having made myself comfortable on a warm boulder, I took an interesting adventure story by Mayne Reid out of my pocket and settled down for what I thought was going to be a long reading session, as I did not expect to see any wild pigs before sunset.

A Poisonous Snake (Medyanka)

However, barely half an hour later my reading was interrupted by a shrill bark of our hosts' dog. I put aside my book in a huff and got off the boulder to survey the surroundings. What I saw was truly amazing: two medium-sized grey-brown boars were casually following each other across the field, followed by the brave pooch whose head could be seen among the soy bean plants. It seemed that the pigs despised their antagonist and nonchalantly continued on their journey, their tails twisting in unison with their trot.

When the procession was within about forty paces from my hiding place, I fired two shots in rapid succession, --"Pow! Pow!"—instantly slaughtering both beasts.

The farmers heard my shots and jubilantly raced to the scene of the carnage.

They dragged my victims into the yard of our hut, gutted them, hung the carcasses in the shade and threw the pig hearts into a vat, in preparation for a feast marking their deliverance from the marauders.

My companions ran towards me after hearing the shots and then went back to their lair to continue the vigil. An orange flame surged from there towards the sky around sunset, accompanied by a mighty pig squeal, signalling the demise of another member of the herd which came down from the hills for an evening meal.

In the morning we hired a two-wheeled carriage driven by a red bull, which delivered the three carcasses of our young prey to Novina….

…. But back to my main story…

Having returned from the hunting expedition we went for a swim in the river after which we changed and resumed our normal life.

Gleb went into the nearby settlement of Ompo to see the Chinese contractors who were building his mother's "dacha" (summer house) and I, having armed myself with a racket, repaired for the tennis court.

It so happened that on the same fine July morning two pretty "Harbinovites", holidaymakers from Harbin by the name of Goolya Ilyina and Zhenya Peacock were scaling our steep local gully called "Uetegi". The higher they climbed the more spectacular became the panorama of "The Land of The Morning Freshness". Beneath them they saw, as if on a giant map, a wide valley surrounded by high hills and a clear river flowing past giant granite boulders, and forming numerous lagoons surrounded by sandy beaches.

A part Japanese, part Korean holiday resort of Ompo with its single-storied buildings was located on the bend of the river, with the Russian resort of Novina situated one and a half versts (one versta is approx. equal to one kilometre) upstream from Ompo.

The hamlet of Novina was the result of many years of effort of a large family. Elaborate and ordinary dachas (holiday homes), together with a theatre (it also served as a canteen), the resort kitchen and office---stood along a straight road lined with poplars and acacias. A suspension bridge spanned the river and the whole area was surrounded by fields and fruit gardens. A compact church built out of river boulders stood on a nearby hill, surrounded by pine trees. An apiary surrounded by a wall nested under the hill, and an enclosure for spotted deer, constructed out of larch boards, were located nearby.

On a plateau on one side of the road stood a volleyball court, with tennis courts occupying the opposite side. A large tiled winter residence built in the shape of a Korean dwelling (fanza), a garage and a water well sporting a long rod for the raising of water completed the picture which the girls saw from their vantage point.

Looking further afield they could just glimpse the ocean on the eastern horizon, with endless mountain ranges visible to the west.

The nearby mountains were green, changing to blue and lilac in the distance, whereas on the western horizon they saw the white peaks of the "Bald Mountains" ("Lysuye Gory" in Russian) which form the Korean dividing range and which are covered in snow for most of the year, losing their white cover only by the end of summer. These snow-covered peaks give birth to the clear River Ompo, which flows through Novina.

The girls were racing from fabulous red and yellow lilies, known locally as "sarankas", to violet irises and burgundy-coloured star-shaped flowers called "Maltese Crosses". They picked some of them and merely smelled the others, covering their noses in orange-coloured pollen in the process and filling the air with laughter.

The flowers attracted numerous varieties of butterflies with showy wings, such as Parnaciusses and dark blue, almost black, Monarch butterflies. A lot of them were highly prized by entomologists.

Time passed very quickly and it was getting quite hot. The girls found themselves high above the valley and decided to make their way back to Novina so as not to miss lunch. Zhenya was spending the summer in a large imposing residence of well-to-do former residents of Harbin by the name of Korenevsky, where she was employed as an English coach of their flighty daughter Irma, with Goolya keeping her company. The Korenevskys were strict hosts, intolerant of late meals—hence the need to rush back!

The descent was very steep indeed and the lasses were racing with ever increasing speed clutching the bouquets of fresh flowers. They galloped like young does in their light shoes worn on bare feet, jumping over clumps of bushes and grassy knolls, paying no attention to any danger on the ground, with Goolya leading the way.

Suddenly she heard a blood-curdling scream from her friend and turning around saw her lying on the ground among a scattered bouquet of flowers. Zhenya sat up, clutching her foot:

"Goolya!" –she yelled –" watch out! A copperhead ("Medyanka") --there it is –crawling away! I must have stepped on it! It bit me! I am in terrible pain and can't get up!"

Goolya ran towards her friend who was trying to squeeze the poison out of the wound on the top of her foot, and tried to suck it out of Zhenya's wound because she heard somewhere that that was the way to remove the poison before it gets into the bloodstream. However, she had to stop that procedure after realising that she was going to absorb the venom through some cracks in her lips.

"Goolya!" --Screamed Zhenya—"I think I am about to die! I feel absolutely dreadful! Hurry up—run to the highway to get some help from a passer-by, and, failing that, hurry to Novina to see if somebody there can come to my rescue!"

Goolya scampered down the hill scattering the flowers and ignoring any danger. It was a sight to behold: a well-built rosy-cheeked maiden racing like a superwoman!

The Uetegi Gully and the creek by the same name join the highway almost exactly halfway between the holiday resorts of Ompo and Novina, which presented a problem to Goolya when she made it to the intersection.

Which way should she go? Ompo is slightly closer and it has a police station but how is she to seek help without knowing a single word of Japanese or Korean? Novina is a little bit further away and the road to it is on an upward slope but at least help is easier to obtain from one's own crowd…Luckily, at that very moment she saw a tall figure of a man, accompanied by a dog, walking in her direction. Good God! She was in luck!

"Gleb! Gleb! Zhenya….Snake…Medyanka!"

……..I should mention here in passing that even though many people referred to poisonous "Copperheads ('Medyankas')" in those days, the correct name of those reptiles is "poisonous copper-brown coloured vipers"………

"She is on the mountain—over there—lying down—unable to walk…"

Even though, as I mentioned at the beginning of my story, Gleb was on his way to meet some builders, he did not hesitate for a second and called out to his dog:

"Geba! Here! Quick!"

"Goolya! Hurry! Lead the way!"

They rushed uphill following Goolya's tracks, walking and running as fast as they could until Goolya recognised a large stone near the path, which led to the highway. But where should they go next?

Goolya was completely lost because in her rush on the way down she took no notice of the surroundings, did not look back once and remembered nothing of the terrain.

"She is probably over there. There were some grey stones…."

Alas, stones and grass look the same everywhere and the poor girl started to cry out:

"Zhenya! Zhenechka (Russian diminutive for 'Zhenya')! We are here! Can you hear us? Let us know where you are!"

But the green mountain was indifferent to their voices as they kept climbing ever higher, calling their friend's name on top of their voices and cringing every time they tripped over a rotting branch of a tree.

….Zhenya was lying in the thick grass, which was obscuring the sky. She barely managed to tie a string around her swollen leg and was unable to get up or to shout to her friends, although she could hear them as if through a cotton wool wall. Her body became limp and immobile and she felt as if she was swimming towards a precipice….

Luckily, Gleb suddenly remembered his four-legged friend, jumped on his feet and shouted to the dog:

"Geba! Search! Dear Gebooshka (diminutive), please search a little!"

His hunting companion was a solidly built dark brown Danish pointer female which was a clever and hard-working animal. It immediately responded to the familiar command and started to walk in wide circles, wagging her tail in the process.

A minute or two later she stopped dead a short distance from Zhenya's friends, "pointing" towards something.

…Here I have to explain that in those days dogs were an integral part of a hunting family. We had a large pack of hunting dogs which was used during the pursuit of large game and which consisted of mixed breeds of Korean and Manchurian origin, but in addition to that each one of us had a personal dog, most of which were Danish pointers.

They were used to hunt ducks, geese and pheasants. But even when hunting pheasants those dogs helped to track foxes and to catch wounded deer. Also, quite surprisingly, the pointers used to be quite good at hunting large game such as wild pigs and predators. For example, a hound called Largo, which was completely black from birth, managed at different times to chase up a tree three large snow leopards when they were trying to attack our caged deer, giving us a chance to shoot the predators…

Getting back to my main story, noticing that Geba was motionless, Gleb and Goolya hurried towards her and saw under a shrub the motionless and silent form of their lost friend. They picked her up and dragged her towards a path. Gleb crouched down and lifted her on his broad back.

"Hang on, Zhenya! Goolya, give me a hand! I am going to carry her to the road and want you to run as fast as you can to Novina and get the boys to bring the motorcar. They are all playing tennis at the moment!"

Zhenya tried her hardest to hang on to Gleb's shoulders…

Summertime in Novina attracted numerous tourists from such far-flung places as Harbin, Shanghai, Tientsin and Seoul. It was a polyglot society of Russians, Britons, Germans, French and Spaniards who bathed in the hot springs, the river and the sea, danced, hiked in the local mountains, went fishing and hunting and played volleyball and tennis. Tennis was very popular, with a Novina Cup being contested at the end of every season.

It so happened that the Sunday morning I am describing saw a vigorous match between two strong players on the tennis court located near the acacia-lined road. The umpire kept the score from his elevated chair and the spectators were noisily supporting their favourites. Being one of the players, I was about to serve, when I saw a pathetic, exhausted figure of a girl walking through the trees towards the court, with head bowed and helplessly dangling arms. She caught a glimpse of me through the foliage and muttered almost incoherently:

"Valery! Help! Zhenya---Medyanka-over there---hospital, hurry!"

Goolya was pointing backwards in the direction of a bend in the road.

The players immediately threw away their racquets and balls and all able-bodied young men made a dash for the garage. Barely five minutes later the former contestants were sitting in the open blue sedan with two folding seats, which we nicknamed "Golubok" ("The Dove"). I started the engine, and being almost new, the car roared out of the garage, raced passed the by now empty tennis court, effortlessly took the bend and flew towards the gully….

We saw Gleb and poor Zhenya a short distance from the bend, on a downward incline of the road. The poor fellow put the patient on the ground and slowly stood up, giving the impression that he could barely stay on his feet. By the time we drew level with the couple and raced towards them, Zhenya was sitting on the side of the road, with the head in her lap and the body twisted into a tiny bundle. She obviously found it difficult to look up, after hearing the sound of the motorcar and of our voices, and we were shocked into silence at the sight of her pale lifeless face, her colourless eyes and swollen purple lips….

Several pairs of strong hands lifted Zhenya's limp frame into the back seat of the car, tightly gripping her to ensure that she did not slip, and once again our trusty "Golubok" made its famous flying start.

We tore through the resort of "Ompo", over hills and dales, villages, past people, carts and motorcars. I ignored most traffic rules and took little notice of the condition of the road. My companions were supporting the patient in deathly silence. Our common aim was to reach medical help whilst there was still life in Zhenya's body, and we arrived in the township of Shuotsu in record time.

Our car raised clouds of dust when I finally came to a screeching halt outside the surgery of Dr. Rhee, a well-known local medico. Dashing into the reception, I confronted the sleepy figure of his attendant:

"Where is the doctor? I have a victim of snakebite in the car! She was bitten by a "mamoosi" (the Japanese word for 'viper')!"

"It is Sunday", --said the sleepy fellow---"and we have not had any patients. 'Sensei' (Japanese for 'Teacher') let his assistants have a break and went home himself. He said to call him if necessary".

"All right! Let's go to his house together! On the double!"

We were in luck: the luminary was resting in his white bungalow and took only a few minutes to get ready, whereupon he picked up his large black bag resplendent with nickel-plated fasteners and joined me in the front seat, exuding an air of authority. Rhee used the short time it took us to get to the surgery to appraise himself of the accident.

Dr. Rhee was an excellent physician and surgeon, a graduate of Berlin University. Possessed of a corpulent well-groomed figure, he gave the initial impression of being too unhurried, but in reality never wasted time or rushed, and did not procrastinate on this occasion. His commands and questions were clear and to the point:

"It is too late to call my assistants. You will assist me. It was a 'mamoosi' (viper)? Was it hot in the mountains? How long ago was she bitten?"

"It was very warm…She was bitten about one and a half or two hours ago."

"Put her on the operating table, tie her body to the table but make sure to hold her tight. Translate my words. It is very important to hold her tight."

Rhee's calm was very reassuring…

Poor pale tiny Zhenya was tied to the table…the doctor administered the local anaesthetic, placed a rubber band around her leg and sterilised the wound and his scalpel.

"I must repeat: hold her tight. I have to make a deep cut because a lot of time has passed and because it was hot during the accident…"

Swish! ---The scalpel confidently cuts across the instep of the tiny foot, through the sunburned skin, through the deep red wounds inflicted by the "Medyanka". The knife wound is deep, so deep in fact that I can see her bones, sinews and the crimson flesh. Zhenya did not utter a sound. She was quite calm and detached. It appeared that the anaesthetic was doing its job.

Zhenya seemed OK but the doctor's amateur assistants did not fare so well…I looked up from the wound at their sweaty pale faces and suddenly felt sick myself. This was very strange because I was used to knifing wounded animals to death, to gutting and butchering the victims of my gun during our hunting expeditions. Neither was I ever sickened by the sight of my own wounds or blood, but this was something different…. My reaction must have been due to either the feeling of compassion for the defenceless prostrate little lass whom I hardly knew or due to the sight of her foot, which was as small as that of a child, which had to be mercilessly carved up.

I ducked out into the yard and took a few deep breaths before returning to the operating theatre.

Professor Rhee was nearly finished. He put in the last stitches and bandaged Zhenya's foot.

"The danger is over, Valery-san, but make sure that you drive carefully on the way home! She needs a lot of bed rest in quiet surroundings. I'll call tomorrow to examine her and to change the dressing."

We carried our patient to the car with great caution and took our time on the way back. The danger had passed and all of us would laugh at the slightest provocation as if to shake off the terrible memories of Zhenya's ordeal.

A Poisonous Snake (Medyanka)

Our ward was resting in the laps of the majority of her rescuers but Gleb and his friend Boris decided to sit on the bonnet (where we usually transported the carcasses of killed animals), so as to give her plenty of room. Observing Zhenya's face in the rear vision mirror, I noticed that her lips regained a healthy pink colour and that she managed an occasional happy smile.

"Golubok's" motor was making soothing noises and was moving quite rapidly, but this time observing the road rules and carefully by-passing all obstacles. It seemed that the poor sedan understood the nature of out mission and lost its voice as a result of nervous tension. Whatever the reason, its horn stopped working, which added an additional element of fun to the return trip.

Instead of operating the horn, I would squeeze either Gleb or his friend, with the "victim" squealing like a stuffed pig. The rest of the healthy passengers would join in, with all of us roaring with laughter. As already stated, such juvenile conduct was helping us to get back to normal.

Upon arrival at the dacha (summer house) of the Korenevskys, Gleb and I lifted their guest out of the car and carried her into the dining room, where we carefully deposited her into a reclining chair.

Yelena Nikolayevna (the lady of the house), her husband Konstantin Phillipovich and daughter Irma welcomed us with open arms and served us some coffee.

Zhenya made a speedy recovery from the venom but the deep wound on her foot required a lot of attention from Dr Rhee and his assistants, who dutifully looked after her until she had completely recovered. It has to be said that Professor Rhee and his assistants were conscientious and able doctors who ministered to the ailments of the inhabitants of Novina during all the years of its existence.

………Forty years is a very long time indeed.

Zhenya (Jenny) Peacock, the petite teacher of English, whose life we saved in Novina, turned into a dignified miniature grey-haired lady. Little wonder, therefore, that I barely recognised her when we met in the town of Suzdal, thousands of miles and a lifetime away from Novina….

Chapter 26. MORE ABOUT MY ANCESTORS.

I feel compelled at this point of my narrative to return to the distant past and to fill the gaps in my previous account of the family history.

My grandfather Michael Ivanovich proposed to his future bride Olga Lukinichna in the house of her uncle Osip Ivanovich Kurtukov, who was the assistant harbourmaster of the port of Vladivostok. Shortly after that event one of Osip Ivanovich's daughters married a recent arrival to The Far East, a Swiss by the name of Yuli Ivanovich Brynner.

Yuli Brynner bought a part of the foreshore of the Sedemi Peninsula from a free settler, a Finn by the name of Friedholf Kirilovich Gek, which led to the establishmemt of a close friendship between our two families. Yuli Ivanovich built two substantial dachas (holiday homes) on that land, where the whole of the Brynner family used to relax every spring and summer. Their graceful cruiser "Voyevoda" used to travel between Sedemi and Vladivostok, in friendly competition with our vessel "Prizrak" ("Phantom"). Likewise, the horses from the Brynners' stables used to contest the Summer Cup in opposition to our mounts.

As already mentioned, the friendship between our clans was very strong and the friendly rivalry helped to enhance it. Yuli Brynner's sons Leonid and Boris were close friends of our father (Yuri {George}) Yankovsky and uncles Yan and Pavel, whereas their younger sisters Maria and Nina were extremely close with our mother Margarita Michailovna (Daisy) and her sister, our auntie Angelina (Gelya). As a result, the dachas (holiday homes) of our two families which were built in the Tabonnaya ("Horse-Herd") Bay bore the acronym of "**DA-GE-MA-NI**" (after **DA**isy, **GE**lya, **MA**ria (Maroosya) and **NI**na), as did the surrounding area.

A family photograph taken in 1911or1912 depicts the whole Brynner clan in existence at the time. Standing from left to right are: The eldest daughter of Yuli—Margarita—Gretel, her husband A.A. Maslennikov holding their son Lyolka. In the centre—Natalia Osipovna Brynner (Yuli's wife), with her son Felix standing behind her; to the right of Felix stand the wife of Leonid Brynner and Leonid himself holding his son Cyril. Seated: Maroosya (Maria) Brynner, next to her father, Yuli Ivanovich (pater familias), with his daughter Nina and son Boris (future father of the actor Yul Brynner) completing the picture.

I have vivid memories of the three-year old Yulka, who looked like a toy doll and his lovely sister Vera (dimunitive: "Verochka") brandishing butterfly nets in pursuit of the colourful creatures which abounded around the flowerbeds in the garden of their dacha. I was three years older than Verochka and uncle Borya (Boris, her and Yul's father) would jokingly tell me: "Look, Lyuka (my childhood nickname), here comes your fiancé". Needless to say, I would turn crimson like a ripe tomato…

More About My Ancestors

We fled Russia in 1922 but the Brynners, being Swiss citizens, enjoyed "extraterritorial rights" (i.e. were subject to Swiss Law) which enabled them to stay on for at least another 10 years.

During a business visit to Moscow in the late nineteen twenties Boris Yulyevich fell in love with a cousin of our mother, Katerina Ivanovna Kornakova who was an actress of the Moscow Arts Theatre and a favourite pupil of the great producer Stanislavsky. That love affair destroyed his family. Boris left his wife Mara and sent her and their two children first to Harbin and then to Paris. That scandalous action caused a major rift in the family. Yuli Ivanovich and his wife were dead but the younger generation was torn apart.

Brothers Boris and Felix married two sisters Mara and Vera and Boris's action turned them into enemies. His new wife auntie Katya (Katerina) being a cousin of our mother, the Yankovskys became the "enemies" of Felix. Fortunately the family feud did not affect Yul Brynner (the future film star) who visited us in Novina and Lukomorye on the way from Paris to the USA, and conquered the hearts of all our young ladies during his short stay.

Luckily we continued to maintain very warm relations with Leonid Yulyevich Brynner, his Russian wife, also an actress, the charming Yelena (Helen) Michailovna and their daughter Ada. If anything, that friendship grew stronger with the passage of time.

The youngest of the Brynner sisters Maroosya (Mary) stayed in Russia where she kept searching for her husband, a White officer who vanished during the Civil War, but her daughter Ninika managed to get to China together with her uncle Boris and aunt Katerina.

Ninika came to Novina when she was sixteen and soon after became involved in a passionate though platonic relationship with my brother Arseny. The romance became so strong that she was being considered as Arseny's fiancé. It is very likely that the young pure couple would have married, had it not been for the intervention of a cruel providence in the person of Olga Ivanovna Sherbakova, the wife of our uncle Paul's wartime friend, a writer by the name of Michael Sherbakov.

Olga came to Novina accompanied by her two children from a previous marriage to take a cure at the Ompo hot springs. Being ten years older she succeeded in bewitching the inexperienced youth to the point where he decided to marry her.

Arseny approached me seeking my support:

"Listen, Valery! The Oldies are against my marriage. I hope that you will support my decision".

My reply was short:

"No way, dear brother! Stop and think! You are just twenty and she is nearly thirty. Don't you realise that in ten years' time you will be thirty and she will be forty!"

"Yes, and in twenty years' time I shall be forty and she will be fifty!", was his supercilious reply.

I am certain that he was unhappy in the subsequent years but, being a man of honour, refused to complain or show any dissatisfaction. Could it be that he preferred to suffer in silence or simply got used to his lot? We'll never know....

As I already mentioned, Arseny was the only male from the Yankovsky family to have escaped the clutches of SMERSH (similar to KGB). (See Arseny's story in Part 1).

He went to Japan where he made a brilliant career with Mitsubishi having become a Commercial Director of that firm. This enabled him to buy a good house in San Francisco and a luxury holiday home in California. His dream was to see me, but it was not to be...However, I finally managed to visit the USA and Canada after his death.

One day before my departure from Vancouver I found out that Ninika resided there. Unfortunately it was too late to pay her a visit but we had a long telephone conversation during which she told me that Arseny rang her shortly before his death and apologised for the past.... Ninika had never forgotten him, and even fifty years after their romance remembered the names of the horses they rode together; they were "Skazka" and "Chingiz-Khan".

Despite the fact that I was quite a few years older, I was very friendly with the son of my aunt, Nina nee Brynner, -- Booroom (Pavel Alexandrovich) Ostroumov. I vividly remember how upset I was when he overtook me in a in a short distance race!

Booroom was a very gentle soul. An old and unfortunately faded family photograph in my possession taken in the dining room of a building we used to call "The Catamaran" shows him sitting a table together with about twenty other people, with my father Yuri (George) at the head of it. In the right foreground of the picture, across the table from a smiling Booroom, sat a blonde girl with two ponytails; neither was paying the slightest attention to the other. That girl was Zoya Vorontsov, the daughter of a Manchurian farmer and industrialist Dimitry Matveyevich Vorontsov. Little did they know that quite a few years later Zoya and Booroom would become man and wife, much to the delight of their distinguished parents, and would bring up two loving children.

During my visit to California in the 1980's I met the lovely couple in the home of my cousin Oleg Shevelev and have kept a photograph depicting that occasion. Shortly after our meeting Zoya and her husband flew to the Philippines to visit their children...

It is hard to believe that Booroom died soon after my trip to the USA, as did my cousin Oleg, cousin Ninika and the mother of my eldest son Sergey, Irma....

Chapter 27. SKIPPER GEK AND HIS DESCENDANTS.

As mentioned at the beginning of Chapter 3, Yuli Brynner bought part of the Sedemi Peninsula from a free settler by the name of Friedholf Kirilovich Gek, with the latter retaining ownership of the northern part, which contained a house built in a Finnish style. The house and all other buildings on the estate were located about one hundred paces from the shore line, with the entrance gate designed in the form of an arch made of whale ribs. The alley leading to the house was flanked with wild pears, which produced pinkish-white flowers in spring. An old whaling boat was lying near the gate. It was the vessel which Gek used in his younger days to harpoon sleeping whales. My father told us kids that when he himself was a youngster, he used to frequently see the old skipper, pipe in hand, transporting a carcass of a whale from the whaling boat. The whaler would sit on the half-submerged huge black body of his prey, with a rowing boat towing him and his victim to the shore.

The alley terminated at a gazebo, which contained a table, made of a shoulder blade of a whale and stools made of its vertebrae. The external walls of his first house were decorated with multi-coloured shells.

Being a famous explorer Gek left a permanent legacy in The Far East. Many promontories, bays and straits of that region bear his name.

As mentioned in the first part of this book, Friedholf's wife and young son fell victims to an attack of the Hung Hu Tse. After that tragedy he married a widow called Pelageya Semyonovna who had two daughters by her first marriage. The only issue of his second marriage was a daughter whom the couple named Yelena (Helen). I remember "Auntie Lena" (short for "Yelena") as a stern mater familias, but she was a daring seafarer in her youth who thought nothing of braving a stormy sea in her yacht....

Yelena Friedholfovna (daughter of Friedholf) married a captain by the name of Nikolai Vasilyevich (son of Vasili) Vasyukevich to whom she bore four sons: Klavdii (Claude), Yevgeny (Eugene), Yuli and Georgiy (George). Zhenya (short for "Yevgeny") and I shared a desk at the Vladivostok Boys' School where we sat for annual examinations (we studied at home).

The Vasyukeviches did not flee abroad and, together with the majority of "byvshy"(members of the so-called "non-proletarian classes"), were "repressed" (imprisoned without trial) at the beginning of the nineteen thirties. My friend Zhenya met his death in a Gulag concentration camp in the Ural Mountains, whereas Yelena served her exile somewhere in the taiga (dense virgin forest) of the Ussuri Region.

Her other three sons survived and later managed to obtain marine qualifications, with all of them becoming captains of ocean liners. "The last of the Mohikans" as he calls himself, Yelena's youngest son Georgiy is currently living in Vladivostok. In company of his grandchildren and nephews he attended in 1991 the opening of the memorial to my grandfather Michael I. Yankovsky. My sister Victoria, he and I were photographed together on that auspicious occasion.

Vandals who had no respect for history have destroyed the historical residence of Captain Friedholf Gek. An identical fate befell the homes of the Yankovskys, the Brynners and the magnificent estate of my other grandfather, a Sinologue and merchant of the First Guild-- Mikhail Grigoryevich Shevelev.

However, the following features remain forever on the map of The Peter The Great Bay in The Sea of Japan: The Yankovsky Peninsula; The Gek Inlet; The Shevelev Promontory, the latter being located in the Sukhodol Inlet of the Ussuri Bay…

The facts speak for themselves.…

Chapter 28. DISCOVERY OF LONG LOST RELATIVES.

After my release from the Gulag and marriage to Irina Piotrovsky which was blessed with the birth of a son we named Arseny, we spent some times in the godforsaken city of Magadan, the capital of the Chukotsky Autonomous Region, in the northern part of the Russian Far East. By the time our son was four we had to move to our third lodgings. It was a difficult time but our last abode was a cut above all previous ones because even though it was a "communal" (i.e. shared) flat, it was located in a solidly constructed sewered building near the centre of the northern capital, and had hot water and a telephone.

Irina had relatives in her native town of Saratov (on the Volga River north of Volgograd). It was there that she was arrested. Her arrest was based on Article 58 of the Penal Code. At that time she was a fifteen-year old Grade Nine high school student (see her story at the end of this narrative).

As far as I was aware, I had no living relatives who stayed in Russia after our escape, but, as you will see, I was wrong....

Irina worked as a proofreader in the regional printing house not far from our new flat in Magadan, and I was employed as a forester of the Magadan Forestry Department. As a result, she usually returned home before me.

One fine day when I returned home from work she was already in our fourteen square meter room in the company of a dark-haired stranger who looked like a hero of an American Western. He turned out to be her former fellow prisoner, both having spent some time in a Gulag camp known as "The Fourth Kilometre". His name was Billy Svechinsky and he told us that he got married after his release. He and his wife had a young son and the family lived not far from our communal flat.

However the surprising thing about his visit was that he was a friend of my relatives who lived in Moscow! He visited them during his annual leave and one of them, a lady by the name of Anna Stanislavovna Reznikova, asked him to look up any Yankovskys who might have been residing in Magadan. Her name was not familiar to me but the picture became clearer when Willy mentioned her sisters Zhenya, Klava and Natasha. I remembered that these three lasses who were our distant cousins spent some time in our home on the Sedemi Peninsula.

This is how they came to stay with us…

Our legendary grandfather Michael I. ("Nenooni") Yankovsky had a favourite nephew whose name was also Michael and who worked on the Yeysk Railway (Note: Yeysk is a town in southern Russia located on the shores of the Sea of Azov, approx. 39degE, 46degN). Nephew Michael and his wife Xenia Georgievna had five daughters. Michael died just before the Bolshevik Revolution of 1917 and his widow, having found herself in grave financial difficulties, decided to send her daughters to the Far East to stay with their uncles. (Note: This is the Russian way of referring to their second cousins who were the first cousins of their father, i.e. my father Yuri {George} Yankovsky and his brother Yan).

Zhenya and Natasha stayed with our family on Sedemi, with Klava taking up residence on the Gamov Promontory with "uncle Yan".

Klava married a manager of a local estate by the name of Ivan Izosimovich Kornilov and Zhenya tied the knot with a merchant, one N.M. Fomenko, who was a resident of Vladivostok. Natasha fled with our family to Korea but later decided to return to Russia where she settled with sister Anna in Moscow.

Anna never made it to the Far East but, being the eldest sister, had been always very interested in the history of our clan and knew the background of all her relatives who lived in the Far East. Being a nursing sister by profession, she was engaged in that capacity during the Russian Civil War of 1918-1922, where she met her future husband Aaron Israelevich Reznikov. At the end of that conflict the Reznikovs settled in Moscow. Being kind and compassionate people they were eager to help the unfortunate Yankovskys as soon as they found out that most of us had been imprisoned in the slave labour camps of the Gulag.

Anna and Aaron had a daughter called Irina and a son Boris, the latter having gone to school with Billy Svechinsky where the boys attended the same class. It was almost a miracle that Boris was not imprisoned with his mate. The Reznikovs stayed in touch with Billy's family during his incarceration. As I already mentioned, Billy found a job in Magadan shortly after his release, and soon after that visited his friend Boris and his family, who gave him the task of locating the Yankovskys. As a result of these fortunate circumstances I acquired a whole host of relatives in European Russia.

Irina and Arseny were the first ones to pay them a visit, with yours truly following suit. During all our visits we were made to feel at home, staying in the city apartment and the suburban dacha (holiday home) of the couple.

The Reznikov seniors have passed on, with Aaron surviving till his 99th birthday. Irina is an artist and has a daughter called Anna and a grandson Ilya. The three of them live in the Moscow apartment built by the late Aaron.

Boris married one Svetlana Oradovskaya. They have a son Andrew who is a talented mathematician. About ten years ago Boris, his wife and their offspring migrated to Israel but they have since visited us in Vladimir and generally keep in touch by mail and telephone.

Andrew and his family have already had jobs in Europe and the USA. Andrew and his lovely wife Olya have two charming daughters called Masha and Yael, both of whom speak excellent Russian, which is exceptional as far as the younger generation of expatriates are concerned.

Boris and Svetlana also have a daughter Anya who, like her brother, speaks fluent Russian.

Chapter 29. FYODOR PAVLOVICH SOLOMAKHIN.

A group photograph taken in 1935 in Novina against the background of a gazebo covered in vines of actiniae shows a White General Kozmin from Harbin and his wife in the centre, with our friend Fyodor Pavlovich Solomakhin, a former officer in the army of the White "ataman" (a Cossack general) Semyonov, on the left.

Fyodor Solomakhin retreated to Manchuria with the detachments of the defeated White forces and decided to become a professional hunter. He met my father in Harbin and expressed an interest in joining our family in Korea. Being a very successful game hunter Fyodor was making a good living in the Manchurian taiga (virgin forest), which was teeming with wild animals at the time. One of his specialties was the capture of live tiger cubs. However, the taiga was also teeming with the Hung Hu Tse bandits, and Solomakhin felt much safer in "The Land of the Morning Cool", as Korea was sometimes called. It was possible in those days to literally safely sleep in the open because Korea's Japanese masters completely eradicated all traces of banditry.

Fyodor Pavlovich became a very valuable mentor of my brother Arseny and myself. During our numerous hunting safaris he taught us to use an ordinary light summer tent during the harsh continental winter. He gave us a practical demonstration of how to pitch it in a way, which would protect the flimsy structure from the cold winds, and how to keep it warm overnight with the aid of a light tin stove. Here the secret was to heat the tent with dry firewood in the evening and to use damp slow burning logs during the night in order to maintain even moderate heat lasting for many hours. The use of a light tent as a safe and cosy abode throughout the winter was an invaluable asset to our efficiency as hunters, as it enabled us to live in otherwise impenetrable corners of the taiga, situated far from any human habitats, and to easily transport it in pursuit of the fleeing game.

He also gave us a lot of "hands-on" invaluable lessons about the habits of the Manchurian deer, which are crafty and careful animals, quite common in Manchuria but rare in Korea. These lessons were of great benefit to us during our forays into Manchuria, because that species represents one of the most valuable hunting trophies of the Far Eastern taiga.

The most valuable part of a slaughtered deer was of course its soft blood-filled horns known as "pantui" which the stags grow in spring. Their sale usually enabled a hunter to buy at least three or even five cows or horses. This was followed by the embryo of an unborn calf, known in Chinese as "Lootai". A heavy embryo (i.e. one almost ready to be born) could fetch about half as much as the pantui. The third place was occupied by dry horns obtained from stags killed after the September mating season (i.e. in the northern autumn). They were particularly popular with Koreans and cost at least half as much as the pantui.

The fat tail of a doe stood in the fourth place, followed by the dried penis, sinews, meat and a magnificent hide, the raw material for excellent suede.

Fyodor P. Solomakhin was a good friend of another hunter and inhabitant of Novina, Ivan Kuzmich Resnyansky (see Part I, Chapter 12). It has to be said for the record that Solomakhin was by far the more skilled of the two.

I am sure the reader will be interested in the story Solomakhin told us about his service under ataman Semyonov….

Semyonov was interested in an alliance with the half-mad White general baron Ungern who became famous during World War I as the commander of the legendary Wild Division ("Dikaya Diviziya", in Russian) and who operated in the Mongolian steppes during the Russian Civil War. Ungern agreed to the alliance in return for financial help and Semyonov sent his liaison officer Solomakhin to deliver several bags of his government's banknotes to the mad baron. (Note: As Russia had no central government during the Civil War, various regional authorities used to print their own currencies. In the case of Semyonov, his currency, known as "golubki" {meaning 'blueys' in Russian because of its blue colour}, was printed in the town Chita which was the seat of his government).

Accompanied by two mounted Cossacks, the brave yesaul (captain of a Cossack regiment) located with some difficulty Ungern's camp in the Mongolian steppes. When a sentry let the delegation into the baron's tent, Fyodor Pavlovich stood to attention and stated his business to the general who was sitting in the middle of his Mongolian tent near a portable stove. When telling me this story many years later, Solomakhin recalled that the mere sight of that self-proclaimed Tsar of the Mongolian steppes, with his face covered with reddish stubble and his piercing blue eyes, was capable of terrifying the bravest of warriors.

Having listened to Solomakhin's report, Ungern barked, without offering the emissary a seat:

"Have you brought the money? Has Grishka (an insulting diminutive of "Grigory", Semyonov's Christian name) sent the required sum?"

"Yes, your excellency! Here it is – in the bags brought by my Cossacks!"

"All right! Unload it!"

The Cossacks dropped the bags at the feet of the former Tsarist general seated in a comfortable chair. They untied them and the baron took out the first bundle, opened it up… and immediately thrust it into the bright flame of the stove…He proceeded to extract the whole shipment and to despatch it into the flame. Solomakhin was enraged and frightened realising that the maniac was likely to hurt him and his men…

Finally the culprit addressed his guest:

"I want you to understand that one word from me is sufficient for my men to skin you alive! But I realize that you have nothing to do with this. Ride back to Chita and tell Grishka to send me money –yen or, better still, gold. I don't need his paper! I can print this rubbish myself! Away with you, and thank The Lord that I am in a good mood today!"

Solomakhin staggered out of the madman's tent and did not remember how he got on his horse…

A year before the disaster, which befell us after World War II, Solomakhin, his wife Alexandra Stepanovna, and daughter Olga joined my wife Irma and me at the Tiger Hamlet and we managed to spend some time hunting game in Manchuria. I heard later that some time after my arrest he was also seized by Russian security.

Chapter 30. MY COUSIN TANYA.

My cousin Tanya, the daughter of uncle Pavel Michailovich, was arrested on the 5th of September 1946, on the same day as my father Yuri (George) Michailovich and my friend Eugene (Zhenka) Ellers. Her "crime" consisted of listening to Russian radio broadcasts at the request of the Japanese military authorities.

Tanya's mother Natalia Nikolayevna was unable to adjust to the loss of her daughter and died soon after of a heart attack, leaving behind an eleven-year-old son Misha who was being cared for by a woman who used to be his nanny. In 1950, during the Korean War, the new Korean militia arrested him. The day after his arrest the inhabitants of Novina found the bodies of Misha and a Korean boy in a ditch in the settlement of Ompo, one kilometre from Novina. Both bodies were wrapped in barbed wire.

Ttatyana Pavlovna (Tanya for short) was sentenced to ten years penal servitude. She spent the first three years in a women's prison in Vladivostok and the rest of her prison term in Siberia. She endured all possible kinds of slave labour tasks, including the horrifying Siberian timber logging. However, her spirit was not broken, and she even participated in the amateur theatre productions of the prisoners, where she was quite successful as a comedian.

She was released from imprisonment in 1954 from the Gulag camp of the town of Taishet (in Eastern Siberia, about 300 km west of Lake Baikal).

I received the numbers of the post boxes of Tanya, my father and brother Yuri while I was still on the Chukotka Peninsula, which enabled me to help them with money orders. Shortly after that I found out that my father's Gulag camp was located at a station of the Bratsk-Taishet Railway called Chunka, not far from Taishet.

I contacted Tanya who at the time was already working as a "free person" and we decided that she would wait for "Papa –Tiger's" release to accompany him to Magadan where I bought a house consisting of three rooms and a large kitchen and where I intended to house all my relatives, including my younger brother Yuri who was completing his term of imprisonment in a Gulag camp somewhere near Karaganda, in Kazakhstan.

I got married soon after buying the house and got a job as a forester. My new bride Irina and I were allocated a new flat that went with that position, consisting of two rooms. It was unsewered but had central heating. We were the first of the former prisoners to receive such favourable treatment!

I sold my house to a Korean called Yugay and we began our wait for father and Tanya. However, Tanya informed us by telegram in May of 1956 of father's death and arrived to stay with us in June of that year.

1956 was the year of mass exoneration and release of political prisoners. Hordes of former "zeka" (an acronym of the Russian word "zakluchonny" ---"prisoner") streamed into

Magadan and obtained temporary shelter with friends who had been released before them. Our flat was no exception, with several people sleeping on the floor on any given day.

A woman by the name of Yevlaliya Georgiyevna Okhotina, known as the "Chinese Consul of Magadan," owned a long barrack-like building nicknamed "The Headquarters," which housed a large transient population of former slave labourers. It has to be said in passing that nearly half the houses in Magadan were constructed in that style at the time.

One of that lady's lodgers, a young man from Manchuria by the name of Georgiy Fyodorovich Bordovsky, appeared in our flat and started courting our Tanya. The two former prisoners could hardly wait to taste their newly found freedom and after a courtship lasting barely a week asked me to bless their intended marriage. Irina enthusiastically supported their plans, which left me no option but to bless their union.

Soon after the nuptials the newly-weds received an invitation from Georgiy's father to join him at a collective farm in the Ural Mountains. It transpired that the old man got a job as a bookkeeper in that establishment after migrating to Russia from Harbin a couple of years prior to his son's release. Tanya and her husband left Magadan for the port of Nakhodka near Vladivostok from which they travelled to the poverty-stricken farm in the Urals.

They spent several miserable years in that outfit, finally managing to settle down in a small town in the Bryansk district (in European Russia, near the Belarus border) called Novozybkovo. Georgiy showed remarkable energy at the new place, having built a cosy three-roomed house and established a fruit garden and a vegetable patch.

I met my brother Yuri seventeen years later in Moscow, and he and I travelled to the Crimea. We paid a visit to the Bordovskys in Novozybkovo on the way back from that trip. Their back yard was covered in flowers and they grew their own fruit and vegetables. We made our acquaintance with Tanya's father –in-law Fyodor Georgiyevich and their two little boys Fyodor and Pavlik.

It is to the eternal credit of their parents that both sons were well brought up and received a good education. Fyodor is currently living in Volgograd with his wife Anna and daughters Yelena and Tatyana; the other son Pavel and his wife Vera are residents of St Petersburg.

Fyeda (abbreviated form of Fyodor) is a motor mechanic by trade. He is a kind and compassionate lad and an excellent handyman. When he and his mother visited friends and relations in California, he volunteered to repair the domestic appliances of the wives of his hosts, which earned him their eternal gratitude.

It can be said that Fedya is a typical Bordovsky by nature, whereas Pavlik (short for Paul) has to a surprising degree inherited the appearance and the business acumen of his maternal grandfather Pavel Yankovsky and the latter's brother. He is an energetic and successful businessman whose modus operandi is reminiscent of his great-uncle, our "Papa Tiger"--Yuri (George) Yankovsky. Pavel married Vera, a girl from the town of Sverdlovsk (Note: Now known by its pre-revolutionary name of Yekaterinburg), whom he met in St

Petersburg and who is his reliable business associate. She is a good house manager and a confident driver. The young couple have paid us several visits in Vladimir.

I stayed with cousin Tanya in St Petersburg on the occasion of the interment of the remains of the members of the Russian Royal family, and took that opportunity to see their magnificent flat and dacha (holiday home) in that city.

Chapter 31. MORE ABOUT LIFE IN NOVINA AND ITS ENVIRONS.

I can't help thinking that the description of life in Novina given in Part I of this novel needs to be augmented.

Life in a new and strange environment had to be conducted without any outside help and was based only on our own efforts. The daily routine was based on the motto: "Heads down—tails up".

For example, when we bought Novina, we had only one milch cow left out of the eight we brought with us from Sedemi, and even that beast was kept in the town of Seisin, some 50 kilometres to the north. We waited till spring and walked it all the way to our new abode, camping like gypsies by the roadside overnight. Having built a shed for our "provider" near the river, the children were given the task of taking turns in looking after the cow. The person on duty had to get up at dawn, to wash the cow's udders, to milk it, to deliver the milk to the kitchen and to put the animal out to pasture. All the former idle gentlefolk quickly mastered these rather complicated chores.

All the kids, with the exception of the one on shepherd's duty, had to cross the river and go to the forest growing on the side of a tall mountain called "Listvennitsa" (Russian for "The Larch"). There we cut down young trees and turned them into poles for the building of the first primitive dwellings and fences. We dragged the poles to the banks of the river and transferred them to the other side by hauling them through the water, or over a small bridge when the river was in flood after a few rainy days. The children also helped with carpentry and the digging of trenches for the foundations. In other words, after a carefree childhood spent in a white castle we turned into little labourers. Needless to say, all the adult inhabitants of Novina: our father, uncle Paul, uncle Victor, brothers Gusakovsky (whom we regarded as our relatives)--shared the daily work equally. Some of the adults' time, however, was taken up by business trips, and the children were required to devote a considerable time to academic studies.

Our mother was hoping to give us a tertiary education, whereas father felt that a secondary education was perfectly adequate for the needs of a hardworking landowner. He often used to tell his wife during their frequent debates on that subject: "I met many utterly useless layabouts with two degrees who were absolutely incapable of handling ordinary day-to-day problems."

Mother found his attitude distressing but there was nothing she could do in the prevailing circumstances, and all we were able to achieve was a level of education equivalent to a higher school certificate by home study. Unfortunately, none of us received an official certificate from an accredited school but most of us benefited from our education. My eldest sister Musa became a stenographer and secretary and held responsible positions in large firms first in Shanghai and later in Santiago de Chile and in the USA. The second sister Victoria became a well-known poetess. I have written several books in my mature years, and brother Arseny made a brilliant career as a commercial director of the Japanese giant Mitsubishi.

The only member of the family to miss out on secondary education was my poor youngest brother Yuri (nicknamed "Lyulya"). Our mother Margarita Mikhailovna died when he was fifteen and his education stopped after her death. He was released from the Gulag after ten years of slave labour and decided to become a builder but a lack of basic education proved to be a handicap. Nevertheless, he completed a building foremen's course at the age of forty, and did become a foreman. Yuri told me with some sadness that he could have gone much further if he had an education equivalent to a school certificate. As it happened, all he had to his name after his release were nineteen roubles and a "certificate of release from imprisonment"…

Getting back to our day-to-day life in Novina, it has to be said that our family quickly adapted to the ways of our new "homeland". The youngsters took little time to gain the knowledge of the language and customs of Asia. During our hunting expeditions in the "taiga" (virgin forest), we would take off our shoes when entering an Asian hut, sit down on the floor with folded legs, eat with the aid of chopsticks and flat bronze spoons, and sleep on warm but hard "kans" (<u>Note</u>: A "kan" is a floor heated by the flue gases from a stove which are channelled under it on the way to the chimney).

Our kid brother Yuri could even get a good night's sleep while resting his head on a hard wooden Korean pillow. This did not apply to father who always embarrassed us by his requests to our hosts to supply him with a bail of soft straw, which he used as a mattress.

Our household furniture and way of life in Novina were essentially European but the food was mixture of Russian, European and Asian dishes.

We ate a lot of rice garnished with hot Asian condiments such as soy sauce and Korean "kimchi" (pickled Chinese cabbage mixed with red chilli). But we also ate a lot of Russian soups such as "borsh" (beetroot soup) etc. Meat and fish were very popular as well. A lot of meat came in the form of legs of ham and various smoked portions of wild game. These and wine made from wild grapes were prepared in Novina, with most other provisions being purchased in the nearby township located on the railway station of Shuotsu ("Churon" in Korean). During the holiday season we bought bags of flour and cereals from the Korean and Japanese merchants in Shuotsu, as well as crates-full of tins of vegetable oil, kerosene and petrol. Butter, cheese, sausages and many delicacies were unknown in Korea and had to be imported from Harbin.

There was no shortage of alcoholic beverages such as beer, sake (Japanese equivalent of vodka) and brandy. We often used pure alcohol available from chemists, costing only 45 sen (cents) for half a litre, to make a fruit punch. During dances or after theatre performances we served that punch in bucket-sized silver goblets brought from Sedemi.

Clothing and footwear came mainly from Harbin or Shanghai because although the Japanese cotton and woollen fabrics and leather shoes were very cheap, their quality was very poor at that time. However, women's cotton and velvet shoes made in Japan were of high quality, as was a unisex boot called "Jikatabi" which is a very light and durable moccasin-like shoe made of thin canvas with a soft rubber sole. The rubber prevents the foot from slipping during mountain climbing.

When hunting in winter we stitched soft leather over our jikatabi and protected the shins with dry puttees made of thick cloth. The other items of clothing used during winter safaris consisted of suede coat and trousers made from a deer hide. My brother Arseny and our friend Kolya (Nikolas) Gusakovsky became very skilled in the manufacture of waterproof suede, which they achieved by soaking it in fish oil.

Not only was the clothing made from treated suede waterproof and durable, lasting for many years, but it was also extremely light and quite warm when equipped with a suitable lining. One of its main advantages was that, unlike most conventional materials, woollen cloth included, it made practically no sound when scraping against a stone or a tree, allowing the hunter to noiselessly approach his prey.

Chapter 32. DE TEMPORA ET MORES.

1. KOREAN CUSTOMS

Upon arrival in Korea at the beginning of the 1920's we found its society steeped in traditions, which, alas, will never return.

Men in villages and towns used to wear beige homemade trousers and shirts, with more affluent males adding a black vest to the ensemble. On their feet they wore "posons" (stitched socks) made of fabric, with shoes being either "sins" (straw sandals) or rubber sneakers.

Women wore long skirts made of the same material as men's trousers and very short bodices, so short, in fact, that they exposed the milk-filled breasts of young mothers. The children were carried on their mothers' backs, with any other loads being carried on the women's heads, supported by a specially woven straw ring. Occasionally a load would be astoundingly heavy, requiring two or more helpers to place it on the lass's head. However, once the burden was put in place, the girl would carry it with no apparent effort, with a peculiar rhythmic step and without touching the load, the gait giving the impression of a smooth "swim".

Single boys, particularly in villages, had long plaits. As a matter of fact, they used to get married at 10, 11 or 12 years of age to much older girls of between 16 and 18, who were able to help around the house. We were told by our interpreter, a happy-go-lucky Korean by the name of Chkhon Chan Guyn whom we called Ivan, that many a young husband was too scared to go to the toilet on his own in the middle of the night because village toilets were usually located far from the "fanza" (peasants' hut), on the edge of the vegetable garden. Fearing an attack by a tiger, the "lord and master" would start to cry, and his bride was required to take him by the hand and escort him to and from the outhouse...

2. A KOREAN WEDDING

On the day of the wedding several burly men carried the heavily made up bride on a special stretcher from her village to the village of the groom . Weddings were usually celebrated following the September harvest season, which corresponded to the splendidly hot Korean Indian Summer. The heat did not bother the tipsy carriers who practically ran all the way, with the solemn-looking under-aged groom accompanying them on a skinny-legged Korean pony. He no longer had a plait, as his crown was cut short on the wedding day, with the surrounding hair gathered into a two-inch bun. A narrow brimmed translucent hat made of horsehair was placed over the bun and held in position with a silver needle. The bun was meant to signify that its owner was no longer a boy but a husband. One can only guess about what transpired during the first few years of the couple's married life.

3. RESTAURANTS AND BATH HOUSES.

Marriages were invariably arranged by the parents of the bride and groom and were celebrated with great pomp and circumstance following a long preparation period, even though the young couple would often have only met on their wedding day. The reception took place in the large clean yard of the groom's fanza (hut) sheltered from the wind. A large number of low tables arranged in a long row were placed on straw mattresses covering the ground. The newlyweds sat at the head table, with the guests occupying the rest of the row. No toasts or shouts of "gorko" were involved (Note: this is a Russian custom: when any guest shouts "gorko" {'bitter'}, the bride and groom have to kiss).

Food consisted of boiled chicken and pork, peeled boiled eggs, dried fish and salads, featuring radish and Korean cabbage with incredibly hot red pepper and garlic. Yellow and white-coloured flat cakes were served instead of bread. The yellow ones were made of sorghum and the white ones –of pounded rice.

Clear fragrant Korean vodka called "suri" was served in teapots and consumed in fairly large bowls. This Korean custom differs from the Japanese and Chinese practice of using tiny cups.

Money was the only acceptable form of a wedding present. Guests placed their donations in envelopes and deposited them into the slot of a "ballot box".

4. HANGYABY.

It was not customary in those days to celebrate a man's birthday, with "Hangyaby", a man's sixty- second birthday, being the only exception, signifying as it did the end of his working life and the beginning of retirement. If the retiree belonged to a well-to-do family, he was given the "top" room of the house, i.e. the one furtherst from the kitchen, as a birthday present, The guests at a hangyabi usually comprised only highly esteemed old people whose presence was signified by a collection of footwear and an array of ornate walking sticks left on the entrance porch. However, our family was very much respected for help given the farmers in combating the onslaught of bears, wild pigs and deer, and therefore young descendants of the "Nanooni-The Four eyed" were often invited to these feasts.

Discussion among the score of white-bearded patriarchs, solemnly sitting cross-legged behind a long table set on warm straw mattresses, generally centred around hunting, fishing and the crops. The eldest son of the host was given the task of filling the bowls of the guests with "suri" (Korean vodka). Teapot in hand, he would approach each of the old men and offer a refreshment. Each guest was obliged to respond in the following terms: "A ige mise? Ige suri?" ("What is this? Is it suri?")—As if a teapot could contain water on this occasion! It was a ritual hypocrisy, which, however, was very tactful and appropriate for the occasion.

At the end of the dignified feast the elders lit their pipes consisting of small bronze bowls on yard long reed stems, filled with unbelievably powerful homegrown tobacco. At the same time the fifty-year-old son of the host, in a demonstration of his respect and subordination to the old man, would sit in the corner with his back to the gathering, unobtrusively smoking a rolled cigarette hidden in the palm of his hand.

5. RESTAURANTS.

Korea of the nineteen twenties had a lot of indigenous and Japanese restaurants but the most popular eating-houses belonged to the Chinese. We used to refer to them by the Russian name "kharchevka" (a slang word for a small and cheap eating place). Instead of straw mats on which one sat in a Korean or Japanese restaurant, a kharchevka had primitive wooden tables and long benches, each seating two or three clients. Any of these establishments served quite sophisticated dishes, such as pork and mushrooms or sea cucumbers, but Russian customers preferred the famous fried Chinese dumplings, called "yaki tsiaotsa" in Chinese. A normal portion consisted of twenty oblong fragrant fried dumplings filled with meat, Chinese cabbage and various spicy herbs. Instead of bread, customers were served "mantow"-- hot steamed buns made from white flour. The dumplings were served with a variety of hot sauces and washed down with "ho-dju", a powerful Chinese spirit that would ignite from the flame of a match!

At the end of a lengthy stay in the taiga (virgin forest) we normally emerged at a village or railway station and immediately repaired for a "kharchevka," where each of us would devour two portions of the dumplings. Naturally enough, we used chopsticks during the feast and spoons when eating Chinese soup. However, soup in Japanese and Korean establishments was drunk directly out of the bowl, just like European tea.

Residents of Novina frequented Japanese hotels in the nearby township of Ompo. The visit started with a just bearably hot bath in blueish water filled with a characteristic fragrance, and followed by a dinner consisting of the universally beloved dish of Japanese "sukiyaki", served at a low down polished table, with a hole in the centre.

A "hibachi" (a charcoal grill) is placed in the centre of the table. Two or three Japanese geisha girls dressed in long "kimono" (Japanese gowns) girded with an "obi" (wide belt) flit around the guests, while the ceremoniously cooking the meal on the hibachi. The ritual is worth describing in detail….

The chief geisha places some fat into a wok (Asian frying pan) and waits for it to melt. She then uses chopsticks to place the ingredients of the sukiyaki into the boiling fat. Sukiyaki consists of thinly sliced lean meat, onions, bamboo shoots, and parsley and "tofu" (bean curd)...The cooking meal exudes a fragrant aroma and makes a delicious hissing noise. The other geishas squat along each of the guests in turn, filling one of his two bowls with snow-white rice, and the other- with a selection of freshly cooked ingredients of the sukiyaki. Hot sake (Japanese rice wine) is served during the meal in small porcelain cups filled from miniature porcelain bottles.

If the dinner is hosted by a Japanese, it is important to follow Japanese drinking customs. The usual way of showing one's respect for a person is to place an empty cup on the palm of one's hand, face the recipient and to offer it to him. The recipient accepts it with a bow, while the nearest geisha kneels and fills it with hot sake. The recipient is not obliged to return the cup to the person who offered him the drink. Instead, he rinses it in a vase filled with water and repeats the ritual by handing it to another guest. In addition to the individual exchange of drinks, senior members of the gathering propose common toasts, in response to which all members of the congregation lift their cups level with their foreheads and "skol" (drink in one gulp) the toast without clicking their glasses with anybody. This is easily achieved as the cups are designed for one gulp. It has to be said that the Japanese seldom get inebriated.

6. BATH HOUSES.

Bathing is an integral part of Japanese culture. A Japanese always takes a hot bath before supper. This applies even to villagers who always wash in a back yard hut after a day in the fields, and douse themselves with water out of a bucket instead of taking a bath.

There were public baths in towns, which charged seven sen (cents) admission and consisted of a male and a female section. A visitor to one of these establishments used to take off his shoes and step up on the floor of a disrobing area, containing benches and boxes for the storage of underwear. Having disrobed, the visitor proceeded to the general hall which usually contained two pools: the first one filled with ordinary hot water, with the second one containing the warm scented one. A partition reaching part of the way between the floor and the ceiling separated the two sections of the bathhouse, with a cold-water tank positioned underneath the partition. Such an arrangement enabled the males to hear the goings on the female side. In addition, it was a well-known fact that when collecting cold water from the tank when its surface was undisturbed, it was usually possible to see the reflections of the belles on the other side...

Large copper taps supplied clean hot and cold water for the visitors. A new visitor picks up a small washbasin and takes a seat on a bench where he applies soap to his body and douses himself with warm water, repeating this procedure at least ones. At the completion of this ritual the customer enters one of the pools.

Members of a family often communicate across the barrier in a manner, which is unusual by European standards. For example, a husband can ask his wife to enter the male section to rub his back. I still remember how crazy it appeared to us when we observed this custom for the first time when sitting on the benches of a bath house…

One of the married guys yelled out: "Oi, Fumiko, kochi koi!" ("Hey, Fumiko, come here!") . The master's shout was immediately followed by the opening of an unobtrusive door in the partition and the appearance of completely naked well-endowed Japanese lass, shielding her nether regions with a little towel used by the Japanese! (Such a towel replaces the European loofah). The dutiful wife squatted behind the man and proceeded to wash and vigorously rub her spouse's back to the accompaniment of his satisfied groans.

Young lads that we were, we found that scene severely embarrassing and sheepishly sat on our benches not daring to wash off the soap and not knowing where to look. The awkward situation continued until the husband barked: "Yoshi, yoshi! Ike, Ike!" ("Enough, you may go!") After we hurriedly finishing our ablutions and scampering outside, all of us burst out laughing, with one lad saying: "Well, fellows, when in Rome, do as the Romans do! Next time I'll enjoy the scene without any compunctions!" He was quite right—we soon got used to the quaint custom and, frankly, always eagerly anticipated a command from a self-indulgent husband.

This story brings to mind another amusing episode involving a bathhouse…

I was told that some Chinese living in a remote hamlet in Manchuria were keeping a number of caged spotted deer and, being interested in a purchase, went there one late autumn to investigate the rumour. I stopped in a Japanese guesthouse because they were invariably cleaner than Chinese establishments, and also because my Chinese was quite poor. The trip was a great success: on the day after my arrival I purchased and dispatched to Korea a score of magnificent spotted deer.

It is necessary at this point to explain the circumstances prevailing during the Japanese occupation of Manchuria…

Having occupied that region and created the state of Manchukuo, the Japanese failed to adapt to the unusually harsh climate of their new possession, and built all houses in accordance with the construction codes of their much warmer homeland, with thin clay walls and floors lacking a Chinese-style "kan" (a flue pipe mounted under the floor and carrying exhaust gases from the cooking stove). Light paper-covered doors and windows added to the discomfort. For that reason my hotel was unbearably cold that late autumn.

I had a decent room and, having barely managed to get warm, heard a polite knock on the door followed by the appearance of a young lady carrying a tray. "Thank God", I thought, "a hot supper at last!"

But as the lass got closer I realised that she was actually carrying a flat basket containing an evening "kimono" (a dressing gown worn instead of pyjamas by the Japanese), a cake of soap and a "taoro" (a wash towel). "The bath is ready", murmured she,   "would you want me to wash your back?"

Frankly, I was somewhat taken aback but the mere thought of having to undress in a cold room sent shivers down my spine. My reaction was quite reasonable, bearing in mind my Russian background:

"No thank you, I had a bath last night! Please bring me supper instead!"

" Hai! (As you wish)", said the young girl politely, putting aside her basket and delivering a very palatable standard dinner shortly afterwards. I declined her offer to serve the food, as I can't stand people hanging around and looking in my mouth.

My unhurried enjoyment of the meal was wrecked by the sound of girls' laughter and chatter, which I could clearly hear through a thin partition. It seems that the belle who offered me a bath and later brought the dinner was telling her girlfriend about the demeanour of the new client. "The Russians are just as grubby as the Manchurians! Ha-ha –ha! They don't wash in the evening! Ha-ha-ha!"

I cursed my hunger and fear of a cold bathroom, which made me refuse the invitation of the enchanting Japanese, and resolved that, in future, I would never retire for the night in a Japanese inn without taking a bath.

7. BUSINESS ACUMEN.

If the client of a Chinese eating house left a tip, which could be substantial or as small as 20 or 30 cents, the waiter would acknowledge it with a war cry: "The guest has left thirty cents! 'Samochen!' (Thank you!)". If the client were descending the stairs on his way out, a chorus would accompany his exit from the kitchen: "Samochen!"

I think that such vocal expression of gratitude also served as public acknowledgement of the sum involved for the benefit of the whole staff, and made it impossible to pocket a tip without sharing it with one's workmates. Consequently, all concerned were interested in pleasing the guest. This is in marked contrast with the present-day Russian salespeople who often engage in lively conversation, ignoring a customer, who is forced to stand around, patiently waiting to be noticed.

The word "fatsai" (profit, earnings, yield) was very popular in pre-maoist China. Most enterprises distributed their earnings in accordance with the basic salary of an employee—from the managing director right down to the cleaner. This created an interest in giving one's best in order not only to keep one's position but also to contribute to the profitability of the company. I think that the new Russian capitalists could benefit from this ancient Chinese custom. Who knows, may be our shamefully indifferent salespeople will learn the art of an efficient service, which was the order of the day in old Russia and later amongst the émigré community, a service attested   to by former Russian inhabitants of the Chinese cities of

Harbin and Shanghai. What are needed are real incentives and not mere "encouraging" platitudes, which fall on deaf ears. People must be made afraid of losing a valuable position, and the position, in turn, must offer a lifetime career.

8. THE YANKOVSKY LEGACY.

Our main land holdings in Novina were bought from an old Korean by the name of Kim who owned a small soy bean field. It contained one solitary hut built beneath a small rock, which was located at the foot of a hill, overgrown with young pines, oaks and hazel nut trees. A single huge old wild apricot tree growing near Kim's abode produced small but fragrant and sweet fruit at the end of summer. There were also some cultivated apricot trees a short distance down hill from the hut yielding huge yellowy-pink fruit on their overloaded branches.

We built our first apiary consisting of only a few beehives underneath those trees, and ignoring painful bee stings helped our father Yuri (George) to kill the drones, to install and change the frames and to pump the honey. It was unbelievably lovely to break in half a freshly picked ripe apricot, to break it in half, to remove the stone, to fill the hole left after that operation with honey, and to despatch the whole thing into the mouth!

Our family friend Ivan Kuzmich Resnyansky took over and developed the apiary increasing its size to forty beehives and its yield to several hundred kilograms of honey. We surrounded the apiary with a wall and enclosed it in a large shed. The beehives and a row of eighteen litre tins stood against one of its walls, with the winemaking equipment of our farm manager Anton Pavlovich Kozak placed near the other wall. Anton Pavlovich used to make a dark purple-coloured wine out of wild grapes. They were supplied daily during the autumn harvest season by Korean women from nearby villages, who brought them around in huge timber tubs, made out of hollowed logs, carried on their heads. Our manager used to issue the ladies with credit notes, which they cashed in the office of the Novina resort.

Yankovsky senior devoted a lot of time to the planting of ordinary and fruit trees. In autumn and spring he used to order apple and pear trees from large nurseries of the nearby regional centre of Kyongson. The trees made the twenty-five-kilometre journey from there in two-wheeled Korean carts driven by powerful red oxen. We also planted several trees on each of the blocks of land of the "dacha" (holiday-home) subdivision. Most of these blocks were later sold to European residents of Harbin and Shanghai.

Some time later we bought part of a garden on the banks of our river from its Japanese owner, Mr.Sato, a shopkeeper from the nearby settlement of Ompo. It contained about two hundred young and established fruit trees of different varieties, which yielded a substantial harvest every autumn.

In addition to fruit trees, our family planted pine trees, two varieties of poplars (the fragrant and pyramid-shaped poplars) and white acacias, the latter being used as hedges along the roads and around various blocks of land. Some of these trees came from the surrounding forests, with others being purchased from nurseries.

The valley adjacent to our land holdings contained a lot of abandoned arable land, and on it we planted thousands of seedlings of Daurian larches (Note: Dauria is a region in Siberia), which by now, over half a century later, must have turned into a large forest...It is possible that some of the locals know of its origins.

I made numerous applications to the North Korean Embassy for permission to visit Novina and to pay my respects to the graves of my mother, grandmother and our Japanese nanny Osada-san, such visits being regarded as sacred by the peoples of the East, but I never once received even an acknowledgement of my requests. It seems to me that the new communist doctrine, which has been forced down the throats of the inhabitants of the northern part of "The Land Of The Morning Cool", killed its historical ideals, its noble traditions and even elementary human decency. That new "morality" has produced a young generation of heartless cynics.

Our family enjoyed a great respect of the Korean people for the selfless way my father and my grandfather before him defended them from the Manchurian Hung Hu Tse bandits, without any regard for their own lives or safety. The legend of Nenooni-The-Four-Eyed lived in every village and God-forsaken hamlet of Northern Korea and was passed on by the old men to the younger generation. I can attest to it, as I personally heard them relate that legend.

Right throughout his life in Korea my father visited Seoul, Harbin, Tientsin and Shanghai with the object of acquiring things which could be useful for the land which became the home of the descendants of "The Four-Eyed". He engaged useful and hard-working people, each of whom made a valuable contribution to the region. The fruits of these labours, which lasted a quarter of a century, have been inherited by the present-day generation. Doesn't all of this deserve a lasting gratitude? I am certain that these noble deeds live in the memory of the ordinary working people, but that the powers-that-be have erected an impenetrable barrier against any expression of thankfulness.

Chapter 33. THE SHEVELEV FAMILY.

My cousin Oleg Shevelev, was a champion of China in boxing and was well known in Shanghai in the nineteen thirties under the professional name of "Baby Russ". In the nineteen eighties he published his memoirs in San Francisco, in Russian, calling the book "The childhood and youth of Oleg Shevelev". In it he gives a very touching description of those distant times. Let me quote from his foreword:

"Whilst tidying up the papers in my study, I came across a few faded sheets of paper which constituted my 1923 diary…I reread it for almost an hour and relived the memories of my childhood and youth. Not many people have been blessed with such an interesting life…"

Oleg's father, Vladimir Michailovich Shevelev, inherited a five hundred "dessiatina" (fourteen hundred acre) estate from his father, Michael Grigoryevich. The estate was located on the shores of the Ussuri Bay, near the present-day town of Vladivostok, bearing the Chinese name of "Kangouza" (**Note**: A "dessiatina" is a Russian measure of land equal to approximately 2.7 acres or 1.1 hectares).

The Shevelevs used to spend the summer in Kangouza, moving to Vladivostok in winter, to take up residence in several homes left by the grandfather to his wife, son and two daughters. The daughters, called Margarita and Angelina were married to the two Yankovsky brothers—Yuri (my father "George") and Yan Yankovsky.

It was also customary for the Shevelevs to spend part of a summer in the Yankovskys' estate of Sedemi and for the Yankovskys to be house gests in Kangouza.

The estate of Kangouza, which was Oleg's birthplace, boasted a massive homestead consisting of fifteen rooms, one of which was a huge lounge-dining room forty arshin long and twenty arshin wide (**Note**: An "arshin" is a Russian measure of length equal to approximately one yard or two thirds of a metre). My cousin never saw a room of this size in any other private homes.

The dining room contained a grand piano, an ordinary piano, a three thousand-book library, settees, easy chairs, a dining table for twenty five guests, two cupboards, a trapezium, a large table for Russian billiards and a dancing area for twenty five couples. Heating was provided by two Dutch-style stoves, which were located in the basement.

Seven windows of the house were overlooking a veranda, which extended along the whole length of the building and contained a table capable of accommodating 40 people. The table was frequently used in summer to seat the numerous guests who descended on the estate. Vines of wild grapes twined around the veranda protected it from the summer heat. The structure was overlooking the Ussuri Bay and a garden, which contained the surname of its owners written in ten-foot high Chinese characters, composed of white bricks laid on the ground.

An old cannon standing on the slope of a hill near the bay was fired once a year, on the wedding anniversary of my cousin's parents. Two large rowing boats equipped with sails were suspended underneath the roof of a wharf jutting into an inlet. A cleverly constructed winch enabled even the children to lower the vessels into the water and to raise them at the end of an outing.

A huge yard containing a croquet field and a merry-go-round was situated in front of the main entrance to the house, with barns and two small Japanese houses located on both sides of the building. It is interesting to note that these houses were bought and dismantled in Japan and rebuilt on the estate.

A two-storied house designed for fifty Chinese labourers also formed part of the Kangouza estate as did a cowshed, a piggery and a yard housing 200 deer. Its final feature was a large garden on top of a hill.

Grandfather Michael Grigoryevich Shevelev was a great friend of the Chinese. He had an excellent command of their language and knew many thousands of Chinese characters. The dreaded Chinese Hung Hu Tse bandits guaranteed the safety of his possessions, and their famous "ataman" (head) Lin Gooi, was a frequent guest of the Shevelevs.

On one occasion a minesweeper sailed into the bay, and a group of officers decided to pay a visit to Oleg's father, who introduced them to his Chinese houseguest as a "Mr. Lee, a buyer of the pantui (deer horns)". After a sumptuous dinner the fun-loving Vladimir Michailovich Shevelev asked if any of his guests would care to cut a burning candle in half with one stroke of a sword, making sure that the candle did not go out in the process. The obliging guests destroyed many candles without success, until it was the turn of "Mr. Lee". "I'll never forget the glint in the old bandit's eyes", related later Oleg's father. Lin Gooi rolled up his sleeves, wielded the sword and cut the candle with one mighty stroke, without extinguishing the flame! Later that night he was taken to the other side of the Ussuri Bay in the Shevelevs' motor boat and disappeared into the Chinese crowds…

Among other of Oleg's interesting memories were the night time fishing trips to the inlet near Kangouza where the fishermen used torches to catch scores of skates and similar marine creatures, including occasional sharks and even sturgeon.

When Oleg turned ten, his father became a business partner of Yan Michailovich Yankovsky (the brother of my father Yuri [George] Yankovsky). Shevelev Senior rented out the Kangouza estate and moved to the Gamov Promontory, in the vicinity of the Korean border, where he started building a house on the eastern shores of the Vityaz ("Knight") Inlet. His partner Yan had by that time erected a very attractive three-storied castle in the deepest corner of the same inlet.

Unlike the patriarch of the Shevelev family, the Yankovskys had always been on the side of the Koreans, and the Hung Hu Tse bandits were their implacable enemies. For that reason uncle Yan's castle was built as a bastion in the war against the Manchurian gangsters. All the windows of the lower floors had iron grills and the roof and the balconies were protected with gun emplacements. Oleg said in his memoirs that my uncle's house "looked like a crusader's castle". Some of its windows were narrow and long, with others being T-shaped or octagonal.

Oleg Shevelev remembers that his first visit to the Yankovskys took place late one evening. After he had dinner uncle Yan took him to a bedroom and said pointing to a small bed: "This bed belongs to Fialka ('Violet'—the nickname of his daughter Geliana). She is away at the moment and you can sleep in it". The uncle told Oleg that, unlike in Kangouza, any night could bring an attack from the armed Hung Hu Tse bandits. Handing a rifle and a box of cartridges to the boy and pointing to a corner of the room he continued: "I'll wake you up in case of an alarm, in which case I want you to take up a position in that corner of the room, near the window, pressing your body against the wall, so that you cannot be seen from outside. Don't be afraid –you have to get used to danger." The old man spoke very seriously, and the youngster felt almost grown up and not at all frightened.

There was a battery-powered telephone communication between the Gamov Peninsula houses of the Yankovskys and Shevelevs. Guardhouses located on the hills and manned by armed huntsmen provided further protection, and a motor cruiser moored in the lagoon provided a means of escape, if all else failed.

Oleg continues:

"A few days after my arrival a band of Hung Hung Hu Tse attacked a Korean village in the vicinity of The Holy Trinity Bay. Uncle Yan sent a telegraphic SOS to his brother, my uncle Yuri (George), on the Sedemi Peninsula, and in the evening called in my cousin Andy and myself. 'Your watch is from now till midnight, lads!' –he said- 'Take the guns, the ammunition and torches. Don't be afraid, and may God be with you!' With these words he escorted us to the roof to start the watch. Luckily, all was quiet that night.

"As soon as uncle Yura (George) received the SOS from his cousin, he chartered a boat called 'Batareya' ('The Battery') carrying a crew of his bodyguards, most of whom were former White Army officers fleeing to the Far East from European Russia. 'Batareya' docked in the Vityaz Inlet the day after the declaration of the emergency and its men, led by uncle Yura (George), chased the bandits all the way to the Manchurian border.

"Several days after that episode Andy and I were again summoned by uncle Yan. 'You turned out to be brave fellows'—he said 'and I have decided to give you a treat by showing you the secrets of my home!' He took us from the second floor to his first floor bedroom where he stopped near a built- in wardrobe, pressed on something, lifted a floor tile, picked up a small torch from his pocket and stepped into the wardrobe. The wardrobe had an opening with a small but very sturdy ladder, which took us into a secret basement consisting of a fifteen by twenty foot room! That room was not connected to the rest of the basement and had a tunnel leading to a waterfall about two hundred metres away from the home. We were completely enchanted by all this. The whole idea of the secret tunnel was absolutely brilliant! A lot of people today would find my story hard to believe, but it is the absolute truth…"

An old Korean visited the building site of uncle Yan castle when the construction work was about to begin. He spent a lot of time gazing at the hills and dales surrounding it, walked around the perimeter of the sight, took a deep breath, shook his head and said: "The site has been chosen incorrectly. It is sitting on the neck of the spirit of the mountain. The spirit won't tolerate that and the owner will not live long…"

Nobody took any notice of the old man's words but, alas, uncle Yan Michailovich died early in January 1920 leaving behind a widow and two young daughters Geliana and Marianna.

At the end of his memoirs Oleg recalls that when he was eight years of age his father took him to a shooting gallery and asked the proprietor to select a well-adjusted rifle for his son. The proprietor assured him that all his rifles were well adjusted producing as proof a small target with bull's eye shots peppering its centre. "Just have a look at what the five-year-old son of Yuri Mikhailovich Yankovsky has done to this target!"-He exclaimed. Oleg's father spent a long time examining the target and finally said, scratching his head: "Well done! Valery is a fine marksman!" These words referred to me….

Chapter 34. HISTORY OF THE PIONEERS OF THE USSURI REGION.

A group of devoted historians employed by the V.K. Arsenyev* Regional Museum of Local History in the town of Vladivostok have formed a club called "Rodoved" ("Student of the Motherland"), with Galina Alexandrovna Aleksyuk as its chair. (***Note:** V.K.Arseneyev was a famous explorer of the Far East who lived and worked in that area from the beginning of the twentieth century to the nineteen thirties).

The aim of the club is to reconstruct the family histories of the pioneers of the Ussuri Region. The painstaking and selfless work of the group has "brought to life" many half-forgotten names. The Chief Curator of the Museum Nina Boguslavovna Kerchelyayeva and her deputy Boris Alexeyevich Dyachenko collected a huge number of documents and exhibits, whereas club members Svetlana Sergeyevna Rusnak and Tatyana Karpovna Kushnareva sent me quite a few questionnaires.

So far the Museum has organised four so-called "Yankovsky Readings" (in 1992, 1994, 1996 and 1998), which included trips to Sedemi, where the participants visited the memorial to my grandfather, Michael Ivanovich Yankovsky. As already mentioned, he pioneered horse breeding and deer farming on the Yankovsky Peninsula. The program of the 1998 "Yankovsky Readings," which took place between the 23rd and 25th of September of that year, is included elsewhere in this novel. Unfortunately, I was unable to participate in that conference and had to contend myself with a letter and a telegram expressing my thanks.

This year (2000) I forwarded to the Museum a copy of an irreplaceable typewritten magazine called "Teremok" ("Small Tower"), a single copy of which was published in Seisin during the first few years of our emigre life in Korea. My sister Musa miraculously retained a few editions of that magazine when she migrated to the USA. It is indeed remarkable that my mother and auntie Tata (the wife of my uncle Pavel Michailovich) found the spiritual strength to produce a literary magazine during the first, difficult, years of our exile (1925, 1926, 1927), when most other émigrés were preoccupied with far more mundane problems of personal survival….

The pioneering Yankovsky family adopted several Korean children whose names I have decided to include in this chapter…

The Korean stepson of uncle Yan and auntie Angelina was called Tom (Indis Ivanovich Tsoi-Yankovsky). As he wrote to me much later, he "owed a debt to comrade Stalin" in the notorious year of 1937 and spent ten years in the Gulag. (**Note:** 1937 was arguably the worst year of Stalin's murderous regime. Millions of people lost their freedom or lives). After his release Tom got a job with a building organisation in Karaganda (a town in Kazakhstan, about 73E, 50N) and one day came across a name which greatly surprised him: "Yuri

Yuryevich Yankovsky". Having made enquiries, he realised that its owner was the son of his adoptive uncle, Yuri (George) Michailovich Yankovsky. At the time Yuri Junior had just been released from the Gulag. The two cousins met. Having found out my address during that meeting, Tom wrote to me in Magadan and kept up the correspondence for the rest of his life.

Uncle Yan and his wife also had an adopted Korean daughter called Asya (Anastasia Yanovna –"daughter of Yan"). I met her in the home of our mutual friends, the Reznilkovs, in Moscow.

My parents Yuri (George) and Margaret Yankovsky adopted a Korean girl whom they called Zosya (Zlata Yuryevna—"daughter of Yuri"). She became a talented ballerina, married a Serbian officer, Zlatko Mirkovich Tsar, and left with him for the town of Tientsin in China a short while before our escape to Korea. Unfortunately, she died there in childbirth.

Chapter 35. OUR JAPANESE AND KOREAN FRIENDS.

When the cruiser "Prizrak" brought us into exile in Korea, we discovered that our young Japanese friend Kobayasi Masao was employed by the police department of the town of Seisin as an interpreter of the Japanese and Russian languages. Kobayasi used to visit us in Sedemi during his student days, when he was gaining practical experience in the Russian language, and continued to call on us in Seisin. Our friend made a good career, first becoming the Assistant Chief of Police of his province, and later-- a prominent member of the Japanese Military Mission in the town of Mudanjiang in Manchuria.

Having survived imprisonment in Russia after WWII, he returned to his native Japan, and managed to locate my sisters in the USA. They gave him my address in Russia, and we began to correspond. My friend sent me several parcels containing foodstuffs and clothing to my Vladimir address. Particularly valuable were warm gloves, which I still wear in winter. Masao Kobayasi died at the age of 96, having left a warm memory in our hearts.

My friend Kim Ryo Ho is a native of the Korean town of Kanko. He spent all of 1946 as a political prisoner in his native town. Some time later, he joined a group of three hundred Korean students who went to study in Russia as a result of an agreement between Stalin and Kim Il Sung. The young student married a Russian girl and managed to stay in Russia. He and I started a correspondence, which developed into a friendship. Kim tried to help me to visit Novina, but as already mentioned, the North Korean Embassy did not even bother to acknowledge any of my written requests.

A native of North Korea, my friend now only visits South Korea, Japan and the USA. He writes on many topics, one of them being our family. About two years ago he brought a group of South Koreans to visit us in Vladimir. During the course of the evening our guests asked me to sing a very popular Korean patriotic song "Ariran". Unfortunately, unlike my late brother Yuri who used to sing many Korean songs very well, I am not much of a singer at all. Nevertheless, helped by alcohol, I did my level best, first singing solo and later in a chorus. Surprisingly, the guests were ecstatic and gave us many valuable presents as a token of their appreciation.

I consider it my duty to give a copy of this book to my new Korean friend and hope that he will find it worth translating, at least in part, into Korean. At any rate, he hinted at such a possibility.

I would like to add a few more words about my new Japanese friends...

A contributor to the "Yankovsky Readings" in September of 1998 and a secretary of the Japanese Consulate-General in Vladivostok by the name of Yamamoto Chisuko contacted us in Vladimir some time ago to let me know that she translated my father's book "Half a century in pursuit of tigers" into Japanese. She rang again this summer (1999) from

Vladivostok and said that she wanted to visit us in Vladimir. Soon after her last call, our home was graced by a visit from this charming lady from "The Land of The Rising Sun," who spoke very good Russian.

Chisuko spent two days with us during which time she visited the nearby ancient town of Suzdal. Upon her return to Vladivostok she sent a delightful letter of thanks to our family, which we are keeping as a treasured memento.

Our recent visitor translated my father's book at the request of an entomologist by the name of Endo Kimio, a very attentive and gentle person, a typical representative of his people. Endo visited us three times in his quest for material for a book he is writing about our family and its connection with tiger safaris. Unfortunately, unlike Chisuko, he only knows a few Russian words.

There was a time when I spoke fluent Japanese, albeit confined to everyday subjects. In the year of our arrival in Seisin my brother Arseny, our two cousins Fiala (Geliana) and Malina (Marianna), and I attended a Japanese school in that town, where we picked up "katakana", the simplest version of the Japanese alphabet. I still know it very well. So good was my command of spoken Korean and Japanese that on occasions I even used to think in one of them. I used to think in Korean in the company of Koreans during hunting safaris, and in Japanese when conducting business with the Japanese in a city.

Alas, that was half a century ago! True, I spoke Japanese with Endo during his visits and, much to the surprise of my wife and son, even on the telephone, but found it devilishly hard to translate Russian texts into the dictaphone he left with me. I felt as if I was lugging a hefty burden up a steep hill! I was absolutely hoarse at the end of the day and was dog-tired.... However, Endo was more than satisfied with the result and gave me the dictaphone in appreciation of my efforts. I have since been corresponding with him using the trusty "katakana".

The idea of the book captured my partner's imagination to such an extent that he went to the USA and Canada after visiting me. He saw my sister Musa in San Francisco and my son Sergey in Vancouver, asking questions, looking through old albums and packets of photographs. Endo also borrowed a bunch of old photographs of Korea and Sedemi from me, copying and returning them in perfect order. It is a pity that his book will only be published in Japanese.

In conclusion, I must relate an amusing story about the extent of my and brother Arseny's proficiency in Japanese and Korean.

We often lapsed into Japanese or Korean during private conversations or used them to quote somebody's remarks verbatim so as to preserve the fine points of a conversation, which would be lost if translated into Russian.

In this particular instance he and I were sitting in our room in a Korean hotel in the town of Maygetsko in Manchuria and engaging in idle chatter, which involved quotations in

Korean and Japanese. The partitions between the rooms being thin, hotel guests could easily hear each other's conversations. It seems that one of our neighbours became interested in our conversation and decided to join us. We heard his footsteps along the corridor, followed by a knock on our door. The stranger poked his head into the room, paused and said in utter amazement: "Oh! Europeans! What happened to the Koreans and the Japanese?" Arseny and I burst out laughing, with the hapless questioner beating a hasty retreat to the accompaniment of some incoherent muttering….

Chapter 36. BEYOND GULAG. I REVISIT VLADIVOSTOK AND SEDEMI.

Having survived the Gulag and having been "exonerated" (regained citizenship rights), I was first granted permission by the authorities to visit Central Russia, Moscow and Crimea during my 1962 annual leave. This I did, spending my leave with my brother Yuri. I worked as a forester in the town of Magadan and arrived in Khabarovsk on the way to that city a few days before I was due to go back to work. (Note: Khabarovsk is a city in the Russian Far East {135E, 48N} approximately 1200 km/ 800 miles southwest of Magadan {150E, 59N}).

That being the case, I decided to risk a trip to my birthplace of Vladivostok. This required a special permit, which I obviously did not have. Nevertheless, I boarded a train and sneaked into my hometown after an 800- kilometre (500 mile) trip, without any repercussions.

I knew from my old friend from Harbin, pianist Shoora Dzygar, who had served his imprisonment in the Kolyma Lowland (150E, 70N-above The Arctic Circle), that his uncle, a "People's Actor" (a title given to talented artists by their Communist masters) by the name of Andrey Alexandrovich Prisyazhnyuk, lived in Vladivostok. Shoora told me that because his uncle had fond memories of the Yankovskys going back to his teens (he used to spend many a day at the racecourse admiring the beautiful mounts, some of which belonged to our family), he would be happy to accommodate me.

Shoora was right. The distinguished actor, his wife and daughter met me like a long lost relative, despite the risk associated with my unauthorised arrival. Upon hearing that I wanted to visit Sedemi, the host told me where to catch a ferry for the township of Slavyanka, which made an intermediate stop on "our" peninsula. His only advice to me was not to wear a beret and a cloak, which made me unnecessarily conspicuous in the Soviet setting of that era. "Do you want me to lend you an old padded jacket?"—he enquired. He felt that a more proletarian appearance was more appropriate on that occasion…I declined and managed to make the trip in my own clothes.

One of my travelling companions on the way to Sedemi told me in considerable detail that the peninsula I was about to visit used to belong to a squire by the name of Yankovsky and still bears the name of its founder, and that the owners maintained their possession in perfect order. I nodded sagely, while floating towards me was the Gek Bay, full of bittersweet memories, and the gentle hills of my childhood covered in lush growth. Somewhat to my surprise they looked considerably smaller than in the days of yore…I spent the night in the hold of my ferry, which had to undergo minor repairs before continuing on its way, stepping ashore only the following morning.

Exactly forty years had passed from the day since I walked upon that land as an eleven-year-old lad…I visited the ruins of the ancestral castle and made a safe trip back to

Vladivostok to the immense relief of the kind Andrey Alexandrovich. The poor man ran a considerable risk when he agreed to put me up.

After all, meetings were held on the 25th of October of every year to commemorate the anniversary of the capture of Vladivostok by the Red Army. They were invariably accompanied by ritual denunciations of the Yankovskys, Brynners and Shevelevs—"the blood-sucking capitalists who exploited the toiling masses". The proceedings of those cabals were also broadcast over the radio…

Upon my retirement in 1966 our family moved from Magadan to Vladivostok where we managed, albeit with some difficulty, to acquire a "communal" (shared) flat. Unfortunately, the moist climate of The Maritime Provinces turned out to be unsuitable for our seven-year-old son Arseny who was suffering from chronic pneumonia acquired in Magadan. Nevertheless I managed to pay two visits to Sedemi. I was accompanied by my wife Irene and some friends during the second visit, but made the first visit on my own, after finding out that the former manager of my uncle Yan's estate was living on the Gamov Promontory.

The man's name at the time was Alexander Alexandrovich (son of Alexander) Lensky. However, he was born with the surname "**Bogoyav**lensky" ("The one to whom **God** appeared") and, though a decent person, decided to remove the reference to God ("Bog") from his name after the arrival of the Communists, leaving behind the politically correct ending of "Lensky". Thus, the descendant of God-fearing ancestors became a "comrade Lensky", the owner of a name derived from the pseudonym used by the "proletarian leader" and "deity" -- "Lenin".

Lensky met me very cordially. He told me about the time he spent in the service of my uncle and enquired about the life of the members of our family. Though already a pensioner, Alexander invited me to inspect the estate, which he had been managing only recently. We paid a visit to the cemetery where we saw the graves of one of my uncles, Sergey, who died in infancy, and of my father's and uncles' mentor (see page 13), Platon Fedoroff. (I described in the first part of this book how he was mauled by a tigress). We also looked in on the deer farm and a new venture—a mink farm.

At the end of the inspection Lensky invited me to meet the management of the estate, which operated from a new building erected behind the ruined castle. The new edifice comprised a two-storied grey brick house. The castle was completely destroyed and I only recognised its powerful brick foundations. The director of the enterprise was polite enough, whereas his "Zampolit" ("Political Assistant" –usually a KGB stooge) started circling me as if I was a rare museum piece.

"Yankovsky?" –he finally ventured. "That one? The Old Man's son? Most of us in Primorye (Maritime Provinces) thought that you had all been exterminated root and branch! Fancy that! A live heir!"…

Another ten years passed during which I kept suggesting to brother Yuri that he should visit the place of his birth. I think it appropriate to make a slight digression to describe his birth and early years…

…Yuri was born on the second floor of our home on the Yankovsky Peninsula and not in a hospital, like the rest of us. Mother was forced to give birth at home because Yuri arrived somewhat prematurely, when it was still early January. Although the bay was covered with ice, it was not strong enough to support a motorcar, which was to take her to hospital.

During her labour the rest of her children were told to play outside, but we came back after a short while and gathered in the ground floor drawing room discussing the expected arrival of a sibling. Our meeting was interrupted by an unfamiliar sound, which prompted the following response from Arseny, the youngest of our group:

"Listen! Somebody is singing Sharaban in a hoarse voice!" "'Sharaban"- 'The Chariot" in English – was a popular song at the time. It was performed in most nightclubs in Vladivostok and people sang and hummed it at home.

The little performer of the "Sharaban", my kid brother Lyulya (Yuri), and the rest of the family, left Vladivostok for Korea on our cruiser "Prizrak" when he was two and a half years old. The vessel was towing two heavy barges and struck a severe storm by the time we were sailing past the mouth of the border river Tumangan. It was rolling from side to side, with water spraying over the captain's bridge, where the whole family gathered so as to escape the stifling air of the cruiser's cabin. Little Lyulya, wearing a red overcoat and a red beret with white pompons, was hanging on for dear life to the railing of the bridge the top of which was level with his head. The poor child was sea –sick but not understanding what was happening to him, kept crying out: "Mum! I am coughing!"

In the meantime, our "Prizrak" kept doggedly fighting against the howling wind and relentlessly sailing south- west, carrying our family to a new and unknown life…

…Fifty five years after that fateful day, in August 1977, we met again in the same area, having arranged our meeting after numerous calls between my Vladimir residence and Lyulya's abode in Karaganda in Kazakhstan. We decided to visit the nearby Partisan (formerly known as Suchan) Valley, the home of a well-known ging-seng grower by the name of Porfiriy Yevstigneyevich Yelizarov first. My brother was a passionate collector of stalks and roots of a medicinal plant called "Tsimitsifuga", which was popular at the time. He had also searched for a medicinal substance called "Moomiyo" in the rugged vertical rock outcrops of Kirgizia and published a fascinating account of his adventures in the Moscow magazine "Okhota" ("The Hunt").

Yelizarov acquainted us with his work and introduced us to his pupil Nikolai Ivanovich Kovalchuk with whom we struck a friendship. A few years later Kovalchuk took part in the opening ceremony of the memorial to my grandfather on the Yankovsky Peninsula. He praised Michael Yankovsky's choice of location in his speech, calling it "the most remarkable site in Primorye (Maritime Provinces)".

Our next destination was the Sedemi Peninsula, where we were accompanied by Klavdii Vasyukevich, the eldest grandson of the legendary Skipper Gek.

We took an early ferry from Vladivostok, and I immediately went to the office of "The Amursky State Deer Farm", which is the present owner of our estate. I introduced myself to the director of the farm and stated the purpose of our visit. The official was very polite and offered a chauffeured motorcar to take us to our destination. I politely declined, asking only to be given a letter of introduction to the overseer of the most remote part of the peninsula, a place called "Dlinnaya Pad" (Long Dell), where uncle Yan and auntie Gelya had their home before they moved to the Vityaz Bay.

We donned our rucksacks and, having scaled a small pass leading to the "Tabounnaya Pad" (Horse Herd Dell), arrived at the Dagemani Beach, where our "dachas" (holiday homes) stood half a century ago. After a refreshing swim we had lunch by a campfire. There was no sign of the dachas, the only remaining structure being a set of stone steps leading to a brook. By the evening our party made it to the striking Torpedo Boat Cove (some torpedo boats used to be stationed there) from which, in total darkness, we finally reached Dlinnaya Pad, having hiked across a chain of hills on the way.

Our arrival disturbed the guard dogs that started to bark. The overseer was suspicious at first, but, having been reassured by the letter of introduction from his director, allowed us to spend the night in one of the empty cottages on the estate. In the morning we looked around the place and observed a stroppy stag in his enclosure. I took photos of Klavdii, brother Lyulya and the overseer against the background of the ruins of the wall of the once hospitable home of uncle Yan and auntie Gelya. I vividly remembered how I used to play there with my cousins Fiala (Geliana) and Malina (Marianna). Looking at the ruins I remembered a "scandalous" prank, which took place (I could scarcely believe it) sixty years ago!

…Accompanied by a grown-up member of the family, a group of Yankovsky youngsters was delivered to Dlinnaya Pad in a horse-driven carriage to play with their cousins. Everybody had lunch, after which the adults left the kids alone in the dining room. My first cousin Fiala, who was the same age as I, was an incorrigible prankster. On this occasion she got hold of a large box of tiny liqueur-filled chocolate bottles belonging to her mother. We hid under the table, using the tablecloth as a tent, and started savouring the unbelievably tasty chocolates. Biting off the white bottle tops, we ate the sweets and drank the fragrant sweet liquid. I am not sure how many bottles we managed to devour. All I remember is that when the adults finally managed to discover the whereabouts of "the alcoholics", we were peacefully asleep, with a half-empty box of chocolates resting in Fiala's lap…

Getting back to my main story, we left the precious ruins and made our way through a well-preserved forest to the "Lebyazhya"("Swan") Lagoon, which separates the Yankovsky Peninsula from the mainland. Throughout that trip, I could not keep my eyes off the slender trunks of the Manchurian nut-trees, Maak acacias, ash-trees, elms, hornbeams, oaks and lindens—that collection of fabulous representatives of the Far-Eastern fauna. Unfortunately, not many such forests remain on the foreshores of the present-day Primorye (Maritime Provinces). To top off the nostalgia, towards the end of our journey we met a young enthusiastic kid –an angler by the name of Kesha-who was catching small redfish with the same enthusiasm as I, in the days of my far-away childhood….

We completed our journey through the land of our forebears by midday when we arrived at the wharf on the shores of the Gek Bay, where we encountered a group of people we knew from Vladivostok. A short time later a ferry took us back to Vladivostok.

Although our trip into the past was completely innocent, it gave rise to a legend among the good folk of the Sedemi Peninsula…It seems that, according to my informant who had been a member of our group, the burghers of Sedemi "knew" that under the guise of an ordinary trip the Yankovsky brothers were searching for a treasure buried by their father before the family fled to Korea…I suppose it had to be expected, as such fantasies spice up an otherwise dull life of the average citizen….

When I returned to Gamov at the invitation of the then director of our former estate by the name of Y.D. Chugunov, he told me another legend: "Everybody knew" that at one time there existed a submarine tunnel, which led from uncle Yan's castle to the other side of the Bay, and he used it for secret trysts with his mistress!

I met Yuli Nilkolayevich Vasyukevich, the brother of Klavdii, in Vladivostok, forty-five years after we said goodbye to each other in that city, by which time he had the rank of a captain of ocean-going liners. Yuli told me many anecdotes from the past of which I have not been aware. I found out from him that my father dismounted his horse before leaving for our cruiser and, in a farewell gesture, kissed the land of his forebears…

Shortly after our departure rumours swept the area that Yankovsky Senior was coming back to rescue the caged deer he had to leave behind on the shore, because they would not fit on the boat. This prompted a group of heavily armed "Chekists" (members of the called "Extraordinary Commission"—the precursors of the KGB), equipped with powerful binoculars, to spend several days on the rocky shores of the Yankovsky Peninsula, scouring the surface of the stormy seas for the avengers.

Another of his accounts is very illuminating…

During the terrible years of "de-kulakking" (a term used by the Communists to justify the confiscation of the farmers' land and possessions—**see Part I, bottom of p.57, for a more detailed explanation**), the Vasyukevich family were thrown off the property developed by their grandfather, which had been nationalised. In addition, the members of the family were sent into internal exile.

The family comprising the mother Yelena Fridolfovna and her two sons returned from exiles many years later. The boys managed to graduate as sea captains but for many years were not game to visit the seat of their family. However, Yuli finally overcame his fear and caught a ferry to the bay bearing the name of his grandfather, to catch a glimpse of the spot where he spent his childhood. He easily located the gates made out of whale ribs and started walking towards his grandfather's whale-boat which had been lying in the vicinity for many years but was stopped in his tracks by an ugly sight of two troglodytes vandalising the vessel. These creatures were hacking pieces of timber off the historical structure to light a campfire and make themselves a pot of tea!

Unable to contain himself, Yuli remonstrated with the hooligans: "What are you doing, comrades! Don't you know that this boat belonged to a famous whaler?" He was not game to say, "It belonged to my grandfather" but hoped that the hoodlums would be embarrassed into desisting from the vandalism. However, the response was far from conciliatory:

"Get lost, Brother! Haven't you heard the proletarian slogan: 'Rob the robbers?' Your famous whaler was sucking blood of the toiling masses, and it is our revolutionary duty to avenge his victims! Shut up and get out of here! You obviously don't know who you are dealing with!"

Yuli Nikolayevich lowered his head, retreated towards the shores of the bay where he used to fish as a little boy, and sat down on a nearby rock. A local resident who evidently heard the exchange and the threats, and clearly sympathised with the grandson of the famous captain Gek, left his boat, which he had moored nearby, and walked towards him.

"Don't become involved with these 'gentlemen', friend! I tell you who they are: they are members of the Vladivostok judiciary; one is a judge and the other one-- a public prosecutor. This is not their first visit here either—these scoundrels are quite fond of this place." All Yuli could do was to wait for the next ferry which took him back to Vladivostok…

The grey-haired captain of ocean liners had tears in his eyes when telling me this story…

Chapter 37. FALSIFIERS OF HISTORY.

It is a matter for deep regret that such well-known Russian writers as Lidin and Prishvin succumbed to the political pressures and trends which characterised their shameless era. Having spent a very short time indeed in the Far East, that pair managed to produce a farrago of lies about people they had never met. They produced a string of inventions consisting of twisted and distorted "facts".

Let me, for example, quote from Lidin's book "Three Novels" (printed in 1967 in Moscow by "The Soviet Writer" Publishing House). The present quote is from the novel "The Great Pacific." The author starts with the following preamble:

"This novel describes the first 'Pyatiletka' *(the first of the Stalin-engineered so-called 'Five Year Plans of Socialist Development of Russia')*, when The Far East was going through a difficult and at times painful transformation, a transformation whose vibrant forces were often hindered by indolence, inability to do an honest day's work and, occasionally, by direct sabotage from hostile forces".

Lidin introduces the hero of his novel, a native of Vladivostok and a former Red guerrilla fighter by the name of Sviyazhinov who became a prominent party apparatchik on the Kamchatka Peninsula (in the Far East about 160E, 55N).

The Communist Party decides to send this hero to Vladivostok where he is told that his long-time flame, Varya Vilkidskaya, is living on a deer farm on The Yankovsky Peninsula. The ardent Lothario takes a steamboat "Zhelyabov" heading for the town of Posyet, which drops him off, together with a few other passengers and several bags of mail, at Sedemi, and continues on its way to the Slavyanka and Vityaz Bays.

Sviyazhinov repairs for the deer farm where he meets his buddy and former fellow-partisan, a Latvian by the name of Paukest, who lives in the home of the former owner of the Peninsula. "The house with a large belvedere stood on top of a hill"—writes Lidin—"which provided a splendid view of the surrounding hills, the bay and lagoons surrounding the Peninsula. The structure with its gazebos and turrets was the product of the fertile imagination of the deer-breeding squire."

It has to be acknowledged that the general description of the edifice and its location are sufficiently accurate. Improvisation begins with the names of the owner (Yaroshevsky instead of Yankovsky) and his neighbour (Siemens instead of Brynner). If the reader survives till page 24, he is confronted with the following gem: "The last owner of the flowering land of this peninsula, the madcap animal and horse breeder Yaroshevsky, fled from it ten years ago, at the very height of the Revolution."

And elsewhere:

"John Siemens and the gold-prospector Yaroshevsky were among the first people to come to the shores of the Bay (The Peter The Great Bay -- V.G.Yank.). Siemens' remains were entombed in the family necropolis on the Peninsula, which was built in a Gothic style and had stained-glass windows. His family owned the best homes and the best yachts; it owned mines, dachas (holiday homes) and ships, which plied the oceans of the world.

"Kazimir Yaroshevsky started off by developing the gold mines on the grim island, but, being a hunter and trapper at heart, gave up that pursuit. He moved to the peninsula, becoming its joint owner with Siemens, built a house with a turret and started to breed deer. His son inherited the father's passion for animal husbandry and the old man's temper. He wore a bekyesha (a padded overcoat) in winter and a tussore (strong coarse brown silk) "poddyovka" (a man's long tight-fitting coat) in summer, and was passionate and arrogant. He quarrelled with Siemens over a trivial matter and cut off the water to his neighbour's estate by changing the course of the brook flowing through their properties. After the advent of the revolution Yaroshevsky formed an officers' detachment, which he equipped with his best horses. He hosted visits by "ataman" (Cossack leader) Kolmykov and fled to Korea at the last possible moment, narrowly avoiding capture. The Siemens family stayed behind and continued to work the mines …But The Revolution continued on its inexorable way, and one night the family fled to Japan in its yacht, leaving behind its homes, mines and farms…"

And yet another jewel:

"While still a student of the Vladivostok "Gymnasium" (select public school), Sviyazhinov (hero of the novel—**V.G. Yank.**) Found out that one of his school friends, a dark-eyed girl called Varya Vilkidskaya, was Yaroshevsky's daughter. Yaroshevsky seduced her mother and wounded her father because he had power. Half of the peninsula belonged to him and he could afford to be extravagant, to breed thoroughbred stallions and keep herds of deer. Merchants from Swatow and Shanghai beat a path to his door in search for expensive pantui (deer horns). He raced around the bay in his brilliant white yacht. He bought a collection of whale vertebrae from an old whaler and used them to build a grand fence. He managed to beguile Varya's mother. She was fifteen when her girlfriends told her the truth. Dad, her dear prematurely grey dad, was not her father. Two years after she heard that news she was fully grown and matured.

"The revolution was approaching like a distant storm. The windows were thrown open and a fresh violent wind blew in, the wind of an approaching holocaust. The doors of Yaroshevsky's home opened to a procession of officers, and with them--everything she hated: the glitter of shoulder straps, the shining personal weapons, the faultless military bearing….

"A long grey destroyer was the next one to arrive, disgorging a company of naval cadets, resplendent with white short daggers, who took up residence on Yaroshevsky's spacious estate. As a welcoming gesture, the host slaughtered ten deer from his farm to feed the cherished visitors, organised hunting safaris in their honour, and pleasure cruises on the bay in his yacht and motor vessels.

"Four families lived in the Siemens' dacha (holiday home), comprising married daughters and sons, their children, governesses and tutors. Theirs was a large noble family of country squires, which seemed to be indifferent to the vulgar din of history. Flowers, as always, blossomed in the magnificent garden and luxuriant rose bushes adorned its paths. White yachts were gently rocking on the blue waters of the Lebyazhya (Swan) Lagoon, with large indigo swallowtail butterflies flitting about, and migratory birds landing amongst that splendour.

"The days were too short for the Siemens Seniors who lived in Vladivostok. It was impossible to fit in the multitude of business deals, contracts, movements of ships carrying army supplies, uniforms, American tinned goods and frozen lamb from Australia. Warehouses, stores and open wharves were jam-packed with equipment meant to strangle The Revolution.

"All that incensed Varya, who joined an underground group…"

Who was that "hard-done-by dark-eyed Varya" invented by Lidin? Was it Zosya, my parents' Korean adopted daughter? Or was it Panna Savitskaya, who, with her parents, worked on our estate? But in either case, there was never a hint of any hostility. For example, Panna was a frequent visitor in our home, and relations between our families were extremely cordial. The Savitskys spent many years on Sedemi…

Despite all of that, the author found it necessary to blacken the name of the "bourgeois class enemy" –Yaroshevsky-Yankovsky. However, in my opinion, by resorting to such deliberate lies, he only succeeded in lowering his own credibility and sullying his reputation. The undeniable truth is that the two "evil heroes" of Lidin's tale—Yankovsky and Brynner— left a bright and indelible memory in the history of The Ussuri Region.

The name of my grandfather is occupying a place of honour on the plaque outside the building owned by the Historical Society of The Amur Region, sharing it with such luminaries as Admiral Makarov, Governor-General Unterberger and other famous people.

As for Yuli Ivanovich Brynner, homes built by him to this day grace the Aleutskaya Street, one of the main thoroughfares of Vladivostok leading to the railway station. Brynners' family home housed for many years the Political Branch of the Ministry of Far Eastern Shipping, and the Head Office of their family firm served as the Headquarters of the Far Eastern Merchant Fleet. A comfortable camp for Young Pioneers (a Communist League Organisation for pre-teenage children) was located for many years in the dachas (holiday homes) of the Brynner family on the Sedemi Peninsula.

And finally, on the blasphemous statements about the necropolis….

The "coloured windows imported from Italy" were smashed by vandals a long time ago and the necropolis itself is neglected and desecrated. The author writes with low irony about the "bricked up" remains of Brynner-The-Elder, his spouse and their son-in-law Maslenikov.

In fact, their remains were laid to rest in lead coffins, which were thrown into a gully by some thugs.

To quote Lidin: once again: "The revolution was approaching like a distant storm. The windows were thrown open, and a fresh violent wind blew in, the wind of an approaching holocaust". It was indeed "the fresh wind," as represented by the new Communist masters, which savagely disposed of the remains of the people who created beauty and harmony, by throwing them into a gully. Luckily, there appeared decent humans on the scene of the carnage who did not abide the sacrilege. As a further indictment of that barbarity, it was left to some unknown Koreans (not Russians!) to rescue the desecrated coffins in the dead of the night, and to bury the remains in another, as yet undisclosed, location…

Let us now say a few words about the second falsifier of history –the unabashed purveyor of slanderous inventions –Michael Prishvin.

In one of his novels Prishvin waxes lyrical about the beauty of the "hua-lu"—the so-called "deer flower", and yet lacks the courage to give even a short historical reference to the exiled Polish nobleman who, after years of penal servitude, managed to establish himself in the Far East and to save the precious deer from extinction, actually considerably increasing their numbers.

The same literary hack spent many years in Sedemi and on The Gamov Peninsula, where the sons of Michael Yankovsky put in an enormous amount of effort into the preservation of their father's legacy, but did not find it expedient to favourably mention their achievements. The only thing he had to say about my uncle Yan was:

"Yan Michailovich was actually quite a nice fellow. One day he was served a bad rissole in the local restaurant which made him very sick, so sick, in fact, that he could not shake off the food poisoning and eventually died from it".

The only reference to my father is:

"Yuri Michailovich scuttled across the border."

And that's all! Not one word about the brothers' efforts for the benefit of the Region! To top it off, Prishvin's long story about the deer is entitled: "A Bad Rissole". **(Prishvin, M.M.—Zolotoy Rog ['Golden Horn'] Publishing House—Khabarovsk—1955, pp 135-138).**

Both Lidin and Prishvin had only one purpose in mind: the use of flowery language coupled with flights of fantasy. Historical truth was absolutely unnecessary. The aim of the Communist Party, as conveyed to The Soviet Writers' Union, was to blacken the names of the old owners and to extol the virtues of the new masters. The bitter irony here is, though, that our successors had indeed been very successful in mismanaging and thoroughly fouling the legacy of their predecessors! It is quite unbelievable that everybody, including undoubtedly talented authors, was mortified by the threat of reprisals by the inhuman Soviet regime. Nevertheless, that's how it was, and, I suppose, people like Lidin and Prishvin are only to be pitied!

Chapter 38. THE TRUTH

I can't help thinking that Prishvin would not have dared write in such derogatory terms had he been aware of the letter of condolence the greatly revered explorer of The Far East V.K. (Vladimir Klavdiyevich) Arsenyev wrote to my aunt on the occasion of death of her husband, my uncle Yan Michailovich Yankovsky.

Here it is, written in Vladivostok and addressed to her on The Gamov Peninsula:

V. K. Arsenyev's letter to A.M. Yankovsky, addressed to her estate in Vityaz Bay.

(Published in the magazine "Rubezh" ['The Border'] Far Eastern Almanach,1992. No1/863 pp. 347-348)

Vladivostok, 6th Of February 1920.

Greatly esteemed Angelina Michailovana!

I was greatly distressed when I read in the press about the death of your husband Ivan Michailovich Yankovsky (**Note: Arsenyev used to call my uncle by the Russian name "Ivan" instead of the Polish "Yan"**). It took me a long time to recover from the grief occasioned by that sad news. The death of I.M. Yankovsky deprived me of the company of a man for whom I have always experienced feelings of sincere friendship.

How can I adequately attempt to console you?! We all have our moments of grief. Some of us are destined to drink from the cup of sorrow in our childhood, others-- in their youth, with yet others destined to suffer in their old age. You have been destined to drink that cup to the bottom, and now is your moment of destiny. It is left to you to find the spiritual strength to overcome that grief and to rise above it. It is my ardent wish that you should find that inner strength, and I hope most sincerely, from the bottom of my heart, that you will overcome your suffering.

I have extremely happy memories of I.M. Yankovsky. He possessed rare spiritual qualities: he was a person of ready sympathy, he was kind, full of energy and extremely capable. He was interested not only in agriculture but also in intellectual pursuits (science). He was extremely interested in my accounts of the history and archaeology of our remote region. I derived an immense pleasure from talking to him. I.M. Yankovsky was involved in putting together the diverse written material, maps and articles belonging to his late father and father-in-law, M.G.Shevelev. The will of the Almighty was to call him to this world and to allow him but a short life during which he fulfilled his destiny prescribed by Providence, and was returned to the other world, leaving it to the others to complete his tasks and, likewise, depart for the unknown yonder. Indeed, it is the destiny of one of us today, and the turn of the next one tomorrow! The laws of life and death are inseparable. There is no such thing as absolute death! Birth and death are the two important events in our existence, which bind us together with our ancestors and our descendants. Philosophy, being the realm of abstract thought, sometimes offers us a modicum of consolation…..

Please accept my best wishes, dear Angelina Michailovna! I shall be very happy to repay you, at this difficult moment in your life, for the cordial hospitality extended to me by you and I.M.Yankovsky during my visits to the ging seng plantation on the Yankovsky Peninsula.

Please convey my respects to Margarita Michailovna and Yuri Michailovich.

Sincerely and faithfully yours,

V.ARSENYEV.

Arsenyev's respect for out family is further illustrated by the foreword to his book "In the Mountains of Sikhote Alin" (138-140E, 45-50N)where he writes:

"The list of the explorers of the region would be incomplete without the inclusion of two pioneers who arrived at the time when swans were still common in the Vladivostok Harbour and tigers were roaming the nearby hills. I am referring here to M.I. Yankovsky and M.G. Shevelev. The former performed a lot of work in the field of ornithology and entomology of Northern Korea and the Posyet Region, whereas the latter was an intellectual who lived most of the time on the Bay of Kangouza.

"Shevelev's name is intimately connected with the study of local history. He spoke Chinese, was well conversant with Chinese characters and owned a large number of ancient manuscripts. The only criticism that can be levied at that distinguished figure, is that he made no effort to disseminate his knowledge, taking it to his grave instead. We are in possession of only some fragments of his work, which are, nevertheless, extremely valuable. They offered a considerable help in establishing that The Bohai Kingdom (which existed between the 7th and the 12th Century) occupied the region bounded by The Pacific Ocean, Eastern Manchuria, Northern Korea and The Ussuri Region." (*Arsenyev, V.K. , Selected Works in two Volumes. Vol.2—'In the Mountains of Sikhote Alin. Walks in The Taiga{virgin forest}')* . *Moscow, 1986-- p16).*

The following episode illustrates the true feelings of my father's employees to their boss and his attitude to them.

My wife Irina Kazimirovna and I were living in Magadan after our release from Gulag where she received a visit from a fellow inmate, an old Korean who had just been released. Irene offered the old fellow a cup of tea and engaged him in light conversation.

"Say, your man –Yankovsky?"—asked the old chap.

"Yes", she replied.

"And what his name?"

"Valery".

"Ah, yes, yes, I remember when he still little boy".

"You remember him from Korea?"

"No, I am farm labourer his father at Sedemi. His father name Yurike." (Many Koreans in Primorye called my father "Yurike").

Upon hearing the word "farm labourer" ("batrak" in Russian—a slogan-like tag used by the Communists to label the so-called "exploited members of the rural proletariat"), my poor wife was taken aback, expecting a standard Soviet-style denunciation by the "oppressed proletarian" of his former "cursed exploiter"!

Noticing her discomfort, the old boy started to laugh:

"You afraid? You silly! I never live better than when I work for Yurike!"

Chapter 39. THE NEAREST AND DEAREST OF MY AUTUMN YEARS.

1. MY WIFE IRINA AND HER FAMILY.

Irina Kazimirovna Yankovsky (nee Piotrovsky) was arrested at the beginning of World War II (in 1941) in accordance with the articles of the penal code which were "fashionable" during Soviet times, namely: "Law No 58-10 Part I and No 58-11 and 17-58-8 in the Criminal Jurisdiction of The Russian Federation." These laws punished citizens for "Anti-Soviet agitation and membership of an Anti-Soviet group". My wife's "group" comprised senior high school students (they belonged to years 9 and 10) and her crime consisted of reading of a poem by Sergei Yesenin, a "prohibited" poet (*Note: The insane system of the day used to prohibit not only the reading or reciting of certain works but even the mention of the names of "prohibited" authors*). The poem read by the "criminal" Irina Piotrovsky at one of her classmates' birthday party was entitled: "Return to The Motherland". Fifteen years later, i.e. in 1956, the members of the "criminal children's group" were exonerated by the State. Regrettably, some of the youngsters did not survive till 1956 and had to be awarded a posthumous certificate of innocence.

Irina's father was a Polish nobleman, who, not unlike my grandfather, had been sentenced to penal servitude by the Tsarist Regime, only to commit suicide during the Communist rule in 1934. He chose what seemed to him as an easier way, because he was due to be arrested by the precursors of the KGB (known as NKVD) after the political murder of one of Stalin's potential rivals by the name of Kirov. Irina's widowed mother, Margarita Ivanovna Piotrovskaya, was a well-known teacher in the town of Saratov **(on the Volga River in Central Russia –46E 52N)** who had a younger daughter called Natasha. After her eldest daughter's arrest Margarita and Natasha sent parcels to Irina, which helped to sustain the young inmate of the prison camp.

Natalia Kazimirovna (Natasha) married an engineer by the name of Boris Alexandrovich Zorov. They have three sons. Michael, the eldest, is a medical doctor and his two brothers, who are twins, are engineers who currently run their own businesses and pursue interesting hobbies.

One of the twins, Mitya, writes poems, whereas his brother, Pavlik, is a keen traveller. Business interests permitting, he takes his family on various trips and expertly records his adventures on film.

Since early childhood the twins have been visiting us in Vladimir. They have read all of my books and show a keen interest in the history of the Yankovskys, their relatives who hail from The Far East. I find it very touching, because most young people tend to be preoccupied with the day-to-day affairs of their immediate families.

2. EXTRACTS FROM IRINA YANKOVSKY'S MEMOIRS.

(i) Academician Vavilov.

In winter 1942, whilst an inmate of Buildings 3 of the Saratov Penitentiary For Political Prisoners, I fell ill and was waiting for a "Black Raven", a prison van which was to take me and some others to the prison hospital. We were all taken from our cells and lined up facing a prison wall. I stared crying, perhaps because I felt ill, or maybe because I was afraid.

Standing to the right of me was an old very thin man wearing a long black coat. Prisoners were not allowed to talk but he did say to me: " Don't cry! You are still a child, and they won't give you a long sentence. Will you please remember who I am? My name is Academician Vavilov *(Note: He was the brother of another Academician Vavilov, The President of The Soviet Academy of Sciences).*"

Soon the "Black Ravens" arrived to pick us up and to cram pairs of prisoners into tiny compartments designed for one inmate. I was in luck, having found myself sitting in the Academician's lap. He repeated his surname and added: "When you get to Moscow tell the people there that you saw Academician Nikolai Ivanovich Vavilov in the Saratov Prison. Make sure you do it! You are still just a little girl, and I know that you will survive, but take care of yourself!" The journey to the hospital was short, and we soon arrived at our destination, but Nikolai Ivanovich cheered me up by telling a few funny stories during our trip.

Regrettably, I was so terrified of the regime that it took me sixteen years, i.e. till 1958, to tell anybody about that meeting.

(ii). GULAG'S "First Circle".

I served my first sentence (between 1941 and 1947) as a member of a construction team, which was building a railway branch line near the town of Stalingrad *(Note: Formerly known as Tsaritsin, currently named Volgograd. On the Volga River, in Southern Russia, 45E, 48N).* The prisoners were kept behind barbed wire in a village, which previously belonged to some "Volga Germans". They were descendants of German migrants who had been invited to Russia by Catherine The Great in the eighteenth century. The twentieth century descendants of those pioneers were expelled to Kazakhstan, because they had the "honour" of having been born on Russian soil ten generations later. The walls of the confiscated homes bore cheerful inscriptions: "Barracks of the Trotskyites". That was our official designation.

Our "nourishment" consisted chiefly of thin soup made from dill left behind by the deported Germans. As a result of that diet, the "Trotskyites" soon turned into live skeletons. Such was their pitiful condition that the authorities no longer had to distinguish between sexes when squads of "dokhodyagy" *("those destined to soon die of starvation"—a nickname given to starving prisoners of the GULAG)* were being shaved and washed in the prison bathhouse.

In order to ensure that the "'dokhodyagy' did not swing the lead (stay idle)", we were forced to collect stones in the precincts of the slave labour camp and to put them in neat heaps one day, only to demolish the results of our efforts on the following day, and to start new heaps nearby.

Our attire came from the bodies of slain German soldiers, except for the headgear which consisted of old peaked Soviet Army caps, known as "Budennovky" *(after Semyon Budenny, a Soviet Marshal during WWII, who was also a famous Commander of the Red Army in the Civil War of 1918-1922)*. However, in our case, the red stars were removed from the military caps.

I remember how one day I was sent to clear a pile of corpses of German prisoners of war. I was just a little lass at the time but I was given a carriage driven by a lazy ox, which for some ungodly reason only understood two commands, both in Ukrainian! Thy were: "Tsob!" ("stop") and "Tsobey!" ("go"). I also remember how light the corpses were—so light, in fact, that I had no trouble in unloading them from my cart and throwing them into a ditch, which has been specially dug for that purpose. However, I lost my "Budennovka" (cap) in the process and was too weak to jump into the ditch to retrieve it. Therefore, upon return from my assignment I was charged with an offence, which was called "promot" (deliberate loss of government property) and punished by several days of solitary confinement.

(iii). GULAG'S "Second Circle", or Man's Inhumanity to Man.

Even though I had been sentenced to five years of penal servitude in the so-called "corrective labour camps" *(Note: Their Russian acronym is **ITL**- "**I**spravitelno **T**rudovuye **L**agerya")*, I was kept in confinement a few extra months pending "a special directive".

I was then released for a short time, only to commence "The Second Circle" of GULAG, i.e. a repeat imprisonment for a period of, this time eight years of ITL, without any additional charges being laid! In addition, at the expiration of that sentence, **I** was to be exiled to "The Far North" (Magadan [60N] and areas to the north of that city) for the duration of my natural life.

I spent the eight years of the "second Circle" as a slave labourer of a state timber company on The Kolyma Lowland (approx. 70N) and on the construction of the City of Magadan. Work in Magadan included the clearing of the local river called Magadanka of the ice crust, which used to form in early autumn. I belonged to a women's detail, and we worked in shifts, sharing common rubber boots and breaking up crusts of ice with iron bars. Hours had to be spent in ice water on this infernal task, and many women acquired severe rheumatism for the rest of their days…

Our torment was exacerbated by the taunts of specially "trained" guards. These sadistic creatures used to have a great time at the expense of defenceless women. The head guard was the worst sadist of them all. On the way back from a day's draining labours he would halt our column at a muddy puddle, which was a permanent feature of Yakutskaya Street, and make us lie in it for as long as he saw fit. The armed soldiers stood by and stopped all pedestrian traffic during that torture. It was during one of these regular ordeals that we heard a clear innocent voice of a little boy:

"Mum! Mum! Look there! Mum, are they also people?"

I would like to conclude this short extract from my autobiography by pointing out the unprecedented and ugly "campaign" of the Soviet Government against political prisoners who completed their sentences in the years immediately following the Second World War (i.e.1949, 1948 etc).

We were not allowed to have a "Propiska" (a residence permit required by every citizen) at our former place of abode, and our release certificate which indicated the reason for imprisonment as "Article 58 of The Penal Code" ensured that former inmates were blacklisted, i.e. were not eligible for employment…

I went home to Mum because I simply had nowhere else to go, and poor Mother used to hide me in a wardrobe any time the doorbell went, because she feared that neighbours would report my "unlawful" existence… I shook in the darkness fearing exposure of my "crime"….

That ordeal lasted till autumn of 1948 when I was again arrested without any new charges being laid. The charge was still the same: "Violation of Article 58, Section 10, Sections 17 to 58, Sections 8 and 11".

When I was taken to the Remand Prison and thrown into a cell, I realised within very few minutes that I was surrounded by the same unfortunates as myself… We called this Second Circle of GULAG --"The Second Stage of Stalin's University of Untold Millions of Victims"….

14th of February 2000.

3. MY SONS.

My eldest son Sergey grew up in Canada.

My first wife Irma went to Harbin, China, five years after my arrest and imprisonment in the GULAG. There she married a German citizen by the name of Yuri (George) Schneider. The couple left Harbin for (as it was then known) West Germany and later migrated to Vancouver in Canada.

I first met Sergey when he was forty years old. By that time he no longer spoke Russian, and he and I conversed in English. These days we keep up a correspondence, naturally also in English. In his younger days Sergey was known by his stepfather's surname but changed to the surname "Yankovsky" when he grew up, and cherishes the history of his forebears. He has one daughter called Maree who writes me kind and touching letters.

Irina and I have a son called Arseny who is a fanatical reader of literature and who occasionally writes himself. He won a place at the Maxim Gorky Literary Institute in Moscow on the basis of his very first novel, and for just over three years gave every impression of seriously studying for his diploma in Russian Literature. Such a document gives its holder a very important official title of a "Literary Worker" (despite my literary efforts, I, for example, have no such official qualification).

Unfortunately, it was not to be. Arseny had a difference of opinion about his literary work with a seminar supervisor. This, in turn, led to a failure in a subject and an exclusion from the course. He was given a chance to resume his studies the following year, the only restriction being that he had to complete the diploma by correspondence. He stubbornly refused to go along with that proposal, telling us that, as there had been a change of Management at The Institute, he felt that the new Chancellor was unlikely to accept a student who had been taught by the previous Administration. Such obduracy resulted in Arseny's failure to obtain the desired qualification.

Our son is well conversant with the history of his forebears and helped me with this book. I should add here that his mother also assisted me in my efforts. Despite the fact that she was an unfortunate victim of Stalin's "system", she managed to acquire an occupation as a proofreader during the period of her incarceration. One of her tasks was the editing of numerous articles in an official prison newspaper, published by the slaves of the GULAG. Many of the authors lacked talent and were barely literate.

Arseny's partner, a young lady called Nika, is a capable draftsperson, who used my freehand sketches to produce maps of Novina, Primorye (The Maritime Provinces), Korea and Manchuria included in this book. These maps help the reader to visualise the locations described in my work.

4. BEYOND GULAG.

As far as I am concerned, my literary work, dealing as it does with our family's romantic past, coupled with my love of the nature, which surrounds me, keeps me young at heart. Everything that I have written in my books, and magazines such as "Okhotnik" ("The Hunter") and others in the past thirty years, is the truth and nothing but the truth. And when I write about my past experiences and feelings, I relive them in my mind.

God has been very kind to me since my move to the city of Vladimir in blessing me with very good and loyal friends. I have known one of them, a man by the name of Anatoly Alexeyevich Yevseyenko, for nigh on twenty years. He is an extremely talented person: a poet and author as well as an expert in natural sciences. He is the director of a state-owned National Park, which consists of a forest and lakes where some hunting is permitted.

I have spent a lot of time going for walks in the forest with my friend and exploring numerous local lakes in a rowing boat. Our trips are always accompanied by discussions on various subjects. We have conducted experiments with the transplantation of medicinal herbs from the Far East, and hunted wild ducks and geese. I regard every visit to that Park as a God-sent break and am delighted by my host's attentiveness, which characterises his noble soul.

I have belonged for some years to a small group of lovers of hunting, mushroom gathering and fishing. It consists of four people: an old friend by the name of Mark Solomonovich with his wife Valentina Ivanovna, a former fighter pilot, Vasilly Illarionovich Vinnichyuk, and yours truly. We spend many weeks getting ready for each hunting season, be it in spring or in autumn, because the preparations get us closer to the day when we can finally travel to the wilderness forming part of the National Park, created through the loving efforts of my friend the poet.

I have taken part in many hunting safaris, which my present friends can only read about, and dream of. There is no way I could take part in any of them at my present age, because I no longer have either the keenness of sight or the necessary agility. Nevertheless, I still experience the thrill of achievement when I manage to bring down an occasional "cunning" wild duck. The most precious part of the exercise is the sound of the wayward wind, the scent of the forest and the swamps, the rustle of the wings, the cries of the migrating birds, journeying to far-away lands only they know about. And, of course, the excitement when a flock of birds starts to circle a lake, and one asks oneself: "Which way are they heading? Towards or away from me?"

Those are the moments, when, in the words of the immortal crooner Vertinsky : "Your heart soars and sings like a bird".

A shapely and attractive young oak stands near an outdoor dining room - gazebo in an area called "Gridinskoye", which is a subdivision of my friend Yevseyenko's National Park. I became enchanted with that tree and asked my friend to give it to me. A birch tree obstructing "my oak" was removed at my request, and the gracious plant is basking in the sunlight. I get the impression that it is grateful to me for my help. I always greet my oak upon arrival at the National Park and pat its powerful trunk covered in coarse bark. It is my intention to affix a metal plaque on the mighty trunk, bearing the inscription: **"The tree of V.G. Yankovsky, a hunter and explorer, born in The Far East."**

When I am no longer here, the mighty oak will continue to live for a very long time, reminding friend and stranger alike of the author of books devoted to the description of nature and the noble sport of hunting....

Chapter 40. EPILOGUE.

The tale of the tragic history of the clan of Novina-Yankovskys who took part in the rescue of The Lord's Casket from the "infidels" has come to an end...Many, very many people and events did nor get a mention, because their numbers are so vast. I can't help thinking that some of the narrative lacks proper cohesion and that events are not always described in proper sequence. However, those lingering doubts aside, I am buoyed by the realisation that my generation of that distinguished clan, which grew up in Korea and was subject to the horrors of the Soviet GULAG , managed to achieve nigh impossible.

First of all, we managed to achieve a complete exoneration of my father's name twenty four years after his death in the hands of his captors, and to stop frequent attempts by malevolent guardians of Stalin's traditions to blacken his name.

Secondly, we located if not his grave, but at least a cemetery, by now overgrown by a forest, where our heroically stoic "Papa Tiger" was laid to rest. That feat was accomplished with the aid of some kind inhabitants of a small Siberian town of Vykhorevka and, above all, thanks to the selfless help of Stepanida Ivanovna Merdelina, an émigré from Manchuria, who had also been a victim of a unjust punishment. It was she and her brother who found the abandoned cemetery in response to my appeal.

In 1966, forty years after release from imprisonment, former inmates of a GULAG camp called "Ozerlag" ("Camp by the Lake") gathered together to commemorate that event. Stephanida Ivanovna invited my cousin Tanya, who had been one of the inmates of that camp, to join in these ceremonies.

Tanya (her full name is Tatiana Pavlovna Yankovsky-Bordovskaya) was the last member of our family to see Yuri (George) Michailovich Yankovsky alive. She was released from a prison in the town of Taishet a few months prior to my father's impending release and paid a few visits to him in prison, hoping to accompany him to my abode in Magadan. As we found out later, despite the fact that he was due to be released, the prison authorities were keeping him in prison, due to the chaotic nature of the penal administration at the time. The physically strong old man was being forced to walk through the snow between prisons, carrying a heavy bag containing his personal belongings. This proved too much for him, and he collapsed in the snow without the guards noticing his absence until some time later. By the time they found him he was exhausted and in shock, which resulted in a bout of lobar pneumonia.

My father was unconscious by the time he reached a hospital of the women's prison on the Chucksha station where this distinguished squire, the owner of estates first in Primorye and later in Korea, died on the thirteenth of May 1956, surrounded by female political prisoners, none of whom he knew. They buried him and installed a post on his grave, bearing an inscription, which they showed Tanya when she arrived there having been notified of my father's death. It read: **"This is the resting place of the Ukrainian professor Yankovsky".**

The women told Tanya that her uncle was in a delirium before his death and kept calling out : "Tanya, Tanya, Tanya……"

Forty years after that day, on a fine August day in 1996, Tanya and Stephanida Ivanovna drove the last nail into the coffin of the infamous GULAG by affixing a plaque to a large birch tree standing on my father's cemetery. Prepared by a craftsman attached to the Russian Orthodox diocese of my town of Vladimir, it read:

NOBLEMAN
**YURI
MICHAILOVICH
YANKOVSKY
1879—1956
AUTHOR OF THE BOOK
"HALF A CENTURY IN PURSUIT OF THE TIGERS"**

END OF PART TWO

Chapter 41. APPENDIX.

THE WILL OF MY GRANDFATHER MICHAEL IVANOVICH YANKOVSKY, 1912.

(This is a condensed version of the will, given in "plain English", to avoid legalisms and tautologies).

M.I.Yankovsky's Will is dated 20th of January 1912. It was prepared by a solicitor named A.P. Buzhko and witnessed by V.P. Margaritov (a senior public servant), A.A. Maslennikov (described as a "personal nobleman") and A. A. Trusov (a farmer). The will makes the following stipulations:

The estate called "Konny Khutor"("The Horse Stud") on the Yankovsky Peninsula is to be left to Yuri (George) Yankovsky, subject to the following conditions based on the recognition of the fact that the property was developed with the help of Michael Yankovsky's wife Olga, his son Yuri (George) and, to a lesser extent his daughter Anna:

(a) Olga to be given a lifelong use of the property and to be recognised as its owner.

(b) Anna to have a lifelong right of abode on the property and a reasonable share in its net profit, after proper financial assistance is given to aged and incapacitated relatives. She is also to be given the task of caring for aged and sick relatives. A suitable building surrounded by a sufficient area of land is to be erected on the property for that purpose. Anna is to co-ordinate the extent of the financial assistance to be given in each case and the details of the proposed building with her mother Olga and brother Yuri.

(c) Michael expressed a wish that his sons Alexander, Ivan (Yan), and Paul should make their own way in life. However, if any of them was to fall ill or decided to live on the property, they were to be allowed to do so, with Yuri paying them an allowance commensurate with the profits of the enterprise.

(d) The sale of the property could only be effected as a result of a mutual agreement between Yuri and his mother. In that "unfortunate event" (Michael's words) the proceeds are to be divided as follows:

The proceeds are to be divided into twelve equal shares. Olga is to receive two shares. Yuri is to be given five shares in recognition for his many years of labour as a worker and manager of the property. The sons Alexander, Paul and Ivan (Yan), and the daughters Elizabeth and Anna were to be given one share each.

(e) In the event of any of the heirs wishing to obtain their share of the estate prior to its sale, they would have had to first obtain the agreement of both Yuri and Olga for such a step. The amount and nature of compensation (i.e. money or real estate) had to be ascertained in consultation with those two people. No further compensation or assistance was available after that.

(f) Michael was leaving all the money and all his interest in the publishing firm "Yankovsky and Trusov" in the town of Vladivostok to his daughter Anna.

(g) In the event of his death away from home, Michael did not wish to have his body moved back to his estate. His body was to stay in its original grave.

16-1-2000

Chapter 42. Family Trees

From the Crusades to Gulag and Beyond

The Yankovsky Family Tree
(Descendants of Michael Ivanovich Yankovsky)

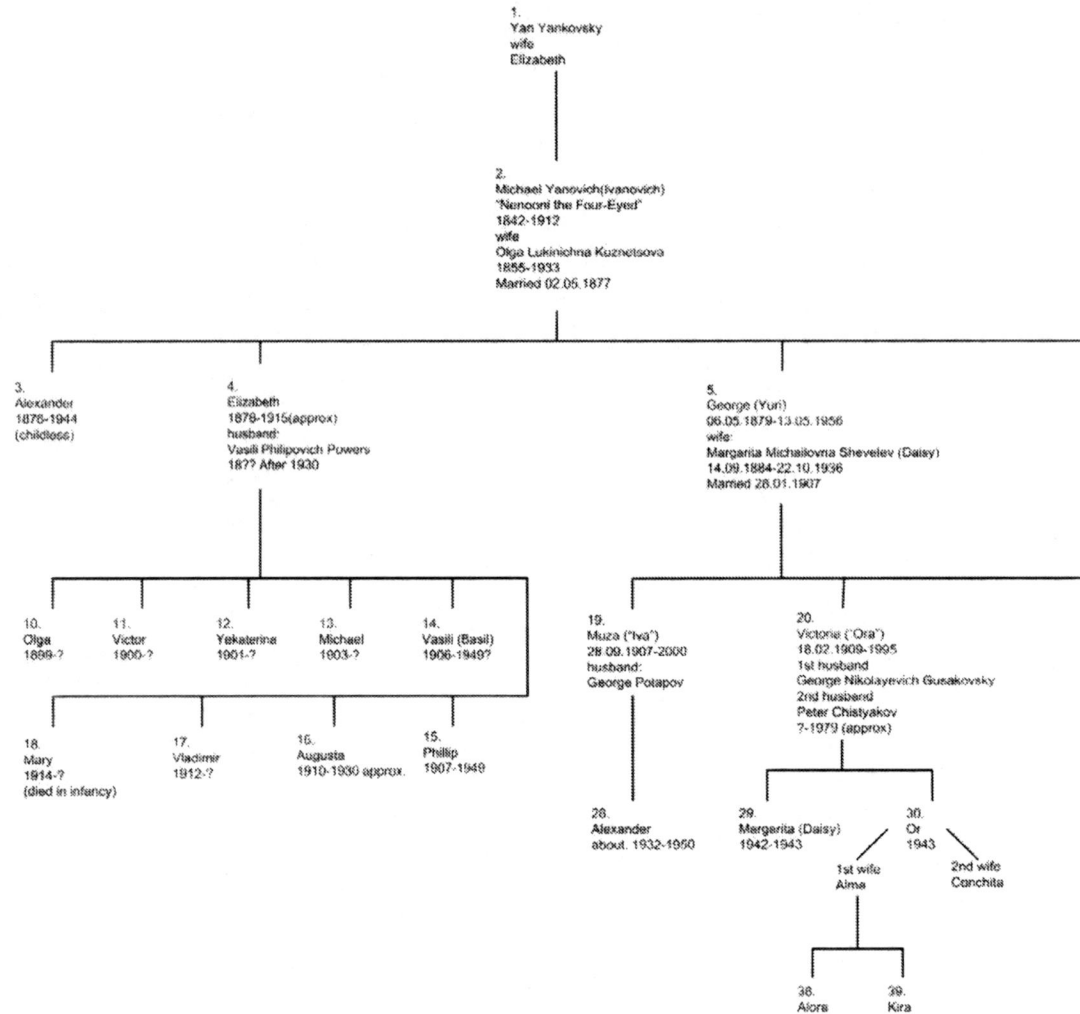

FAMILY TREES

The Yankovsky Family Tree
(Descendants of Michael Ivanovich Yankovsky)

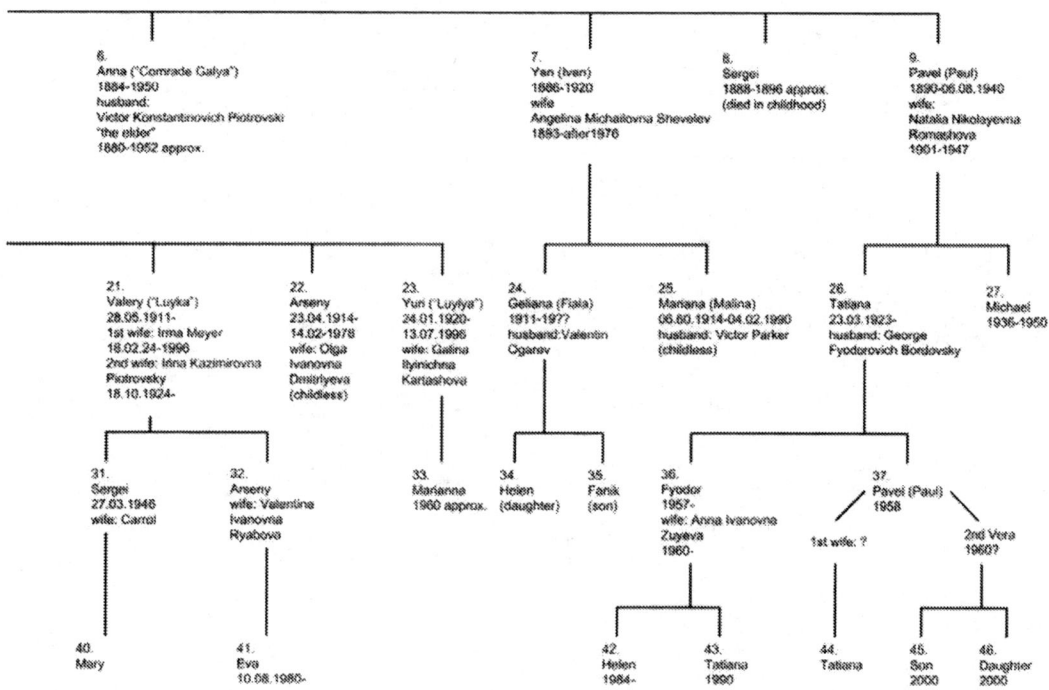

The Shevelev Family Tree
(Descendants of Michael Grigoryevich Shevelev)

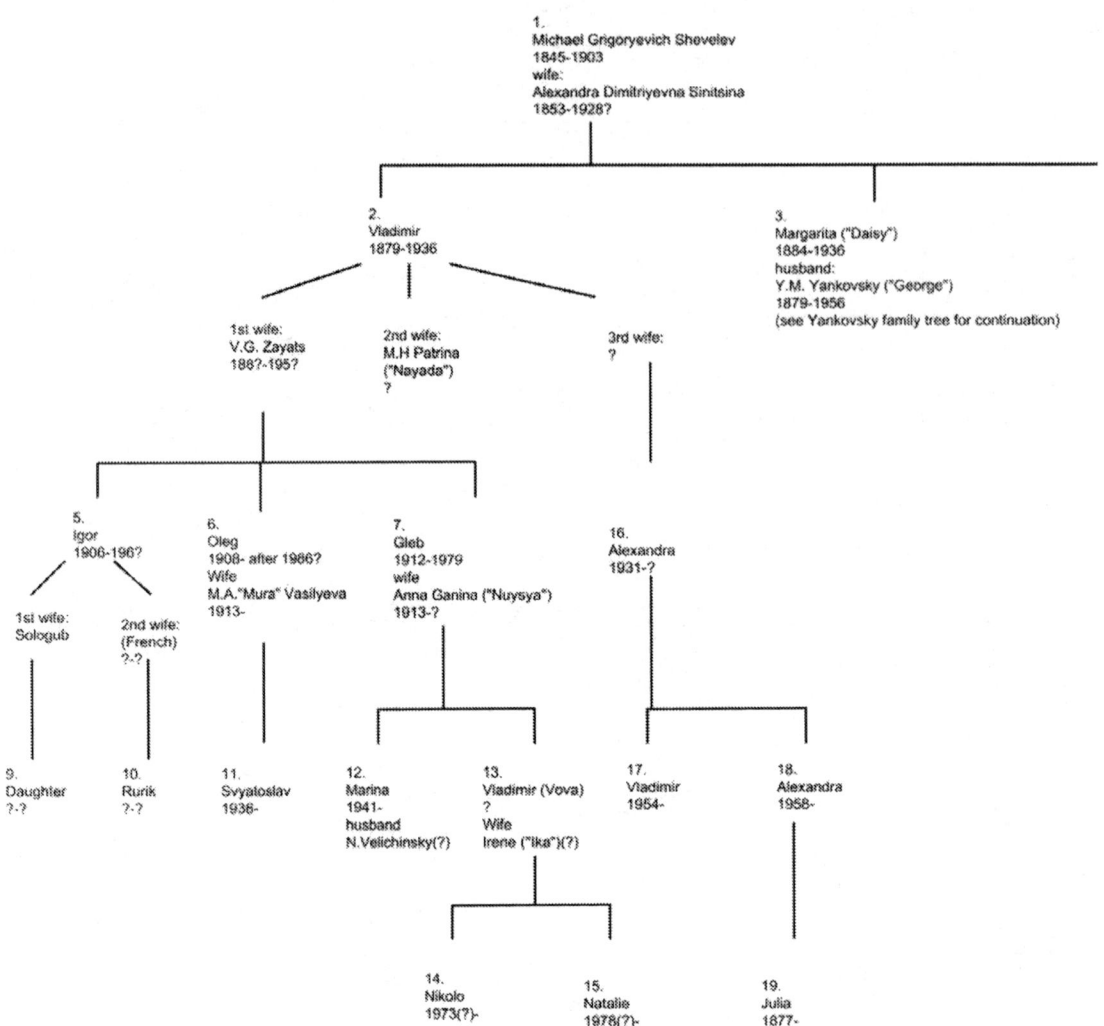

Family Trees

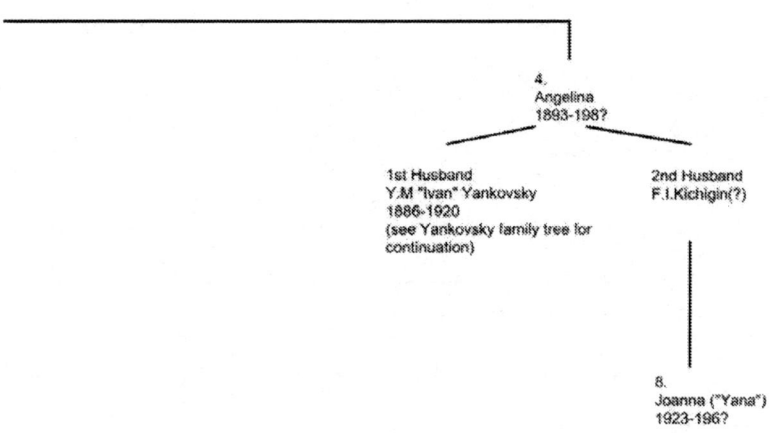

FROM THE CRUSADES TO GULAG AND BEYOND

The Brynner Family Tree
(Descendants of Yuli Ivanovich Brynner)
(From Switzerland)

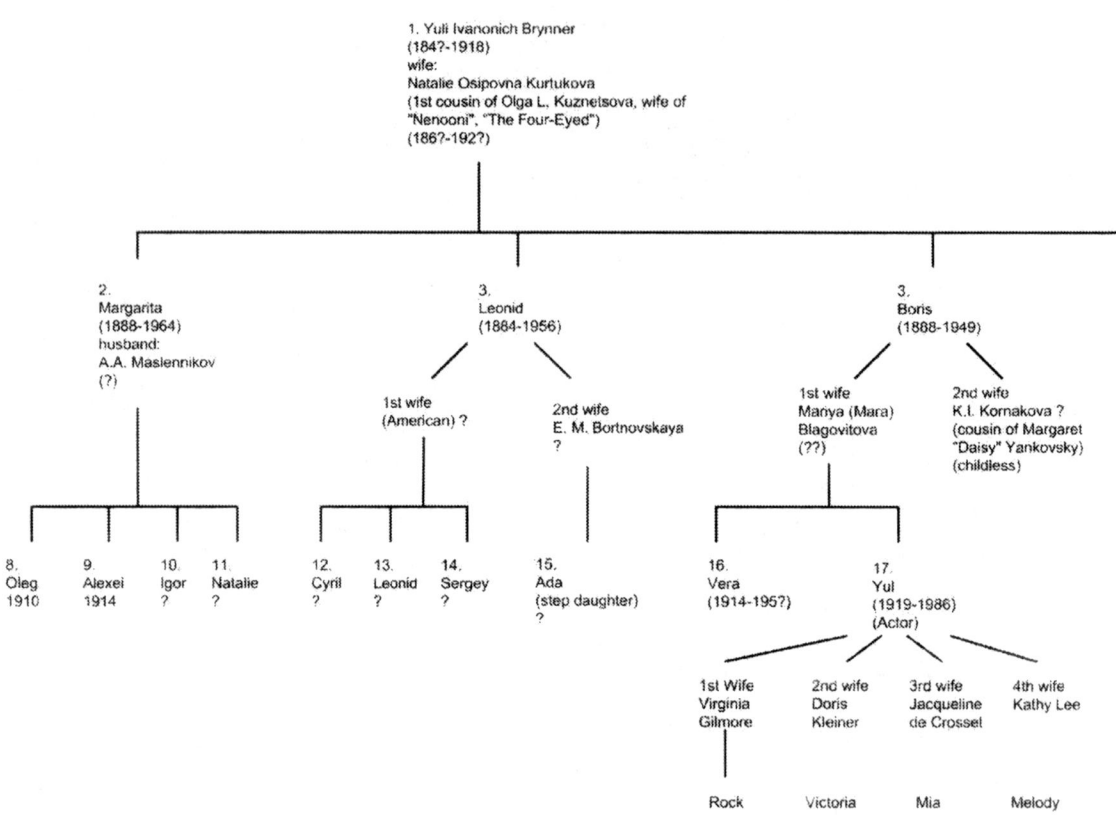

Family Trees

The Brynner Family Tree
(Descendants of Yuli Ivanovich Brynner
(From Switzerland)

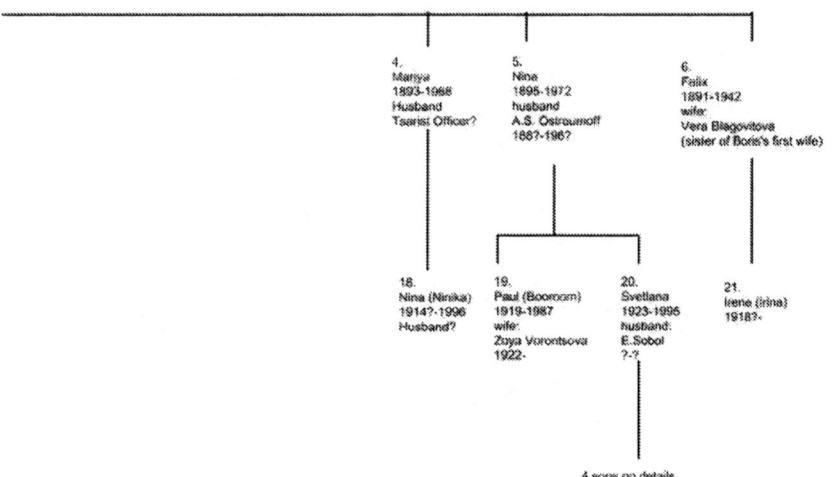

Chapter 43. Photographs

1. 1929. **Early days of Novina**. Ompo River. Top centre –E. S. Kaufman's dacha. Hintzes' block next to it marked xxx. Two Yankovskys' houses -- centre right.

Photographs

2. 1930 (approx.).

2. 1930 (approx.).   **Left--** Arseni Yankovsky.   (Centre ?)   **Right--** Valery Yankovsky.

1932. Novina.   Young spotted deer in an enclosure.

3. 1929 Novina. The dacha of M. and N. Hintze nearing completion. Builders (Left to Right) Valery and Yuri (George) Yankovsky sr.

Photographs

4. 1929. A camping trip near Novina. From left : Geliana (Fiala) and Yankovsky and Michael Natalie Hintze.

5. 1929. Lukomorye Beach. Standing in white singlet ---Michael Hintze. Sitting in the centre-- Natalie Hintze. Standing on the right --Yuri (George) Yankovsky. Children unknown.

Photographs

6.1931. Novina . Yankovskys and friends .

Back Row : From left : Standing --Yuri Yankovsky sr. Sitting in front of him in dark dress --actress Vera Panova . Next to her-- adjusting her hair -Yelena Korenevsky, with Anton Kozak , the caretaker next to Yelena.   Bending down --Arseni Yankovsky .   The last man in the back row----F Solomakhin.

Centre : Victor Pyotrovsky (mop of black hair) . Girl in front of Victor --Tanya Yankovsky. Third from the right in the same row --Mrs Natalie Yankovsky (Tanya's mother)--behind the girl in a floral dress. Lady next tsoVictor---Vera E. Kichigina ,wife of the artist Michael A. Kichigin.

Front.   Sitting on rock --M.A. Kichigin.   Squatting ,with dogs, Shura Nikiforov. Boy with dog-- Kunik, a friend of the Unterberger family. Lady in white dress and dark top--Nina Y.Ostroumova (nee Brynner, sister of Boris Brynner)

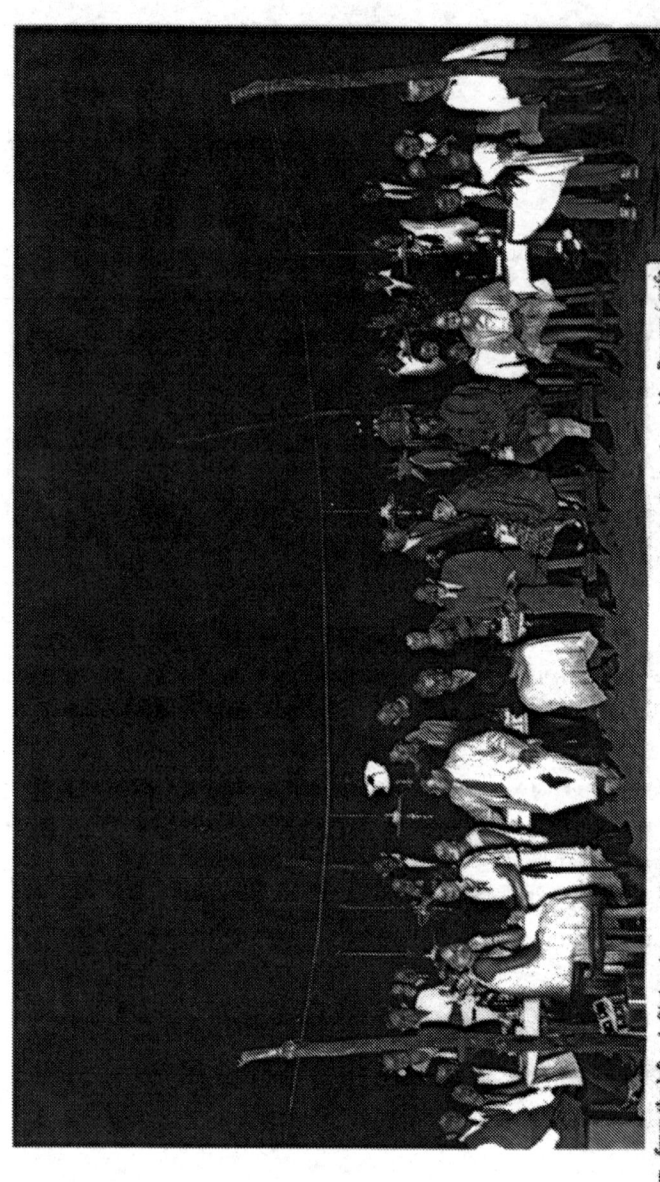

7.1931. Novina. An outdoor party.

Front Row, from the left: 1. Sitting down, with the head resting on her hand --Victoria Yankovsky. Facing her --Alya Powers (wife of Vasili Powers) Sitting behind Alya--Malina Yankovsky (daughter of Yan) 2. Man in long white socks facing camera on the right -- Alexander Yankovsky (Yuri Yankovsky senior's half-brother). Next to him--Sally --wife of George Gusakovsky 3. Little boy sitting down on the right, supporting his cousin on his knees--Yuri Yankovsky jr. The cousin --Tanya Yankovsky. Small boy in white shirt next to Tanya--Dima Chirkin. 6. Paul (Pavel) Michailovich Yankovsky. 7. Botanist N.A. Desualavi (co-worker of the famous explorer V.K. Arsenyev)

Back Row, from the left: 4.Man in a suit and a white shirt (bow tie) standing near a post -- Michael A. Hintze. Next to him -- Natalie Yankovsky. 5.Standing in the centre (moustache) --Yuri (George) Yankovsky sr. Small woman standing close to him (in the centre)--Mrs. Gusakovsky. 8. Painter M. A. Kichigin, facing Mrs. M.Yankovsky. Left to right from the post above Alexander Yankovsky's head, (9)--Viktor'Piotrovsky (white shirt); Natalie Chirkina ;Valery Yankovsky; Ninika Brynner (daughter of Mary Brynner, white dress); Arseny Yankovsky (coat and tie).

Photographs

8.1931. Novina. A game of "gorodki".

1.Mrs. N. Gusakovsky. Sitting next to her--artist Michael Kichigin. 2. Michael A. Hintze. 3.Fiala (Gelüma) Yankovsky. Next to her--poet Val from Shanghai. 4.Yuri Yankovsky jr. 5.Arseni Yankovsky.Next to him (dark dress) --actress Vera Panova. In light -coloured dress next to Panova--Alya Powers. 6. Victor Piotrovsky(sitting down). 7. Valery Yankovsky. 8. Kolya (Nikolai) Gusakovsky (hiding behind No9). 9.Yelena Korzaevsky.10.Yuri (George) Yankovsky sr. (between 9&11). 11. Natalie Hintze. Next to her --a Japanese guest. 12. Nimika Brynner. 13. Mrs. Natalie Tchirkina, wife of the former Russian consul in Korea.

259

9. 1932. Novina. Amateur children's theatre organised by Mrs Margaret Yankovsky.
From left to right: Irma Meyer (Korenevsky). Next to her--Svetlana Ostroumova (daughter of Nina Yulyevna, neé Brynner). Dima Tchirkin in a dress and wig, next to Svetlana, Centre, dressed as a page,--Yana Kichigina. Next to her--Tanya Yankovsky. Extreme right--Nata Yankovsky (Sokolovsky)-- Arseni's step-daughter. Next to Nata --Kiryusha Tchirkin.

10. 1932. **Novina.** Yuri (George) Yankovsky with his victims.

11. 1932. Novina. One of the early settlers Mrs Prince on horseback.

Photographs

12. **1932 . Novina .** Michael A. and Natalie Hintze at their dacha . The nanny is holding Viva , with Michael jr. next to her.

13. **1932. Novina .** In front of the dacha of M. A . and N. Hintze .
First row , L toR : Tanya Yankovsky ; Dima Chirkin ; Sveta Ostroumova ; Yana Kichigina ; Irma Meyer ; Kiryusha Chirkin ; Nata Yankovsky (Sokolovsky) ; Natalie Hintze ;
Standing in the back ---M.A. Hintze with Michael jr. on his shoulders .

14. Novina 1932 Horse-back riding in Novina

L. to R.: Lady in white shirt --Yelena Korenevsky. Blond boy in front of her--Dima Chirkin. Dark - haired boy---Booroom (Paul) Ostroumoff. Man to the right of the first horse-- M.A. Hintze. Next to him- his wife Natalie with Michael jr. on her shoulders. Man wearing a hat next to her --Yankovsky snr. Girl in a Cossack uniform in front of them (next to the dog)--Sveta Ostroumova. Riding second horse - Tanya Yankovsky. Lady holding the second horse --Alya Powers. Dark-haired man next to second horse -- Victor Piotrovsky. To Victor's left--Vera Kichigina, in short breeches (wife of artist M Kichigin) Woman in white shirt holding third horse -- Geliana (Fiala) Yankovsky. Riding 3rd horse --Irma Meyer (Korenevsky). Boy holding the third horse -- Kunik, a friend of the Unterbergers. Little boy in white shirt next to its stirrup--Kiryusha Tchirkin. Boy in a jumper next to Kiryusha--Boomka (Paul) Unterberger. Boy holding the fourth horse --Yuri Yankovsky jr . Girl riding the fourth horse--Yana Kichigina (no relation to Vera Kichigina , the wife of artist M. Kichigin)

15. Novina 1932. Apple harvest.
L. to R.: Michael (Misha) Hintze.   Yuri (George) Yankovsky snr.   Yuri Yankovsky jr.

16. Novina 1932. Two friends.

Natalie Hintze (left) and Victoria Yankovsky.

17. Novina 1932. The young Yankovskys.
Standing, from left: Valery and Arseni.
Front: Victoria (left), Yuri jr and Mooza.

18. Novina 1932. Frozen Ompo River near the Hintze's dacha.

Adults: Michael A. Hintze, wife Natalie and Mrs. Solomakhin.

Children (L to R): Misha Hintze and Olya Solomakhin.

Photographs

19. **1932. Near Novina**. Sukyaki dinner at a Japanese restaurant in the Ompo village.

Standing (L to R) : Victor Pyotrovsky. Natalie Hintze. George Gusakovsky. Mrs Margaret Yankovsky. Valery Yankovsky. Michael A. Hintze.

Sitting down (L to R) : Japanese waitress. Nikolas (Kolya) Gusakovsky. Mr Chirlkov-- a senior salesman of a shop in Seisin. Yuri Yankovsky jr. Mrs. Gusakovsky. Sally, wife of George Gusakovsky. Yankovsky snr. Japanese waitress.

20. Lukomorye Beach 1936.

Michael A. Hintze and an unknown girl.

Adults (L to R) : Yura (George) Dorian. Natalie Hintze. Two others unknown.

PHOTOGRAPHS

21. Lukomorye Beach 1932. Hintzes on the beach.

L to R. : Nanny holding Viva. Michael A. and Natalie, holding Misha.

22. Novina.

1936.

. The house of the Korenevsky family.

In hat --Konstantin Korenevsky.

1942.

Konstantin Korenevsky nursing daughter Katya

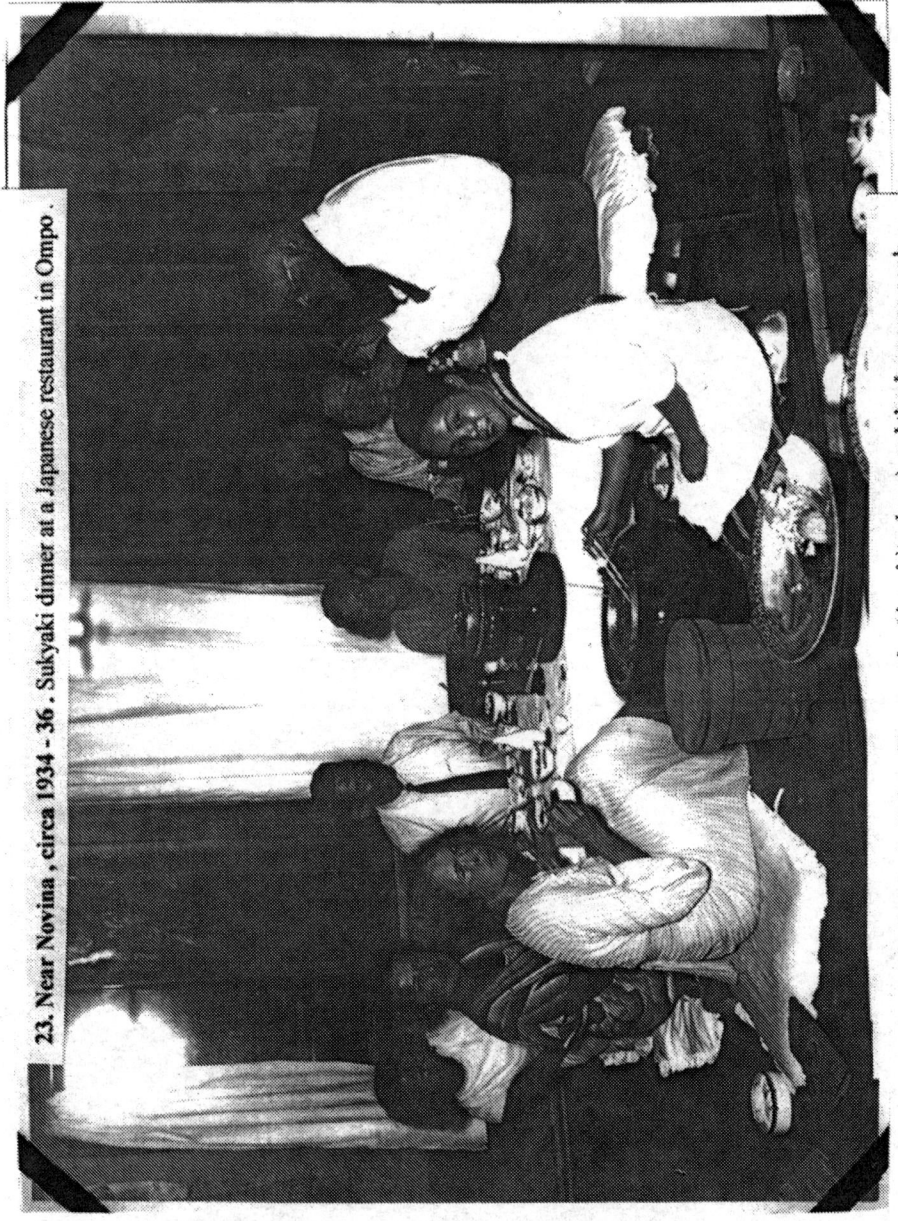

23. Near Novina, circa 1934 - 36. Sukyaki dinner at a Japanese restaurant in Ompo.

Foreground : Yelena Korenevsky (in white dress) and the Japanese cook.
Centre : Michael and Natalie Hintze.
Extreme right : Konstantin Korenevsky (in white shirt)
Extreme left : Vera Kichigina, wife of the painter   M.A.Kichigin

1936. From left:

Viva Hintze . Svetlana Vasilyeva . Misha Hintze . Zhenya Baikovsky . Dima Hintze .

1938. From left:

Olya Bushuyeva (nanny) .   Dima , Viva and Misha Hintze .   Rita Rimsha (daughter of an employee of B. Brynner) .   Bruno Saul.
Svetlana Vasilyeva .   Irma Meyer (Korenevsky)

Photographs

25. LUKOMORYE 1936.

From left:

Viva and Misha Hintze with Zhenya Baikovsky.

Children, from left: Viva Hintze, Zhenya Baikovsky and Misha Hintze.
Adults: Olya Bushuyeva (extreme left).
Natalie Hintze (centre, standing on a stone).
Extreme right: Helen Baikovsky (white blouse, long dress).
Sitting down (holding Zhenya)—Helen's sister-in-law
Irina Nesterenko (nee Baikovsky).
Two others-- unknown holiday-makers.

From left:

A relative of Shevelevs—Vera Koltsova-Mosalskaya (her mother was a Shevelev). Konstantin Korenevsky (beard). Mura Sheveleva (nee Vasilyeva). Irma Meyer (Korenevsky). Yelena Korenevsky. Kostya Vasilyev (Mura's brother).

26. Novina 1937 . Beach on the Ompo River near the Hintze's dacha .

From left : Dima Hintze .   Irma Meyer (Korenevsky) . Nata Yankovsky .
   Unknown holiday- maker.   Natalie Hintze with sons Viva and Misha (extreme right) .

27. "The Bald Mountains", Near Novina, 1937.

Natalie Hintze.

Boris Krivosh (right) and an unknown holiday-maker.

28. "The Bald Mountains", Near Novina, 1937.

Natalie Hintze on the right. Next to her —Eugenie (Zhenya) Peacock.
Left —Goolya Ilyina

PHOTOGRAPHS

29. 1937. Mountains near the Manchurian - Korean border, in the vicinity of the sacred legendary peak "Paektu-San" (2744 m).

Mountain Mist.

Yankovsky Senior with hunting dogs.

30. 1937. Mountains near the Manchurian - Korean border, in the vicinity of the sacred legendary peak "Paektu-San" (2744 m).

Hunting dogs.

Wild Country.

31. Novina 1936.
An old Korean farmer in national dress walking home along the narrow-gauge railway line.

32. Novina 1936. Bird's eye's view from the "Listvennitsa" Mountain.

Ompo River Valley

Novina, with E. S. Kaufman's dacha in the foreground.

PHOTOGRAPHS

33. Novina 1938. A religious procession after mass, usually accompanied by the blessing of the waters of the River Ompo.

1. Valery Yankovsky. 2. "Vera Belaya". Next to her -Mrs Gusakovsky

3. Misha Hintze.

4. Dima Hintze.   Lady holding an icon above Dima's head :
Mary, relative of the Unterbergers who later married
a famous violinist Shoora Dzygar

5. Viva Hintze.   6. Yuri Yankovsky jr (in the back)

7. Fiala (Geliana) Yankovsky.   8. Yuri Yankovsky sr.

9. Valentin Valkov (next to Yank sr). On the other side of
Yankovsky snr (bald)-a holiday maker from Shanghai

10. Nata Yankovsky   11. Unknown holiday-maker

12. Nikolai(Koka)   Gusakovsky.   13. Arseni Yankovsky.

14. Natalie Hintze.

Looking over Arseni's shoulder --Olya Bushuyeva.
Next to her--Natalie Yankovsky.

34. Novina 1938. The same procession as in the previous photograph but on another date.

1. Dima Hintze. 2. Viva Hintze. 3. Misha Hintze. 4. Dima Chirkin.
5. Valery Yankovsky. 6. Arseni Yankovsky. 7. Yuri Yankovsky jr. (between 11&8)
8. Nata Yankovsky. 9. Valentin Valkov. 10. Victor Pyotrovsky.

11. Malina Yankovsky   12. Yuri (G.) Yankovsky sr.   13. Natalie Hintze.
14. Kiryusha Chirkin (between 12&13)   15. Ivan Kuzmich Resnyansky (far back, beard).
16. Fr. John Trostyansky (next to Nata), long hair, beard.

35. NOVINA 1938 . FLOODED OMPO RIVER

36. NOVINA 1938 . FLOODS ON THE OMPO RIVER

From left : Yuri (George) Yankovsky snr . , Gutya Bibinov and Natalie Hintze , with the destroyed Supension Bridge in the background

Photographs

37. LUKOMORYE 1938.

Farewelling mum on a shopping trip :

From left : Olya Bushuyeva (Nanny) ; Viva , Dima and Misha Hintze (white shirt) , with cook Alekseevna in the centre .

Yelena Korenevsky , **left**, with an unknown holiday- maker .

A boxing match outside Kostya Vasilyev's dacha rented by the Hintzes in 1938 :
From left : Rita Rimsha. Misha and Dima Hintze , with Bruno Saul in a white shirt.

A Korean fishing village about 1 km south of Lukomorye

Holiday-makers on the beach (see story " Butamochi").

1. **Standing on the left**   Boris Brynner, Yul's father (in white shirt).
Man next to Boris -English guest from Shanghai.
Arms akimbo (white dress) --Mrs Nekhoroshkova.
Standing next to the dog--Mrs N's daughter
2. Yuri (George) Yankovsky sr.(arms folded).
3. **Extreme right .**   Natalie Hintze

From left, sitting down : 4 , 5 ,6--- Dima , Misha & Viva Hintze.

PHOTOGRAPHS

39. **NOVINA 1939**. The celebration of Michael and Natalie Hintze's 10th wedding anniversary in a Japanese Restaurant in the village of Ompo (near Novina).

1. Victoria Yankovsky.   2. Valery Yankovsky.   3. Gutya Bibinova.
4. Natalie Korenevskaya.   5. A holiday-maker called "Vassa" (sitting up) Lying on the floor -- Vassa's suitor (name unknown).   6. & 7 -Michael & Natalie Hintze
8. Michael Korenevsky--adopted son of Konstantin P. Korenevsky.
9. Y. Yankovsky sr. (leaning back)   10. Yelena Korenevsky (between M. Hintze & Y. Yankovsky.)
11. Moora Sheveleva (nee Vasilyeva)   12. Publisher Y.S. Kaufman (standing)
13. Natalie N. Chirkina   14. Fr. John Trostyansky.   15. Konstantin P. Korenevsky.

40. 1940. A TRIP TO THE THREE CHALICES

Crossing the turbulent stream.

Extreme right --Tosya Wuerfel.
Behind Tosya   Alya Powers

Third from left-- Ora Yankovsky

Fourth--Natalie Hintze

Extreme right --   Tosya Wuerfel   (standing)

PHOTOGRAPHS

41. 1940. A TRIP TO THE THREE CHALICES (see story).

Waiting for the train back to Novina.
Background left, in bikini --Victoria Yankovsky. Korean man sitting on the rails in front of her (glasses)--Chigoni --an employee and long-time friend of the Yankovskys.

Standing on the right -hand rail tracks, in the centre (floral swimming costume)--Jana Kichigina.

A train loaded with timber logs commencing the return (downhill) journey.
Sitting on the logs, from the left : Japanese official of the railway . Next - Tosya Wuerfel and Natalie Hintze. Names of other holiday -makers unknown . Chigoni (Korean , glasses)- 8th from left.
Standing in front of the logs , on the right---Victoria Yankovsky.

42. **NOVINA 1941.** Yankovskys on their estate.

From left: The new bride, Olga Petrovna. Yuri jr. Yuri (George) snr.

Valery. Mooza. Arseni.

Photographs

43. NOVINA 1940. Overall view of the settlement taken from a mountain located on the other side of the River Ompo.
(See also the map of Novina).

44. NOVINA 1938. ANNUAL VOLLEYBALL CHAMPIONSHIP.

From left: Standing, in white singlets, the Novina team: Arseni Yankovsky. Unknown player. Yuri Yankovsky jr. and snr.(sponsor). Gootya Bibinova (manager). Misha Korenevsky. Valery Yankovsky. Referee (name unknown)

Sitting, in black shorts, the Lukomorye team: Booroom Ostroumoff. Victor Pyotrovsky. Boris Brynner. Nikolai Gusakovsky. Valentin Valkov.

TEAMS IN PLAY.

Photographs

45. NOVINA 1939.

VERA BELAYA ("VERA THE BLONDE")

MALINA YANKOVSKY (DAUGHTER OF PAUL M. YANKOVSKY)

46. NOVINA 1940. Valery Yankovsky with cousin Yana (Joanna) Kichigina.

Photographs

47. KOREA 1940.

Valentin Valkov with a ginseng prospector.

Ginseng prospector at work.

48. KOREA 1940. DUCK HUNTING ON "THE DEAD LAKE" (50 km from Novina).

Valery Yankovsky and Natalie Hintze.

Valery Yankovsky and Gootya Bibinova.

49. 1941 . Novina . Wedding of Yuri (George) Yankovsky snr.   On the church steps after the ceremony.

Front Row :   Bride and Groom .
Second Row : Right--Victor Pyotrovsky.
Third Row: Tanya Yankovsky. Ninika Brynner . Valery Yankovsky.
Fourth Row: Svetlana Ostroumova.

50. 1941. Novina. Wedding of Yuri (George) Yankovsky snr. The wedding breakfast.

Centre: Bride (Olga) and groom. Next to Olga --the priest --Fr. John Trostyansky. Next to the priest--Mrs. Unterberger. Next to the bridegroom (scarf)--Mrs Y.I. Brynner (stepmother of Yul)

Extreme Right: Konstantin Korenevsky (beard).

Extreme Left "Matooshka"---the wife of Father John Trostyansky (facing camera).

Photographs

51. 1941 . Novina . Wedding of Yuri (George) Yankovsky snr. The wedding breakfast.

1. Natalie Yankovsky ("Auntie Tata"). 2. Nata Yankovsky. 3. Mrs. Unterberger.
4. Misha Hintze. 5. Mrs Ellers (Eugene's wife). 6. Valery Yankovsky.

52. 1941 . Novina . Fancy Dress Party.

Extreme Right (facing camera) : Olga and Arseni Yankovsky . On Arseny's right (Russian dress) Mrs. Nina Krivosh , Olga Yankovsky's sister

Centre (in white jacket) :   Yuri Yankovsky jr.

On Yuri's Left :   Mrs . Valentina Georgievna Ellers (no head-dress).

Back to camera : Eugene (Zhenka) Ellers . Next to him--Natalie Hintze.

Iva Yankovsky next to Natalie, with Tamara Nechayeva (daughter of the housekeeper of Mr. &Mrs. B. Brynner, Olga Yakovlevna Nechayeva) next to Iva (long plait).

Photographs

53. 1941. Novina. Fancy Dress Party.

Extreme Right: Arseny Yankovsky (white shirt) watching wife Olga in conversation with Eugene Ellers. Natalie Hintze next to Ellers. Valentina Ellers above husband's head (no head-dress).
At the head of the left table (looking into camera): Victoria Yankovsky. Behind Victoria—Brynners' housekeeper O.Y. Nechayeva. Man at the same table, on the right, looking into camera -- Nikolas (Koka) Gusakovsky. Leaning back, next to him--Tanya Yankovsky. Next to Tanya -- Svetlana Ostroumova.

54 . 1941 . Novina . Fancy Dress Party.

1. Mrs . Valentina Ellers.   2. Mrs Olga Yankovsky (new bride of Y. Yankovsky sr.)
3. Olga Yan kovsky (Arseni Yankovsky's wife).   4. Arseni Yankovsky.
5. Tanya Yankovsky.   6. Boris Krivosh (in fancy dress)   7. Victoria Yankovsky.
8. Natalie Hintze.   9. Kiryusha Chirkin.

Photographs

55. 1941. Near the Korean - Manchurian border. Yankovsky sr. with his quarry.

56. 1941. Near the Korean - Manchurian border.

Yuri Yankovsky jr. and Yuri (George) Yankovsky sr. with their booty.

57. 1942. Tiger Hamlet (in Manchuria).

Victoria Yankovsky with husband George Gusakovsky and daughter Daisy, who died in infancy.

George Gusakovsky and daughter Daisy.

58. 1943. Near the Korean - Manchurian border.

The Yankovsky brothers on a hunting safari.
From left: Arseni. Yuri jr. Valery.

The Victim.

Photographs

59. 1943. Near the Korean - Manchurian border.

The hunting brothers.
From left: Arseni.   Valery.

Valery and an innocent victim.

60. NOVINA 1942.

Katya Korenevsky.

Irma Meyer (Korenevsky), future wife of Valery Yankovsky

61. Xmas 1944 THE LAST DAYS OF NOVINA.

From left:
Standing in the back row: Tosya Powers (wife of Phillip). – Phillip Powers. Japanese guest (in kimono). Eugene (Zhenka) Ellers. Unknown guest.
Sitting in the front row: Japanese guest (owner of the hotel "Okurakan" in Ompo) with his son. Mrs. Valentina G. Ellers and unknown child. Irma Meyer (Korenevsky), holding sister Katya. Lera Ellers (bear).–Ellers' daughter. Tanya Yankovsky. Nata Yankovsky (Sokolovsky).

Epiphany (19th Jan. 1944). Service on the frozen Ompo River, under the Suspension Bridge.

Chapter 44. Maps

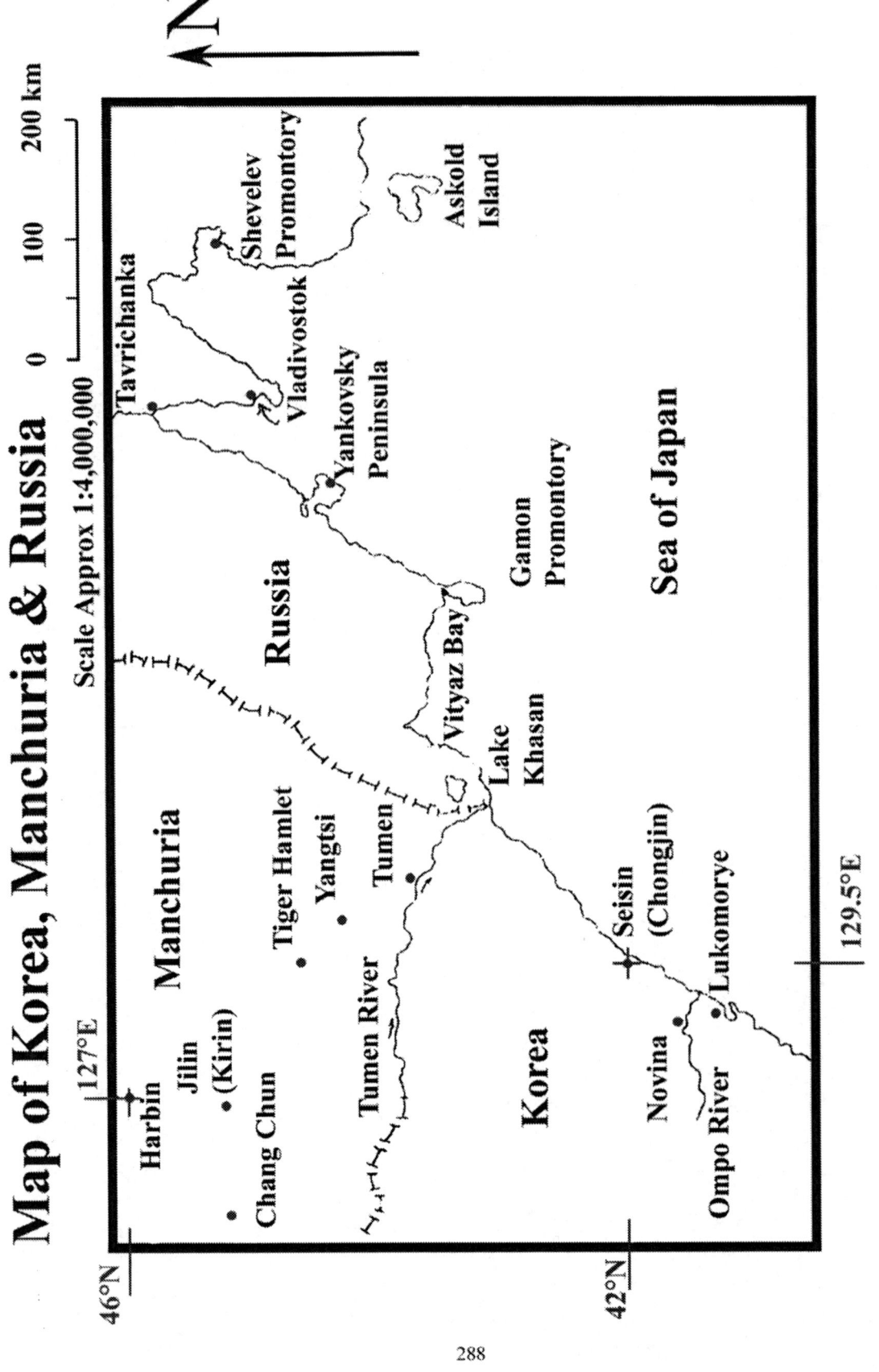

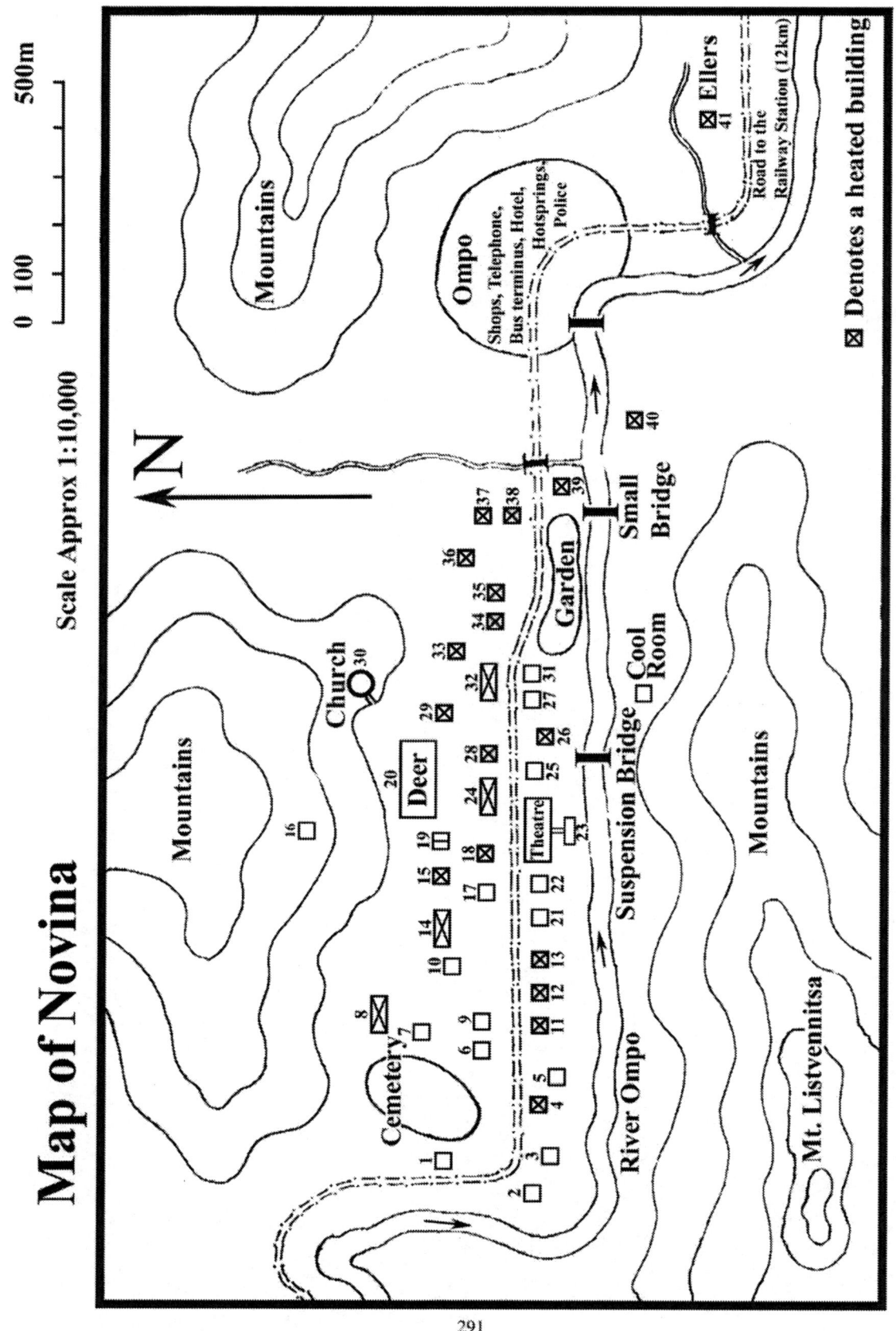

Chapter 45. INDEX

A
Adrianov 76, 77, 83
Africa 92
Alaska 22, 156, 160
Aleksyuk
Galina Alexandrovna 214
America 12, 22, 23, 26, 45, 83, 92, 95
Amur 3, 21, 47, 96
Bay 5, 21
River 3, 4, 5, 8, 11, 22, 76
Amursky 10
Andersen
Larissa 83, 85, 86, 88, 89, 113
Antipov
Afanassy 8
Argun River 4
Arizona 48
Arsenyev 21, 24, 160, 163
Vladimir Klavdiyevich 93, 214, 229
Askold Island 4, 5, 10, 11, 21, 45
Australia 95, 96, 110
Azov Sea 191

B
Babylon 111, 116, 123
Baikal Lake 8, 154, 168, 196
Baikov
Nikolai Appolonovich 96
Bald Mountains 84, 85, 87, 89, 180
Balmont 24
Banionis 110
Belarus 197
Belokrys
M A 46
Benkendorf 46
Bergman 27, 28
Bibinova-Rokotova
Agnya Alexandrovna (Gutya) 83, 166
Bishkek 162
Blagoveshensk 8
Blumenfeld
Dr. 17
Bocharova
Militsa Georgiyevna (Mila) 103, 104, 105, 114
Bolshevik Revolution 191
Bordovsky
Anna 197
Fyodor Georgiyevich 197
Georgiy Fyodorovich 197
Pavlik 197
Tatyana 197
Yelena 197
Boussier 21
Boxer Rebellion 13
Bratsk 160
Bratsk-Taishet Railway 196
Bryansk 197
Brynner 13, 16, 30, 34, 48, 133, 169
Ada 187
Boris Yulyevich (Borya) 83, 94, 96, 103, 134, 166, 186, 187
Cyril 186
Felix 186, 187
Katerina Ivanovna 24, 83, 94, 187
Leonid 96, 186, 187
Margarita-Gretel 186
Maroosya (Marina) 186, 187
Natalia Osipovna 186
Nina 186, 188
Ninika 187, 188
Vera 186
Yelena (Helen) Michailovna 187
Yul (Yulka) 83, 96, 186
Yuli Ivanovich 186, 189
Burke
Edmund iii
Burundin
Vera Petrovna 105, 106, 107
Butsky
Vladimir 136, 141
Butts 30, 31
Buzhko
AP 240

C
California 48, 160, 162, 163, 188, 197
Canada 26, 158, 188, 217, 235
Central Asia 158, 162
Changchun 133
Chile 161
China ..7, 21, 25, 34, 39, 47, 48, 111, 112, 114, 145
Sea 118
Chirkina
Natalie Nikolayevna 36, 37
Chistyakov 137
Or Georgievich .. See Gusakovsky, Or Georgievich
Pyotr (Peter) 128, 133, 161
Chisuko
Yamamoto 216, 217
Chita 4, 46, 194
Chkhon Chan Guyn 202
Chongjin .... See Seisin

Choree
An Yun 86
Chugunov
Y. D. 223
Chukotka 92, 121, 156, 158
Peninsula 19, 196
Chukotsky
Autonomous Region 191
Chuksha 160
Station 238
Chumpeeong 30
Chungou 123, 124
Chunka 196
Churchill
Winston 145
CIA 80
Cooper
Garry 88, 89
Cossacks 194
Crimea 17, 22, 197, 219
Crusades .... iii, 3

D
Dagemani Beach 222
Dalevich 83
Dead Lake 84
Decembrists 3, 46
Delhi 108
Demidov 140, 141
Desuslavi
Numa Avgustovich 83
Dikoy
Alexei 24
Katerina Ivanovna *See* Brynner, Katerina Ivanovna
Diomid Bay 147, 148
Doong Hwa 78, 80
Dostoyevsky's Idiots 18
Dubovsky
Benedict 3, 4, 5, 6, 7
Dyachenko
Boris Alexeyevich 161, 214
Dzu 153
Dzygar
Shoora 219

E
Eldorado Valley 134
Ellers
Valentina 121
Yevgeny (Eugene) Avgustovich (Zhenka)110, 115, 117, 118, 119, 120, 121, 122, 146, 149, 196
Endo 217
England 26, 111, 167
Erdman 5
Europe 3, 45, 48, 78, 95, 116

F
Far East .. 4, 5, 7, 16, 21, 23, 30, 48, 76, 77, 93, 94, 116, 121, 122, 145, 160
Fedishin 166
Fedoroff
Platon 10, 125, 220
Feodosiya 17
Fomenko
N.M. 192
Zhenya 192
Fonvisina 46
Fort Ross 160
France 4, 23, 92, 111
Fulton 145

G
Gamov 47, 223
Peninsula 48, 212, 229
Promontory 22, 192, 211, 220
Ganina
Anna (Nyusya) .... *See* Shevelev, Anna (Nyusya)
Gek
Bay 219, 223
Friedholf (Kirilovich)5, 6, 7, 13, 163, 186, 189, 190, 222
Inlet 190
Pelageya Semyonovna 189
Yelena Fridolfovna*See* Vasyukevich:Yelena Fridolfovna
Geliana 22
Germany 4, 22, 26, 43, 116, 123
Godlevsky
Viktor 4
Gondatti 96
Nikolai Lvovich 96
Gorki 168
Gulag ... iii, 17, 18, 20, 48, 50, 83, 95, 97, 121, 125, 141, 142, 144, 147, 148, 149, 152, 155, 156, 157, 158, 159, 160, 161, 189, 191, 192, 196, 200, 215, 219, 230, 234
Gusakovsky 199
Alora Orovna 163
Georgii (George) Nikolayevich 133
Kira Orovna 163
Kolya (Nikolas) 87, 174, 175, 201
Or Georgievich 133, 160, 163
Guttman
Galya 128, 129
Leonid 127, 128, 129
Gyunn
Chkhon Chan 49

H
Hamburg 43
Hang
Te Djung 94

INDEX

Hankow 47
Harbin 26, 27, 34, 41, 48, 77, 83, 85, 94, 95, 96, 97, 100, 110, 111, 116, 125, 126, 134, 158, 166, 179, 180, 182, 187, 193, 197, 200, 208, 209, 219, 235
Hasabe 153, 154
Henkin 97
Hintze ii
Dimitry Michailovich (Dima) 96
Michael Alexandrovich 96, 164
Michael Michailovich (Misha) 96, 164
Natalia Borisovna (Natasha) 96, 101, 103, 164
Vladimir Michailovich (Viva) 96
Hitler 116
Holy Trinity Bay 212
Horvat
General 48
Irene .... *See* Sheveleva, Irene
Huang
Bong 94
Hun Chan
Lee 47
Hung Hu Tse .. 6, 7, 10, 16, 21, 23, 76, 77, 79, 108, 127, 161, 189, 193, 209, 211, 212

I
Ilyina
Natalya 83, 94, 178
Olga (Goolya) 178, 179, 181, 182, 183
Imperial Russian Geographical Society 3, 4
Inchon 110
India 92, 107
Ingoda River 4, 8
Irkutsk 4, 8, 20, 46, 154
Israel 192
Italy 111

J
Japan 12, 23, 25, 34, 39, 75, 96, 111, 123, 135, 154, 162, 216
Sea 4, 39, 40, 190

K
Kamchatka Peninsula 225
Kaneta 34, 101
Kangouza 210, 211, 212
Kangouza Bay 230
Kanko 216
Kanto 127, 128, 131, 132, 135, 141
Kappel
Vladimir Oskarovich 130
Karaganda 196, 214, 221
Kaufman
Yevgeny (Eugene) Samoilovich 83, 96
Kazakevichevo 4
Kazakhstan 22, 196, 214, 221, 233
Kerchelyayeva
Nina Boguslavovna 214
KGB 18, 48, 95, 135, 161, 162, 166, 188, 220, 223, 232
Khabarovsk 8, 24, 155, 165, 219
Kham
Chi Goni 127, 128, 133
Khanka Lake 4, 8
Khanko 176
Khasan Lake 99
Kichigin 83
Angelina .... *See* Yankovsky, Angelina
Captain 22
Fedor 112
Joanna 22
Kichigina .... *See* Kichigin
Kim 208
Chung Bong 49, 94
Chung Byagi 90
Il Sung 137, 138, 139, 216
Kimio
Endo 217
Kirin 38, 75, 77, 78, 79, 80, 111
Kirov 232
Kobayasi
Masao 216
Kobe 110
Koiso 93
Kojevnikov
Vassili Ivanovich 109
Kolpachevo 17
Kolyma 121, 162
Range 76
Korea ... iii, 3, 12, 16, 17, 18, 21, 22, 23, 25, 26, 27, 30, 34, 40, 41, 48, 78, 79, 80, 81, 82, 92, 93, 94, 95, 96, 99, 108, 111, 113, 114, 117, 119, 120, 123, 125, 128, 136, 137, 138, 146, 147, 149, 154, 159, 162, 165, 168, 169, 178, 193, 202, 221
Korea Northern 209, 230
Korenevsky 180
Irma (Meyer) .... *See* Yankovsky, Irma (Meyer)
Konstantin Phillipovich 185
Yelena Nikolayevna 185
Korf
Baron N.A. 7, 8, 9
Kornakova
Katerina Ivanovna *See* Brynner, Katerina Ivanovna
Kornilov
Ivan Izosimovich 192
Klava 192
Kovalchuk
Nikolai Ivanovich 221
Kovalev 153, 155
Kovyazin 158
Kovzun

Alexander Alexandrovich 164
Kozak
Anton Pavlovich 87, 98, 109, 208
Maria Ivanovna 109
Kozmin
General 193
Krakovsky
Vladimir 164
Krasnoarmeysky 19, 156
Krivosh
Boris (Borya) 110, 117, 118
Kulesh
Nikolai 39, 40
Oleg Stepanovich 161
Kurtukov
Osip Ivanovich 186
Kushnareva
Tatyana Karpovna 214
Kuster 4
Kuznetsk 8
Kuznetsov
Olga Lukinichna *See* Yankovsky, Olga Lukinichna
Simon 7, 8
Stepanida 13
Kuznetsova .... *See* Kuznetsov
Kyakhta 47
Kyongson 208
Kyrgyzstan 17, 162

L
Lange 37, 38
Lavinsky 46
Laylle
Maurice 178
Olga (Goolya) .... *See* Ilyina, Olga (Goolya)
Lazarev
Kostya 106
Vera Pertrovna .... *See* Burundin, Vera Pertrovna
Lazareva .... *See* Lazarev
Lebedev 137, 140
Lebyazhya Lagoon 223
Lee 211
Lena River 3
Lenin 143
Lensky
Alexander Alexandrovich 220
Levchenko 142
Li . 138
Lidin 225
Lin Gooi .... 211, *See* Mr Lee
Listvennitsa 199
London 28, 29, 178
Los Angeles 26
Lukomorye .... iii, 35, 36, 39, 40, 48, 83, 84, 90, 94, 96, 97, 101, 102, 103, 161, 164, 166, 168, 169, 187

Lyoka 175, 176

M
Magadan 76, 121, 158, 159, 162, 191, 192, 196, 197, 215, 219, 220, 234, 238
Magai
Ivan 16
Timothy 43, 50
Makarov
Admiral 21
Manchukuo .... *See* Manchuria
Manchuria 7, 21, 25, 26, 34, 39, 48, 75, 76, 77, 79, 82, 93, 94, 95, 96, 99, 100, 107, 108, 109, 111, 116, 123, 125, 126, 127, 128, 133, 135, 136, 142, 146, 148, 151, 154, 161, 193, 195, 197, 206, 216, 217, 230, 236, 238
Mao 48, 139
Margaritov 21
VP 240
Marianna 22
Maritime Provinces 4, 17, 21, 24, 25, 27, 48, 50, 75, 99, 169, 220
Mark
Ivan 17
Marx 143
Masao
Kobayasi 216
Maslennikov
AA 186, 240
Lyolka 186
Maygetsko 127, 130, 132, 217
Melgunov 96
Merdelina
Stepanida Ivanovna 238
MGB 95
Mississippi 23
Mit
Kiska 115
Mitookov 11, 12
Mitsubishi 188
Modiagou 95
Modji 110
Mogilev 3, 167
Moscow .. 21, 22, 78, 122, 141, 154, 158, 159, 160, 187, 191, 192, 197, 215, 219
Mudanjiang 111, 216
Muravyov 46, 167
Muravyova .... *See* Muravyov

N
Nadezhda 4
Nagasaki 110, 117
Nagayev Bay 76
Nakhodka 18, 156, 197
Naryn 17
Naryshkina 46
Nichols

INDEX

Vera 106, 114
Nikolayev 141, 142, 145
Nikolayevsk 22
Nikolsk 9
NKVD 18, 48, 94, 135, 161, 176, 232
Nonsandon 22, 28
Novikov 143, 144, 145
Novina .iii, 3, 16, 17, 22, 28, 34, 35, 36, 42, 43, 44, 49, 77, 78, 83, 84, 85, 89, 92, 93, 94, 96, 97, 98, 99, 102, 105, 106, 109, 110, 115, 123, 126, 134, 140, 141, 143, 161, 164, 165, 166, 168, 175, 176, 177, 179, 180, 181, 182, 185, 187, 193, 194, 196, 199, 200, 208, 216, 236
Novosibirsk 125
Novozybkovo 162, 197

O
Ob River 17
Observatory Hill 16
Odessa 95
Okhotina
Yevlaliya Georgiyevna 197
Olekma 3
Olsoofyev
Michael 27
Ompo.. 22, 34, 36, 40, 84, 85, 93, 97, 99, 100, 168, 179, 181, 183, 187, 196, 208
River 22, 84, 87, 92, 93, 100, 178, 180
Oradovskaya
Svetlana 192
Osada-san 17, 209
Osavabucho 99
Oslo 159
Ostroumov
Pavel Alexandrovich (Booroom) 188
Ozerlag 160

P
Pacific Ocean. 3, 4, 35, 92, 123, 155, 158, 160, 168
Paektu-San 138
Pak 99
Den Ai 137
Pak-Arai 130, 131, 132, 133, 136
Panova
Vera 83
Paris 76, 95, 97, 113, 114, 154, 178, 187
Partisan Valley 221
Patrina
Mary Alexeevna 47
Patyukov
Michael Michailovich 75, 76, 77
Paukest 225
Peacock
Zhenya (Jenny)178, 179, 180, 181, 182, 183, 184, 185
Pervaya Rechka 121
Peter The Great Bay 190

Petrograd .... *See* St Petersburg
Pevek 156, 157
Piotrovskaya .... *See* Piotrovsky
Piotrovsky
Galya.. *See* Yankovsky, Anna Michailovna (Galya)
Irina Kazimirovna*See* Yankovsky, Irina Kazimirovna
Konstantin 13
Lucy 17
Margarita Ivanovna 232
Natalia Kazimirovna 232
Victor 13, 17, 173, 199
Victor Jnr 13, 17, 27, 100
Podgorny
Nikolai 136
Poland 167
Polish Rebellion of 1863 3
Port Arthur 149
Posyet 21, 23, 225
Region 230
Powers 11, 13, 18
Augusta (Gusta) 13
Katya 13
Masha 13
Olya 13
Phillip 13, 18, 20
Vassili (Basil) 13, 18, 19, 20, 115, 119
Vladimir (Dodik) 13
Primorye 222, 223, 236
Prishvin 225, 229
Prisyazhnyuk
Andrey Alexandrovich 219, 220
Pronya River 167
Puryon 94
Pusan 110
Putung 111
Pyongyang .136, 137, 141, 142, 146, 147, 159, 162

Q
Qingdao 111

R
Rachinskaya
Elizabeth 95
Ranan 93
Razdolnoye 152
Razin 156
Reid 26, 27
Mayne 12, 178
Resnyansky
Ivan Ivanovich 78
Ivan Kuzmich 75, 76, 77, 78, 98, 194, 208
Reznikov
Aaron Israelevich 192
Andrew 192
Anya (Anna) Stanislavovna 191, 192
Boris 192

Irina	192
Masha	192
Olya	192
Tae	192
Reznikova	*See* Reznikov
Rhee	175
Dr	183, 184
Khromonozhka	174
Rokotov	96
Romasheva	
Natalia Nikolayevna	*See* Yankovsky, Natalia (Natalie) Nikolayevna (Tata)
Rosen	46
Roy	30, 32, 33
Rozanov	
Vladimir (Volodya)	147, 148, 149, 150, 151, 152, 153, 154
Rusnak	
Svetlana Sergeyevna	214
Russia	iii, 3, 4, 12, 21, 23, 30, 48, 50, 77, 78, 92, 93, 94, 95, 97, 99, 112, 113, 123, 128, 135, 137, 143, 146, 148, 149, 154, 155, 158, 162, 216
Russian Civil War	192
Russian Far East	191
Russo-Japanese War	12, 21, 135, 154
Ruyken	35, 36, 39
Ryo	
Kim	216

S

Sabashnikov	
Nikita Filippovich	47
Sakhadjan Valley	*See* Eldorado Valley
Sakhalin Island	155
San Francisco	17, 48, 159, 162, 163, 188, 210, 217
Santiago de Chile	200
Saratov	158, 191
Prison	233
Sato	99, 208
Schneider	
Yuri (George)	235
Schultz	
Karl Ivan	5
Second River	48
Sedemi	6, 8, 10, 21, 22, 23, 24, 34, 41, 47, 48, 148, 192, 199, 210, 214, 216, 217, 219, 220, 231
Bay	6, 13, 163
Peninsula	9, 14, 186, 189, 191, 212, 222, 223
Seisin	16, 17, 25, 34, 81, 82, 101, 109, 146, 165, 166, 175, 176, 199, 214, 216, 217
Selenga River	8
Semipalatinsk	22
Semyonov	
General, Ataman	102, 133, 145, 193, 194
Seoul	16, 26, 30, 36, 93, 110, 175, 182, 209
Seryon	90
Shalyapin	97
Shanghai	18, 19, 22, 23, 26, 32, 37, 39, 48, 83, 94, 105, 106, 107, 110, 111, 112, 113, 114, 115, 116, 117, 118, 120, 124, 126, 127, 141, 161, 182, 200, 201, 208, 209, 210
Shelomentsev	
Pyotr (Peter) Fedotovich	133, 134
Shepkin	
Fyedya (Theodore)	147
Sherbakov	
Michael	83, 161, 187
Olga Ivanovna	*See* Yankovsky, Olga Ivanovna
Sherbakova	*See* Sherbakov
Shevchenko	155
Shevelev	46, 48
Alexander	46
Alexandra Dimitriyevna	47, 147
Andy	212
Angelina (Gelya)	47, 186, 210
Angelina Michailovna	*See* Yankovsky, Angelina Michailovna
Anna (Nyusya)	48
Boosya Alya	*See* Shevelev, Alexandra Dimitriyevna
George Alexandrovich	46, 47
Gleb	47, 48, 163, 178, 179, 181, 182, 183, 185
Igor Vladimirovich	47, 48
Irene	48
Margaret (Margarita) Michailovna	*See* Yankovsky, Margaret (Margarita)
Marina	48
Michael Grigoryevich	22, 47, 111, 210, 211, 230
Mikhail	190
Mura	48, 96, 101, 103
Natasha	48
Nikolo	48
Oleg Vladimirovich	47, 48, 101, 114, 115, 159, 188, 210, 212
Peninsula	47
Promontory	190
Svyet	48
Vladimir (Volodya) (Vova)	47, 48, 159
Vladimir Michailovich	210, 211
Xenia Germanovna	47
Sheveleva	*See* Shevelev
Shilka River	4, 8
Shuotsu	34, 36, 85, 183, 200
Siberia	3, 4, 8, 46, 47, 87, 121, 158, 160, 168, 196, 209
Eastern	3, 4, 7, 46
Sinitsin	
Alexandra Dimitriyevna	*See* Shevelev, Alexandra Dimitriyevna
Dimitri	47

INDEX

Sivakovo 4, 8
Slavyanka 219, 225
SMERSH 95, 119, 125, 135, 163, 166, 176, 188
Smolensk 3
Sochi 22
Solomakhin 194
  Alexandra Stepanovna 195
  Fyodor Pavlovich 133, 193, 194
  Olga 195
Solomonovich
  Mark 237
  Valentina Ivanovna 237
Soviet Security Services 80
St Louis 23
  Agricultural College 12
St Petersburg 3, 4, 23, 46, 197, 198
Stalin 20, 81, 95, 136, 139, 144, 216
Stalingrad 233
Stanislavsky 24, 83, 187
Suez Canal 22
Suifunhe River 151
Sukhodol Inlet 190
Sungacha River 4, 8
Sungari River 75, 95, 97
Suzdal 178, 185, 217
Svechinsky
  Billy 191, 192
Sverdlovsk 197
Sweden 26, 106

T

Tabonnaya Bay (Horse Herd Bay) 186
Tabounnaya Pad 222
Tahiti 92
Taishet 158, 160, 196
Taiwan 143
Taki 127, 128, 129
Talon 158
Tavrichanka 149
Tchon Chan Gynn
  Ivan 30, 31
Teggee
  Lee Pok 86
Tetyukhe Bay 30, 169
Texas 12, 23
Three Chalices 84, 86, 88
Tientsin 25, 26, 47, 48, 110, 111, 182, 209, 215
Tiger Hamlet 24, 127, 130, 133, 134, 135, 140, 160, 161
Tikhonov
  Victor 114, 115
Tokmakov 47
Tomon 75, 79
Tomsk 8, 9
Tomsky
  Vassili Ivanovich 83, 100, 101

Torpedo Boat Cove 222
Transbaikal Region 3
Trusov
  AA 240
Tsar 3, 12, 46, 154
  Zlatko Mirkovich 215
Tsaritsin .... *See* Starlingrad
Tsoi-Yankovsky
  Indis Ivanovich (Tom) 214
Tumangan 75
  River 26, 28, 31, 79, 82, 94, 125, 174, 221
Tumyn .... *See* Tomon

U

Uetegi 179, 181
Ulan - Ude .... *See* Verkhneudinsk
Ungern
  Baron 194
United States of America 11, 12, 17, 22, 23, 26, 45, 48, 83, 92, 95, 111, 121, 123, 155, 161, 187, 188, 200, 214, 216, 217
Unterberger
  P. F. 10
Ural Mountains 24, 189, 197
USSR 160
Ussuri 5, 10, 16, 21
  Bay 190, 210, 211
  Gulf 47
  Region 189, 214
  River 4, 8
  South Region 177
Ussuriysk 76, 153, 155
Utesov 173

V

Vakhovich
  Vladimir (Volodya) 41, 162
Val 39, 40, 83
Valkov 102
  Nata .... *See* Yankovsky, Nata
Valentin 101, 103, 133
Vancouver 159, 188, 217, 235
Vasiliev
  Kostya (Konstantin) 96
  Mura .... *See* Shevelev, Mura
Vasilieva .... *See* Vasiliev
Vasyukevich 223
  Captain 13
  Georgiy (George) 189
  Klavdii (Claude) 189, 222, 223
  Nikolai Vasilyevich 189
  Yelena Fridolfovna 189, 224
  Yevgeny (Eugene), Zhenya 189
  Yuli Nikolayevich 189, 223, 224
Vavilov
  Nikolai Ivanovich 233
Venice 120

Verkhneudinsk 46, 47
Vertinsky
  Alexander Nikolayevich 113, 114
Victoria Island 159
Vilkidskaya
  Varya 225
Vinnichyuk
  Vasilly Illarionovich 237
Vita 83
Vityaz 22, 225
  Bay 222
  Inlet 212
Vladimir 159, 160, 163, 164, 178, 192, 198, 216, 221, 236, 239
Vladivostok .. 4, 5, 8, 10, 16, 17, 18, 22, 23, 24, 25, 30, 41, 45, 47, 48, 76, 95, 110, 111, 112, 121, 146, 147, 156, 159, 160, 163, 165, 186, 189, 192, 196, 197, 210, 214, 216, 217, 219, 220, 221, 222, 223, 224, 225
Volga River 158, 191, 233
Volgograd .... 191, 197, *See* Starlingrad
Volkonskaya 46
Vorkuta 78
Vorobey
  Vissarion Ipatyevich 34
Vorontsov
  Dimitry Matveyevich 188
  Zoya (Brynner) 188
Vovchenko 166
Vykhorevka 238

W

Warsaw 4
  University 3
Whampoa River 111, 116, 117

Y

Yamaguchi
  Moichi 24
Yanchen 174
Yang Tsing 136
Yangtsi 127
Yankovsky 24, 26, 45, 108
  Alexander Michailovich (Shoora) 6, 10, 11, 16, 22, 93, 125, 240
  Anastasia (Asya) Yanovna 215
  Angelina Michailovna (Gelya) 22, 111, 112, 214
  Anna Michailovna (Galya) 11, 12, 13, 14, 15, 16, 17, 18, 22, 240
  Arseny (G) Yuryevich 3, 16, 22, 24, 26, 27, 28, 29, 31, 42, 50, 85, 89, 100, 108, 133, 144, 159, 161, 162, 163, 174, 178, 187, 188, 193, 200, 217, 220
  Arseny (Junior) 191, 192, 236
  Elizabeth Michailovna (Lisa) 6, 11, 12, 240
  Fiala (Geliana) 213, 217, 222
  Gelya 222
  George *See* Yankovsky, Yuri (George) Michailovich
  Grisha (Gregory) 162, 163
  Irina Kazimirovna 158, 160, 191, 192, 196, 230, 232
  Irma (Meyer) 24, 128, 134, 141, 142, 143, 145, 159, 180, 185, 188, 195, 235
  Ivan (Yan) 240
  Lisa *See* Yankovsky, Elizabeth Michailovna (Lisa)
  Malina (Marianna) 213, 217, 222
  Maree 236
  Margaret (Margarita) 47, 210
  Margaret (Margarita) Michailovna 22, 24, 83, 186, 200, 215
  Meyer .... *See* Yankovsky, Irma (Meyer)
  Michael (nephew) 191
  Michael Ivanovich 3, 4, 5, 6, 7, 8, 10, 11, 21, 22, 23, 160, 163, 167, 168, 177, 186, 190, 191, 214, 230
  Michael Pavlovich (Misha) 23, 113, 196
  Musa Yuryevna 159, 161, 200, 214
  Nata 133
  Natalia (Natalie) Nikolayevna (Tata) 23, 83, 113, 196, 214
  Olga 5, 6, 7, 11, 21, 161, 162, 163, 240
  Olga Lukinichna 5, 186
  Olga Petrovna 126
  Or *See* Gusakovsky, Or
  Ora 190
  Paul 199, 240
  Paul (Pavel) Michailovich 11, 23, 35, 83, 105, 108, 110, 111, 113, 116, 145, 186, 196, 197, 214
  Peninsula 6, 166, 190, 214, 221, 223, 240
  Serge Michailovich 11, 23
  Sergey Valeryevich 159, 188, 217, 235
  Tadeusz Novina 3
  Tatiana (Tanya) Pavlovna 23, 113, 141, 144, 146, 158, 160, 162, 196, 238
  Valery (G) Yuryevich iii, 7, 10, 12, 13, 14, 16, 17, 19, 20, 21, 23, 24, 25, 26, 27, 28, 29, 30, 31, 32, 33, 34, 36, 37, 38, 39, 41, 42, 43, 46, 48, 50, 75, 78, 79, 80, 81, 83, 84, 85, 86, 88, 89, 90, 91, 92, 93, 95, 96, 97, 99, 100, 101, 102, 103, 104, 105, 106, 107, 108, 110, 111, 112, 113, 114, 115, 116, 117, 118, 119, 120, 121, 122, 123, 124, 125, 126, 127, 128, 129, 130, 131, 132, 133, 134, 135, 136, 137, 138, 139, 140, 141, 142, 143, 144, 145, 146, 147, 148, 149, 150, 151, 152, 153, 154, 155, 156, 157, 158, 159, 160, 161, 162, 163, 164, 165, 168, 169, 178
  Victoria (Ora) Yuryevna 24, 39, 83, 85, 92, 128, 133, 159, 161, 163, 200
  Xenia Georgievna 191

Index

Yan (Ian)(Ivan) Michailovich 11, 22, 47, 112, 186, 210, 211, 212, 213, 214, 222, 229
Yuri (G) Yuryevich (Lyulya) 30, 31, 42, 108, 109, 123, 124, 126, 133, 135, 136, 137, 140, 141, 144, 158, 162, 167, 176, 196, 200, 215, 216, 219, 221, 240
Yuri (George) Michailovich 3, 6, 7, 10, 11, 12, 22, 23, 24, 25, 43, 45, 49, 123, 124, 125, 126, 146, 148, 158, 159, 166, 168, 169, 174, 186, 196, 197, 208, 210, 211, 212, 213, 215, 223, 238, 240
Zlata (Zosya) Yuryevna 215
Yaroshevsky
Kazimir 226
Yekaterinburg .... *See* Sverdlovsk
Yelizarov
Porfiriy Yevstigneyevich 221
Yelkin 166
Yellow Sea 111
Yenchon 109
Yesenin 85
Sergey 158
Yevseyenko
Antoly Alexeyevich 236
Yeysk 191
Yokohama 11, 22
Youshnevskaya 46
Yu Min 30
Yuzefovich 96

Z

Zaozernaya Hill 99
Zaton 97
Zayaz
Xenia Germanovna *See* Shevelev, Xenia Germanovna
Zeya River 76, 77
Zhukov
Pavel (Paul) Kalistratovich 130, 131, 132, 133
Zorov
Boris Alexandrovich 232
Michael 232
Mitya 232
Pavlik 232
Zvezhdovsky
Ludwig 167

CPSIA information can be obtained at www.ICGtesting.com
Printed in the USA
LVOW05s0005171013

357173LV00001B/179/A